blue
rider
press

# JIM
# BROWN

DAVE ZIRIN

# JIM BROWN

—

# LAST MAN STANDING

BLUE RIDER PRESS     NEW YORK

blue
rider
press

An imprint of Penguin Random House LLC
375 Hudson Street
New York, New York 10014

The author gratefully acknowledges permission to reprint excerpts from the
following works: Alex Haley's interview of Jim Brown in *Playboy*, 1968, courtesy
John A. Palumbo. *Off My Chest*, by Jim Brown with Myron Cope, copyright
© 1964 by James N. Brown and Myron Cope. Used by permission of Doubleday,
an imprint of Knopf Doubleday Publishing Group, a division of Penguin Random
House LLC. All rights reserved. *Out of Bounds*, by Jim Brown with Steve Delsohn,
copyright © 1989 by Jim Brown and Steve Delsohn. All rights reserved. Reprinted
by arrangement with Kensington Publishing Corp. www.kensingtonbooks.com.

Photographs: pp. 10, 250 © Bettmann/Getty Images;
p. 32 © Syracuse/Collegiate Images/Getty Images; p. 68 © Focus on Sport/Getty
Images; p. 112 © Tony Tomsic/Getty Images; p. 162 © John D. Kisch/Separate
Cinema Archive/Getty Images; p. 196 © Markus Boesch/Allsport/Getty Images;
p. 290 © Nick Cammett/Diamond Images/Getty Images

Blue Rider Press is a registered trademark and its colophon
is a trademark of Penguin Random House LLC

Library of Congress Cataloging-in-Publication Data
Names: Zirin, Dave, author.
Title: Jim Brown : last man standing / Dave Zirin.
Description: New York: Blue Rider Press, 2018.
Identifiers: LCCN 2017035828 | ISBN 9780399173448 (hardcover)
Subjects: LCSH: Brown, Jim, 1936– . | Football players—United States—Biography.
Classification: LCC GV939.B75 Z57 2018 | DDC 796.342092 [B]—dc23
LC record available at https://lccn.loc.gov/2017035828
p.      cm.

Printed in the United States of America
1  3  5  7  9  10  8  6  4  2

*Book design by Lauren Kolm*

TO LIEUTENANT RICHARD COLLINS III
AND SANDRA BLAND

#SayTheirNames

We always lament in the superficial media culture that there are no heroes, but that presupposes that a hero is perfect and what the Greeks have told us for millennia is that a hero isn't perfect. Heroism is the negotiation between a person's strengths and weaknesses . . . and sometimes it's not a negotiation. It's a war.

—KEN BURNS

# CONTENTS

# JIM
# BROWN

# "IT JUST IS WHAT IT IS"

—

Football is the closest thing we have in this country to a national religion, albeit a religion built on a foundation of crippled apostles and disposable martyrs. In this brutal church, Jim Brown is the closest thing to a warrior saint. Brown is, both statistically and according to awed eyewitnesses, perhaps the greatest football player to ever take the field. At six-foot-two and 230 pounds, running a sub-4.5 forty-yard dash, he was like a twenty-first-century Terminator sent back in time to destroy 1950s and 1960s linebackers. In the gospel of football, defensive demons like Dick Butkus, Lawrence Taylor, and J. J. Watt have carried some of that fearful mystique: transforming their opponents into quivering balls of gelatin. But on offense, the all-time great skill players—Johnny Unitas, Jerry Rice, Walter Payton—have inspired astonishment yet never physical fear.

On that side of the line of scrimmage, the list of true intimidators begins and ends with Jim Brown.

The statistics that define his time in football are still without equal. Brown played nine years and finished with eight rushing titles, a level of consistent greatness no one has come close to matching. He is the only player to average one hundred yards rushing per game over an entire career and the only running back to retire with an average of five yards every time he carried the ball. Then there is the most impressive number of all: zero. That is the number of games Brown missed over his nine years in the National Football League. It would be a stunning achievement for a placekicker. But it is especially remarkable given the ungodly workload Brown maintained and the constant punishment he took, touching the ball for roughly 60 percent of all the Cleveland Browns offensive plays.

In NFL circles, these numbers are spoken with veneration, the same way baseball writers talk about Babe Ruth or NBA fans recall Wilt Chamberlain or boxing writers speak about the young Muhammad Ali or tennis aficionados discuss Serena Williams. Babe Ruth swatted fifty-nine home runs in 1921, more homers than were hit by half the teams in baseball. In the 1961–1962 season, Wilt Chamberlain averaged fifty points every time he took the court, nineteen more per game than the next top scorer. Muhammad Ali fought Cleveland Williams and avoided all but ten punches in three rounds. Serena Williams has won twenty-three Grand Slams as of this writing, and her latest one, in Australia, was during her first trimester of pregnancy. These are not merely examples of great athletes. It is as if they were playing altogether different sports from their peers.

But Jim Brown was also so much more than Babe or Wilt or even Ali. He was in many respects the first modern superstar. In an era before strong sports unions, he organized his locker room to stand up to management on issues great and small, never giving an inch and earning a derisive nickname from team executives: "the locker room lawyer." In an era years before Tommie Smith and John Carlos raised their fists against racism and for human rights at the 1968 Mexico City Olympics, it was Jim Brown who refused to be treated as a second-class citizen just because of the color of his skin. In a time before Muhammad Ali "shook up the world" by joining the Nation of Islam and refusing to fight in the Vietnam War, Brown did so much of his own shaking that Ali, in his darkest hours, turned to him for advice and support.

Brown was the first player to use an agent. He was the first superstar to successfully demand that a coach be fired and that released teammates be immediately unreleased. He was the first athlete to ever willingly quit his sport in his prime, because his "manhood" was more important to him than enduring the disrespect of management. In the words of NFL Players Association executive director DeMaurice Smith, he was the first football player "to walk away on his own terms. To walk instead of limp." He was the first black athlete to be bigger than the league itself. When players from LeBron James to Peyton Manning to Michael Jordan have leveraged their own stardom to assert their will on the direction of their teams and their leagues, it all traces back to Jim Brown.

If that is where Jim Brown's story ended, it would be enough for its own book. But the man's football life was just the opening salvo to a much more sprawling epic. Brown parlayed his athletic fame into Hollywood stardom, where it was thought that he could become "the black John Wayne." When this path was stymied less by his own acting ability than by the racialized rules of Hollywood, he was the first black actor to try to rewrite the script by launching his own big-time production company to make "black films for a mass audience" (in partnership with Richard Pryor, before they had a falling-out for the ages). He was an outspoken Black Power icon in the 1960s and spearheaded a network of Black Economic Unions to build independent hamlets of financial strength in the black community. His decades of work as a truce negotiator with street gangs are why Brown, along with Muhammad Ali and Bill Russell, is considered part of the holy trinity of socially conscious athletes.

Brown has his supporters and detractors. But the common thread that one hears from everybody who has had dealings with him—dealings good, bad, and ugly—is that "Jim Brown is, above all else, a man."

This word "man" might as well have been a birthmark affixed to him when he arrived into the world on February 17, 1936. His nickname as a small child was "Man," and the word "manhood" is the political current that pulses throughout his life.

Kevin Blackistone wrote in *The Washington Post* in 2017 that "Jim Brown, maybe more so than any other black athlete the past 50 years, came to be seen as sort of an emperor of black masculinity and of black power."

Brown's assertion of his unassailable masculinity conjures another legend who was a friend and contemporary, Malcolm X.

In his eulogy for this avatar of black empowerment, actor Ossie Davis said, "Malcolm was our manhood." Davis, in his stentorian voice, was arguing that Malcolm embodied black masculinity, valor, and heroism in a society dedicated to treating and labeling black men as "boys." Yet Brown, because of his athletic achievements, has been put on an even higher, supernatural pedestal. As Public Enemy's Chuck D has said, "Jim Brown is our Black Superman," and he is hardly alone in associating Brown with the son of Krypton.

On the most hypermasculine cultural canvases of the United States—NFL football, the Black Power movement, Hollywood's blaxploitation era, the gang wars both inside and outside prison walls—Jim Brown has made his mark. In the most toxic expression of how our society defines "what makes a man"—the assertion of domination over women—he has left a jagged mark on that landscape as well.

Brown has asserted his fierce sense of manhood as a principle of emancipation. But the history of accusations of violence against women levied against him has scarred his legacy, lumping him in with less than admirable figures like fighter Floyd Mayweather, quarterback Ben Roethlisberger, and pitcher Aroldis Chapman. It has prevented him from achieving the kind of mainstream adulation bestowed on contemporaries like Ali and Russell. Barack Obama—who as president took a particular joy from his regular interaction with black sports heroes of yesteryear—never dialogued with Jim Brown. Donald Trump, however, rolled out the red carpet; accusations of mistreating women—and steadfast, blanket denials—are a point in common for both men. In December 2016, the president-elect sat down with Brown and former NFL player Ray Lewis. Brown left the meeting saying, "I fell in love with [Trump] because he really talks about helping . . . black people."

That night, Brown was on television with right-wing Fox News talker Sean Hannity to sing Trump's praises. People who loved Jim Brown for his pioneer status as a rebel athlete and his decades of Black Power rectitude recoiled. Former NBA player Etan Thomas said, "How could Jim Brown sit down with someone who smiles and winks at the KKK? How can he praise him? It makes my head spin." Jamil Smith, a Cleveland-born-and-raised journalist, wrote, "Seeing Jim Brown praise Donald Trump made my heart stop."

Then, after more than a dozen Cleveland Browns players took a knee during the national anthem in response to events surrounding the white supremacist march in Charlottesville, Virginia, the alt-right website Breitbart trumpeted reports that Jim Brown had gone into the Browns locker room to talk to the team and stop future protests. The headline read: "Every Browns Player Stands for the Anthem After Jim Brown Lays Down the Law."

Former NFL player Shannon Sharpe, now a host at Fox Sports, said, with a catch in his throat, "It's disappointing because all it takes is one big-name person of color to really almost throw a wet blanket over the fire that's being sparked with what Colin Kaepernick and others with the Black Lives Matter movement [are doing]—the positive people who are trying to change and have an impact. You're talking about Jim Brown . . . saying that Colin Kaepernick went about this wrong. That gives them all the credibility they need. That hurts the most and it's so disappointing. I'm so, so disappointed in him."

The anger, confusion, and even feelings of betrayal are all very understandable. But if we try to understand Brown's actual political beliefs over the last fifty years—and not the beliefs we project onto him—this meeting with Trump and Brown's attack on young athletic protesters should have surprised no one. His history shows that in addition to being a great football player, a legendary tough guy, and an anti-racist hero, Brown has had his share of political contradictions; contradictions that crisscross his character like the thick, angry scars that run around his still heavily muscled forearms. He's the paragon of Black Power who endorsed Richard Nixon. He's the anti-racist who condemned Dr. Martin Luther King, Jr.'s civil rights movement as a waste of time. Brown in so many ways wrote the script on masculinity in the Black Power movement, while also being tightly tethered to its most self-destructive minefields. His contempt for younger athletes and their values has been an interview staple for four decades. He is the NFL rebel who has long despised the NFL Players Association. He loves "his people" but has a narrow definition of who his people are, stating at different times in his journey that black women who assert themselves are undermining black manhood and the black family.

It is understandable why so many are transfixed by the icon instead of assessing the human being. Seeing Jim Brown in the flesh, even at his advanced age, is hypnotic. He walks with a cane, but it is a "cane" only insofar as one could call a Humvee a "car." Brown's walking stick is a thick piece of wood designed for holding up a very specific body—a body that, even with age and a pronounced limp, is a physical marvel. The man is built like a series of imperfect craggy cubes. He no longer has the forty-seven-inch chest and thirty-two-inch waist that made him a Hollywood sex symbol; his body has ceased to appear, as John Wooten, his old friend on the Cleveland Browns, described, as if it were "cut like the good Lord said, 'I am going to do this once and not do it again.'" He needs that cane to walk. He cannot turn his neck. His hands can no longer grip objects with anything close to full strength. But he is still unmistakably Jim Brown: sharp as a tack and made of stone, hard and unforgiving.

"I've always occupied a special position and been able to get certain opportunities because the system wanted to use my talents for economic gain," he says. "And as long my talents were relevant, I was relevant. But the greatest desire in my soul was and is to represent myself as a man and carry myself as a man at all times. I wanted to help others and always credit those who helped me. I wasn't 'Jim Brown' always. One time I was eight years old, twelve years old, eighteen years old. So you can't look at me or anybody as just one block, because it doesn't all wrap up like a big box with candy and ribbons around it and shit. And it isn't all negative or positive. It just is what it is."

All the strands of the modern athlete from LeBron James to Colin Kaepernick, from Peyton Manning to Kobe Bryant, can be traced back to Jim Brown. He is tragic and heroic; dragon and dragon slayer.

Forty years ago, feminist trailblazer and onetime Brown paramour Gloria Steinem quoted a friend of Jim Brown's from his pre-Hollywood days in a profile she wrote about him for *New York* magazine. "He doesn't confide in anybody," the friend said. "He doesn't expect much of anybody. Somewhere in his head, he's always alone."

He may be alone, but he isn't being left alone. As a new era of the black freedom struggle has launched under the slogan "Black Lives Matter"—a movement founded by black women— and as a new generation of athletes attempts to use their platform to stand up against racism, the history of Jim Brown has a new currency. As more black athletes engage with the movement, and as America becomes both more diverse and more divided, the legacy of Jim Brown needs to be understood. That means the whole of his legacy. All the lessons are there if we have the courage to examine them.

Most of Jim Brown's contemporaries have fallen by the wayside. Either they have chosen silence or silence has chosen them. But along the way, they have stopped fighting. Jim Brown has not. He's still here: the last man standing.

# ONE

# MAN OF STEEL
# (THE SUPERMAN TRAP)

—

That Jim Brown . . . He says he isn't Superman. What he
really means is that Superman isn't Jimmy Brown!
—*Anonymous opponent of Jim Brown's,*
*who, like most, failed to tackle him*

*You are Dave Meggyesy, a second-year linebacker in 1964 for the
NFL's St. Louis Cardinals. You are six feet, two inches, and weigh
215 pounds. You make $9,500 a year. In the off-season, like a couple
of your teammates, you work in a quarry, breaking rocks to make ends
meet. This week, you are playing the Cleveland Browns. That means
Jim Brown. That means a guy who ran for more than 1,800 yards last
year. These are the days before film study, highlight packages, and even
color television. That means you've heard the stories about Jim Brown—
hell, you even went to Syracuse, as he did, where you heard all kinds of
stories—but you've never seen him in the flesh and on the field. You are
starting to think his on-field exploits are just whispered ghost stories
aimed at scaring young linebackers. You know that he outweighs you by*

*fifteen pounds, but whatever. You're an NFL linebacker. That means you bring the pain, no one brings it to you. Then Jim Brown takes the field and you have to make an effort not to gasp. It's not the size of Brown but the proportions. He's as skinny as a wide receiver in the waist, with all of those 230 pounds in his shoulders and thighs. "He's just a man," you tell yourself. "Just a man." On the first series, Cleveland quarterback Frank Ryan pitches the ball to Brown, who plants his foot and cuts it inside.*

*You see it happening as if in slow motion. You are ready. You slip the tight end and mirror his cut inside to meet Jim Brown head-on, and you hit him. You don't just hit him—you really hit him. You put your head down and aim for the center mass, right in between the 3 and the 2 on his chest. Then you black out. When you open your eyes, your vision has narrowed for some reason. Everything is round and you have no peripheral vision. You can't breathe out of your nose. Disorientation reigns. What the hell just happened? Then you realize: you are looking out the earhole of your helmet, your nose all mushed up against the side of the damn thing. Later, when describing Jim Brown, you can only smile and shrug and say, "He didn't run over me. He ran through me."*

**IT IS A SHORT LIST: ATHLETES WHO WERE LEGENDARY ON** the field of play and then brave enough to risk the ensuing idolatry for a higher purpose. Muhammad Ali was able to turn the world of sports on its head politically only because he had already staked his claim to greatness by upsetting the unbeatable champion, Sonny Liston. Billie Jean King was as principled a political person as we've seen in sports, but her platform was erected on top of thirty-nine Grand Slam titles and the defeat of Bobby Riggs in the Battle of the Sexes match at the Houston Astrodome. LeBron James's recent political statements in support of the Black Lives Matter movement—even if they are less politically bracing than the stinging words and actions of former San Francisco 49ers quarterback Colin Kaepernick—have so much weight precisely because James has cemented his place as one of the finest basketball players to ever live.

To understand how Jim Brown was able to make such an enduring political impact, we have to first understand the awe he inspired inside the lines.

From the moment he stepped onto a playing field, the operative emotion expressed in describing Jim Brown has been reverence. To be clear, that's "playing field," not "football field." In a remarkable variety of sports, Brown dominated, a man among boys. He could drop fifty points in a Division I college basketball game or come in fifth in the National Collegiate Athletic Association track-and-field decathlon without training for any of the events—and was asked to consider competing in that grueling series of ten contests at the 1956 Olympics. He received a request to join the New York Yankees without ever having played baseball and was sent a letter from their manager, Casey Stengel, pleading with him to just give it a try. He never boxed but was offered what was at the time a hefty contract to train for a heavyweight championship bout. One news report from 1957 makes an offhand comment about Jim Brown's remarkable skills at cricket.

But Brown holds another distinction that puts him in the conversation as the greatest athlete of the last one hundred years:

he alone is discussed as the "best of all time" in two separate sports, football and lacrosse. Upon Brown's induction into the Lacrosse Hall of Fame, his old Syracuse lacrosse coach, Roy Simmons, Sr.—a man who had seen decades of players at one of the most storied programs in NCAA history—argued that "Jimmy" was the greatest he had ever coached. Brown himself insists that track-and-field Olympic legend and early football star Jim Thorpe is the top athlete to have played multiple sports. A strong case can also be made for Mildred "Babe" Didrikson, who dominated track and field as well as golf to absurd degrees and could also throw a baseball past Babe Ruth. But Brown, in two major team sports and with a plethora of competition, distinguished himself in a way that still provokes slack-jawed wonder from those who witnessed him in action. This reputation, particularly in lacrosse, was built during a time when most games were neither filmed nor televised. This gives the stories about his ability a Paul Bunyan quality—elders in a room will talk in hushed tones, as if around a campfire. In 1984, when he inducted Brown into the National Lacrosse Hall of Fame, Coach Simmons spoke with *New York Times* columnist George Vecsey about the 1957 college all-star game, and recalled that Brown "scored one goal underhanded with his right hand, one overhanded with his right, one underhanded with his left, one overhanded with his left. There was nobody like him."

In May 1955, Brown's lacrosse team played against Cornell, whose goalie was the late, great sportswriter Dick Schaap. The *Cornell Chronicle* recounted this game upon Schaap's death in 2001: "On May 18, 1955, Syracuse barely beat Cornell, 13–12, scoring the winning goal with about a minute left in double overtime. Syracuse's Jim Brown, who would later become a National Football League legend, scored four goals against Schaap, who made 20 saves in that game."

Schaap, when asked about Brown, said that just because he saved some of Brown's shots, it "doesn't mean that [he] ever saw the ball."

Schaap's son Jeremy, a bestselling author and ESPN journalist, remembered that his father hated playing goalie when Syracuse was the opponent because he was terrified of Brown, as were most people who played against him. Jeremy Schaap said, "Jim Brown was invoked regularly by my dad as the greatest athlete ever. The toughest man in the world."

Famed sports sociologist Dr. Harry Edwards described the way Brown's size and easy grace transfixed his opponents: "The first time that I ever saw him play was in 1965 against San Francisco. I was absolutely astonished at the reaction of the San Francisco 49ers when Jim Brown took the field to stretch before the game. *Everybody* stopped what they were doing, and turned and looked to the end zone at the other end of the field, and the people in the stadium, who were in their seats for the pregame warm-ups, literally stood up. You stand up for two kinds of people in the United States: when the president comes in the room, and when legends appear in this country. So I looked at that, and I said, 'Wow. Already legend.'"

The media during Brown's athletic prime could not contain their purple prose when watching him perform. Their tributes are fascinating to read today, and not only because they are so effusive. In the eyes of the mainstream media—white male journalists—the only way to describe someone with the speed and grace of Brown was by comparing him to an animal. As *Sports Illustrated*'s Tex Maule wrote in 1958, "Jim is a quiet, relaxed human being off the field. In repose, the magnificent body looks loose, the heavy muscles bulging even at rest, the impression he gives one of a great hunting cat asleep in the sun."

Then, with an air of pleasant surprise, Maule said of the college graduate, "He is not talkative, but he is an articulate young man who understands the technique of running with the football and is able to explain it." This astonishment could be because earlier in the piece, Maule described Brown as having "the shoulders of a Miura bull and a 30-inch waist." Sportswriter Bert Sugar said that if he had tried to tackle Brown, Brown would have "dragged me like a plough horse."

Even from the typewriter of the legendary *New York Times* sports columnist Red Smith, who had the sense to eschew comparisons to livestock, we get a description that evokes a respect tinged with terror. Smith wrote, "For mercurial speed, airy nimbleness and explosive violence in one package of undistilled evil, there is no other like Mr. Brown."

With that same combination of fear and bedazzlement, *Time* magazine called him "a fire-breathing, chocolate-colored monster." Brown, armed with a keen intellect, was very aware that this kind of objectification was part of how he was received by the media and the league's predominantly white fan base. In his 1964 autobiography, *Off My Chest*, coauthored with Myron Cope, he wrote, "Although Cleveland fans consistently received me with more warmth than any ballplayer has a right to expect, I can't help but suspect that they admired me as they would a large piece of sculptured stone or a strong draft horse."

Such beastly prose didn't reside just in the distant past. A magazine profile published in 1986, when Brown was fifty, described him as a "sleeping lion" that could awaken and strike at a moment's notice. This appealed to Brown's masculine ego in late middle age. He said wryly, "The old lion is still a bad mother. He just wants to roam. Leave him alone. He's fading, but he's still a lion."

Yet for black journalists and fans, the animal comparisons were not the descriptors of choice. Even though they felt the same awe and spoke of his body as being carved from marble, the point of comparison was not something from a farm or the African savanna. Over and over, so often it is uncanny, the comparison was instead to Superman. In 1992, the black newspaper *Atlanta Daily World* named Brown the best football player to ever live, "the closest thing we will ever see to Superman in this life."

A 1965 article in *The Chicago Defender* put it this way: "Those 17-inch biceps, that 47-inch chest and that 32-inch waist. Superman? Well, not quite. James Nathaniel Brown, 29, fullback of the National Football League's Champion Cleveland Browns, cannot leap over the Empire State Building—or even stop bullets with his chest. But it is sheer nonsense to try to convince the practitioners and patrons of pro football that Jimmy Brown is an ordinary mortal. After nine seasons in the league, Brown is regarded as a genuine phenomenon in a sport that shares the language."

Dr. Harry Edwards, alluding to a star of the moment, Carolina Panthers quarterback Cam Newton, says, "I laugh when I see these guys run into the end zone and all of a sudden pretend like they are opening up their shirt to show the Superman logo. They have no more idea what it means to have literally been mythologized, lionized as Superman, than I do about flying a space shuttle. If you want to go back and really get a sense of Superman in football, go back and study the life, the legend, the mythology surrounding Jim Brown."

Superman is a striking, bracingly evocative name for black men to use when describing Brown. One reason is obviously the absence of black superheroes in the mid-twentieth-century world of comics, but it runs deeper than that. First, and foremost, Superman is a figure of unvarnished patriotism: "truth, justice, and the American way." This has always been an interpretation of Jim Brown—and how Jim Brown has interpreted himself: that he was not a "revolutionary" in the sense of wanting to dismantle the system, but instead was fighting for the black community to have access to the American Dream. This is why sportswriter Mike Freeman subtitled his Brown biography *The Fierce Life of an American Hero* and Spike Lee titled his documentary *Jim Brown: All-American*. As Dr. Robert Bennett, who wrote his dissertation about the Black Economic Unions that Brown launched in the 1960s to promote black-owned businesses, says, "Unlike some Black Nationalists, he embraced the notion of being an American. He didn't distance himself from it. But when a black man embraces that he's an American, he can still face rejection by the broader society, whether he's an NFL player or not."

Perhaps this desire to achieve full citizenship is why the Man of Steel moniker is apt, beyond the obvious associations with Brown's musculature and speed. Superman was created in 1933 by writer Jerry Siegel and artist Joe Shuster, two men who were the children of immigrants. They were young Jews, outcasts in the North America of eighty years ago (Shuster was born in Toronto), and Superman was at heart an assimilationist fantasy. Clark Kent was the nebbishy, awkward Jewish stereotype, brainy but with the coordination of a puppet cut from its strings—more hapless than heroic. But beneath the surface, he was handsome, strong, and the avatar of all things American. It was a tale of acceptance earned through excellence.

Brown, too, believed that individual excellence could be a path toward assimilation. He was attractive and intelligent, and he knew how to speak the language of business entrepreneurship. If he couldn't make it, then who the hell could? Even if those who called him Superman did not know about Shuster and Siegel, there is that idea of needing to be "super" to overcome being the inherent outsider. Brown spoke to this when he said in an interview, "I came up at the crossroads of segregation. . . . It was a blessing on the one hand because there were opportunities, but it was demeaning because you were still looked on as inferior. It was almost as if you'd been given a *favor*. And you always felt you had to perform much, much better."

Yet Brown's legend was about more than assimilation. Former NBA player Etan Thomas says that what makes Jim Brown "Superman" in his eyes is "what he represents: strength, courage, stubbornness, rebelliousness, pride." Brown, according to Thomas, "commands respect even from people who don't agree with his particular stance, unwillingness to be reduced to a clown used only to entertain someone's circus."

Another reason Brown inspired people to reach for the

Superman comparison was that he had the ability to expand the horizon of what people believed athletes could do. His dominance as a black athlete in a segregated country, and in a sports world where teams established quotas for black players, held a political vitality all its own. This was true for football. It was even more true in the world of lacrosse. Black people simply did not—and in many places still rarely—play lacrosse. It was, in Brown's time, an athletic endeavor found either only at prep schools or on Native American reservations. Brown would travel to elite colleges, stick in hand, and leave the field with bodies strewn in his wake. Then he would go to the nearby Onondaga reservation with Syracuse goalie Oren Lyons, a future chief in the Six Nations Iroquois Confederacy, and test himself in an altogether different way. In a 2011 *Sports Illustrated* article on Onondaga lacrosse, journalist S. L. Price wrote, "On the reservation they remember the pickup game in 1957 in which the 155-pound Irving Powless, a future chief, sent the 230-pound . . . Brown tumbling with a brutally precise hip check. 'Brown never left his feet the rest of the day,' [teammate Roy Simmons, Jr.] says. 'He just destroyed them.'"

Brown was bigger, faster, and stronger than anyone the sport of lacrosse had ever seen by a ludicrous margin. It left the established minders of the sport at a loss for words, like having Adele show up at a local bar for some karaoke. In a 1956 article, Gardner Mallonnee, a former Johns Hopkins All-American and coach, said, "Brown is the greatest lacrosse player I've ever seen." Charles Clark, president of the United States Intercollegiate Lacrosse Association, shared that sentiment: "I've never seen a better lacrosse player. It's amazing that a man with his size can be not only so fast but so graceful. The way he whirls and dodges is unbelievable."

One teammate, Roy Simmons, Jr., said that playing lacrosse with Brown "was unique. No one in our sport back then—and perhaps even now—had the size or the physical strength that he had, being six-two and 230 pounds and quick like lightning. But you can't just be a big, quick guy. He also had stick skills. Coming from Long Island, he probably had a stick in his hand even before he had a football in his hands."

NFL linebacker Dave Meggyesy, who arrived at Syracuse after Brown, recalled, "His legend on campus was more as a lacrosse player than [for] football! They would talk about how he had these tight shorts and he'd go down the field, cradling the ball, and the guys would be bouncing off of his massive thighs, and he'd throw it in the goal. That was 'The Legend of Jim Brown' at Syracuse. People said, 'Yeah, he was a great football player, great, but man, you should have seen this guy play lacrosse!'"

There are more than a few quotes from young "Jimmy" Brown that implied he loved lacrosse even more than football. He said such things as: "It sure is a swell game. It's a lot more fun than football overall because lacrosse practices are so much fun whereas football practice is hard work." But today he will only profess equal love for both sports.

Brown dominated lacrosse at a moment when it was transforming from an almost exclusively Native American sport to the status sport of choice at prep schools across the country. He also dominated football as it was undergoing its own transition, moving from a second-tier sport to the country's number-one pastime, thanks to television. And as the game blossomed, Jim Brown was its most dominant force.

The workload given to Brown boggles the mind, especially in an NFL that today eschews every-down running backs and rightfully frets over prematurely ruining young backs with excessive carries. The titular coach and general manager of his team, Paul Brown, had an offense entirely built around Jim Brown running the ball. "[Coach Brown] didn't like to pass," Jim told an interviewer in 1981. "The rest of the league had moved to a balanced game, but there was no bend in him at all. The Browns believed I couldn't be hurt, at least not bad enough not to play, just like everybody else believed. It was that old game, people takin' the best of your ass and leavin' the rest."

Yet despite the abuse, Brown remains razor-sharp between his ears. The road map for how he's been able to hold on to his faculties can be found on those scars on his forearms. Many football players who reach Brown's age have found their brain functions to have slowed dramatically. What used to be called "getting punchy" or "having your bell rung" is now known as the devastating post-concussive syndrome chronic traumatic encephalopathy (CTE). But Jim Brown is still crisply intelligent, and it may have something to do with those scarred arms and the massive hands that are now unable to squeeze hard enough to turn a doorknob. As a runner of unprecedented strength, Brown did not, as many running backs have done before and since, lead with his head. As he described it a few years into his nine-year tenure with the Cleveland Browns, "When a tackler closes in I counteract his force with two blows: one with my shoulder, the other with my free arm. I do not ram him with my head, but I do tuck my body lower to gather my strength. First I knock him off balance with my corresponding shoulder (right against right, left against left). Then I deliver a full, powerful blow with my forearm, aiming it for his chest or midsection." This has saved him from the assorted brain diseases that we now know to be an occupational hazard of playing football. He was ahead of his time in understanding that leading with your head could be catastrophic for your health. In a 1968 interview he criticized players who used their heads as battering rams, calling it an "invitation to disaster" that could "leave you unhinged."

Brown did it his own way, and the Cleveland organization gave him the space to do that from day one. NFL teams have always been notorious for hazing first-year players. As Rick Sortun, who played with the St. Louis Cardinals, said, "The code was, 'If you can't say something nice about a rookie, then speak up!'" The most supportive comment from veterans usually involves helping a player who just had his ass thoroughly kicked and saying, "Welcome to the league, rook." But there was no rocky transition period for Jim Brown, as veterans kept a wary distance. After Brown's first season, 1957, when he led the league in rushing with 942 yards and won the Rookie of the Year and Most Valuable Player awards, Philadelphia Eagles coach Alfred Earle "Greasy" Neale called him "the best power runner in pro football history." The next season Brown was again named MVP after rushing for 1,527 yards in a twelve-game season. (Number two was Baltimore Colt Alan Ameche with 791 yards, slightly over half of Brown's total.) He was just twenty-two years old. It was the second of his three MVP awards over the next eight seasons.

A particular criticism is often used to knock Jim Brown and assert that he is not in fact the greatest football player in history—call it the "Wilt Chamberlain argument." It argues that just as there were few seven-footers in Wilt's day, which accounts for his absurd statistical production, Brown's physical dominance would not translate to today's game, when so many linebackers and defensive lineman are also big, fast, and heavily muscled. When asked about this critique, Brown will throw a look your way, as if you are one of his pet pit bulls and had just piddled on the floor. "People who say that really are showing that they have no idea the caliber of players we had on the field in a league where we were only playing against twelve other teams," he says. "It was the best of the best." He will then name a series of players in his day who were just as big and fast as today's NFL stars, and without the benefit of weight training and nutritional supplements. It is also worth pointing out that a man with his size, speed, pain threshold, and ability to ceaselessly inflict punishment is going to be an athletic freak in any era. But it is also undeniable that being a running back who was physically larger than just about any linebacker in the league was something that had never been seen before and—with the exception of sideshow short-yardage runners like William "The Refrigerator" Perry—is unlikely we will ever see it again.

Brown also faced a series of disadvantages on the field, which make his numbers all the more remarkable. As Gale Sayers, a legendary running back in his own right with the Chicago Bears, said, "Jim ran from a split backfield where you started from about three yards behind the line of scrimmage. He didn't have the luxury of starting from seven yards deep and the advantage that gives you in picking your holes. He was that rare player who combined all the talents desired in a running back. He moved with speed and he also had the power to run over defenders."

With just nine years in the league, and playing only twelve games per season, Brown held records for yards gained in a single season—1,863 in 1963—and a career rushing number—12,312 yards—that lasted for two decades. They endured until a time when the NFL had moved to a sixteen-game season. His record of 126 total touchdowns remained the standard for decades until Marcus Allen broke it in 1994, in his thirteenth season. His record for all-purpose yards, like his rushing mark, was broken twenty years later by the Chicago Bears' Walter Payton.

But it's the stories surrounding his play that animate those sterile statistics. When Detroit Lions tackle Alex Karras was asked how to stop Brown, he said, "Give each guy in the line an ax."

Sam Huff, the Hall of Fame linebacker, commented, "Nothing short of gang warfare is sure to stop Brown. All you can do is grab hold, hang on and wait for help."

As one writer put it, "Lord help the defensive back. At the instant of impact, Jimmy dips a shoulder, slams it into his opponent's pads, and crosses either with a straight arm to the helmet or a clubbing forearm directed at a lower and presumably more tender portion of the anatomy."

But Brown said that despite his physical advantages, he spent most of his time on the mental aspect of the sport. "My game pivoted on having planned ahead of time every move I intended to make on the field. The nine years I was in pro ball, I never quit trying to make my mind an encyclopedia of every possible detail—about my teammates, about players on other teams, about the plays we used, about plays I knew *they* used and about both our and other teams' collective and individual tendencies."

Our footage today of Brown tends to be grainy, filmed from one camera angle. We need descriptions from the witnesses because it is impossible to really grasp what he could do. Dave Meggyesy describes what it was like to play against him in this fashion: "He had such smoothness and grace, it felt at times that he was just running *through* people. He had what I can only think to call 'the strength of grace.' The strength of graceful movement. It's a seeming oxymoron. And so, you would tackle him and he'd always get up the same way."

Excepting the one full season played by Raiders running back Bo Jackson, nobody has been as effusively complimented as Brown for his speed as well as his power. How many players can get such reviews as "He's the only player I know who can run faster sideways than he can straight ahead," alongside comments like "He had the strength of a three-hundred-and-fifty-pound man. If he set his mind and decided he wasn't going to fall down, then he wasn't going to fall down"? Brown once said, not as a boast but as a fact, "My philosophy as a fullback is that five eighty-yard runs in one game are not beyond reach."

This is why, as the expression went, third-and-nine was not a passing down in Cleveland.

The NFL play of Jim Brown's day was dirty as hell. It was not uncommon to have players kicked in the face or kneed in the groin. The bottom of the tackling pile in those days is talked about like a particularly gory Turkish prison. All sorts of things took place on the field that, if they occurred today, would probably lead to a congressional inquiry. Despite the violence and targeting of the tender parts of his body unprotected by muscle or bone, Brown persevered.

Accordingly, one statistic—zero games missed—fills Brown with the most pride. It has allowed him for decades to claim a place not only as a great runner but also as the ultimate badass to be respected: to be "the man." As he said after retiring, "If you come to hurt me and you cannot hurt me, then I have won. . . . My physicality was not being physical for the sake of being physical. It's to inflict pain. . . . Everything is attitude."

Brown's attitude on the field was one of obfuscation. Every time he was knocked down, he made a point to get off the ground in the same gingerly manner and then trudge back to the huddle so, in the words of Hall of Famer Willie Davis, "you didn't know if he was hurt or not."

Now that Brown is eighty-two years old and holding a cane, the macho posturing has surrendered itself, taking the form more of philosophy than braggadocio. When asked in 2014 how he was able to stay healthy and never miss a game, he said, "I don't know. That's an extension of what I've been in my entire time on this earth. No one's going to violate my life. I tell people I don't miss nothing. I take care of everything—body, mind—that I have to take care of. I don't know how to relate how I do that. Being lucky helps. You never know when something crazy can happen, but you have to be in shape."

He also believes, as someone who still goes to the Cleveland Browns training camp to walk among the players, that today's athletes could stand to make some of their own luck. "Players today get hurt too easily. And some of them are fat. I'd say seventy-five percent of them are fat. The player that is two hundred and eighty once was two hundred and twenty. What's that about? They've changed the rules, so now you got these sumo wrestlers up front. They're not throwing a passable block in pro football today. What they do is not blocking, not even close. They just run and push people. They don't make any real contact, they just get in the way."

Brown's ability to run inside and outside—power and speed— would make him naturally averse to today's lumbering, space-eating offensive lineman. This is seen clearly on the two greatest individual efforts of Brown's professional career. On two separate days, Brown ran for 237 yards and four touchdowns. Both games are available in only the grittiest possible film footage, but they still evince what made Brown so singular: the combination of speed and power. These 237-yard totals stood as the Cleveland team record for fifty-two years.

The first game was on November 24, 1957, a 45–31 win against the Los Angeles Rams at Cleveland Stadium. One of his runs was a 69-yard touchdown where Brown took a draw from behind the line of scrimmage and was immediately hit so solidly in the chest by a blitzing linebacker that the guy's helmet popped right off his head. It gives the appearance that Brown's chest was actually stronger than the helmet. After the defender fell in a heap, Brown spun outside and was then simply faster than everyone else on the field. One defensive back, pursuing from an especially advantageous angle, caught up to Brown and tore at his neck as they approached the goal line. Brown's head snapped back violently, but he never fell down, and entered the end zone standing up.

On November 19, 1961, Brown carried the ball thirty-four times for 237 yards against Philadelphia as Cleveland beat the Eagles 45–24. The Eagles had a tough defense, and the win by Cleveland moved them into a tie with Philly for first place. He had four touchdown runs of one, two, three, and eight yards. The two-yard touchdown involved running through people. The three-yard run around the left end created the appearance of someone who, as reported in the Cleveland *Plain Dealer*, "loafed into the end zone with no Eagle within 5 yards."

Today, Brown cannot physically shake his head anymore because of a racquetball injury that exacerbated the wear and tear from football, but he is able to affect the motion. He feels a sense of disgust about the fitness and desire of today's players. Brown has earned that disgust because he not only never missed a game, but also did the ultimate Superman move, walking away from the sport at twenty-nine, in his prime. He didn't limp and he didn't stumble. He walked.

Leaving the NFL on his own terms is another aspect of his mystique. Meggyesy retired from the NFL in his prime in 1969 as an act of protest against the dehumanizing effects of playing in the league. He also believed that football desensitized the U.S. public to violence, particularly the violence taking place in the Vietnam War. Seeing Brown take that step away from the game had a deep effect on Meggyesy. "Jim was the only guy that I knew who quit at the peak of his career voluntarily," he says. "And when he did that, I looked at Jim Brown and thought, 'Hey, that could be a guidepost for me.' . . . What Jim told me is, 'Look, you leave this game as your own choice, of your own volition.' And I said that when I left the NFL, that's what I wanted to do: to leave on my terms, not on their terms. He quit after nine years at the peak of his career. I walked away after seven years at the top of my career. But the whole idea was, I'm gonna leave on my terms."

DeMaurice Smith, the NFL Players Association executive director, says, "Jim is one of the few people that I know of who back in the day actually retired. Not the guys who couldn't play anymore. The guys who could play, but for whatever reason said, 'You know what, I'm done.' Who has done that among running backs? You have Barry Sanders and Jim Brown. To have the wherewithal to say, 'I don't need what you love about this game. I don't need your cheers, I don't need your money, I don't need your adulation.' There's power in that."

There is also power in how Jim Brown retired, saying, "My first year I was Rookie of the Year. My last I was MVP. I did football."

Brown's retirement also cut far deeper than that of Barry Sanders, who left the Detroit Lions in 1999, because of the political motivations and personal ambitions that drove Brown to say goodbye.

Dr. Mark Anthony Neal, an author and academic, says, "Jim Brown ultimately becomes a stand-in for the ultimate feared black male, particularly after Malcolm got killed. Brown created confusion. 'What do we do with this big black man who's not just physically strong, but who clearly has the kind of mental capacity that, even if we've seen it before, we've never had to deal with it up close?' There were no scripts to deal with a figure like Jim Brown. And the fact that he walks off the football field at age twenty-nine crushed the narrative of so many black athletes before him: that you literally die on the field. If you're Joe Louis or Sugar Ray Robinson, once you leave the ring, you have no life left. Jim Brown went against all those expectations. Even Ali stayed in the ring way too long. Jim Brown wasn't about that life."

For young members of a civil rights movement that was barreling north and becoming more urban, it was an act of nonconformity that heightened his legend. Author, academic, and cultural critic Dr. Michael Eric Dyson said the retirement cemented Brown in his mind as "a Greek god in African skin with a free mind."

Several years ago, Brown took out his black Bentley, put the top down, and descended the steep two-mile hill in West Hollywood, on his way to a cocktail party. He rode down Sunset Boulevard, his gleaming bald head sticking up for all to see. Some young-white-executive types gawked and shouted, "Mr. Brown! Mr. Brown!" He looked straight ahead, paying them absolutely no mind. Nonetheless, they stared and bowed repeatedly, mouthing, "We're not worthy!"

Somehow Jim Brown caught all this in his peripheral vision. He said, "Shit. I'm not Superman. I'm a man. Recognize me as a man. Not a damn Superman." Those people on the side, if they'd been in the backseat of the car, would probably have whispered to each other what that anonymous NFL player said so many years ago: "That's exactly what Superman would say."

# TWO

# THE BOY THEY CALLED MAN

—

*You are Syracuse football coach Ben Schwartzwalder. You are a legend. You fought in the Battle of the Bulge and came out the other end still spitting chaw and kicking ass. You love your team and you love your school. You get an adrenaline shiver similar to the best times in World War II when you hear people call Syracuse "Schwartzwalder University."*

*Now there is a nettlesome pressure starting to build to bring Negroes onto the team. There is a civil rights movement brewing in the South, but that doesn't enter your thinking a lick. The problem is more that your competitors are starting to sign Negro high school stars, and all the boosters and candy-ass alumni think you're going to be left behind. With gritted teeth, you tried to integrate the team with a hotshot young quarterback named Avatus Stone, and all your fears came to pass. This Stone fellow wore flashy suits, talked back to you, and for some reason even thought he could date some of the school's beautiful white coeds. You made sure Avatus Stone was out of Syracuse—and fast. You thought the Orangemen were done with Negro players for at least a few years. Let 'em go to the Negro schools. But now a running back from Long Island who averaged fifteen yards a carry in high school wants to play on your team. A respected alum with power and pull is pushing hard for the young man. Fuck him. You can't stop this kid from being admitted to the school, but you'll be damned if he gets a football scholarship. Surely he won't come without a free ride. And if he does, he's going to learn who the boss man is mighty fast. "I try to coach my players as if they are my own children," you like to say, "and a dad has to be tough with his kids once in a while. They have to get spanked." Let's see what happens when this young man from Long Island with the powerful friends shows up without a scholarship and gets spanked. He'll run back home and pick up a mop. "Schwarzwald" means "Black Forest" in German. When Negro players run into the Black Forest, they don't come out the other side. This one won't be any different.*

**JIM BROWN MAY BE COMPARED TO SUPERMAN, BUT THE** story of his childhood and upbringing does not read like any sort of DC Universe origin story. It is a critical road map, however, to understanding how he became the first modern athlete of the twentieth century, as well as how he came to write the intoxicating and toxic script on manhood for a generation of people.

James Nathaniel Brown was born in 1936 in the Gullah

region of St. Simons Island, Georgia. It is immediately striking that the boy who became an avatar of manhood spent the
first eight years of his life being raised by women. Brown's care-
givers were his great-grandmother, grandmother, and aunt. He
earned his nickname "Man" because of his size and the serious
manner in which he handled himself even as an infant. When
Brown was a baby, his teenage mother, Teresa Brown, took a
job as a domestic worker up north, with plans to someday send
for her son. His father, Swinton "Sweet Sue" Brown, was a
part-time fighter and a hustler, a rolling stone who would come
in and out of Teresa's life, much to Jim's rage. There is precious
little information available about Swinton Brown, but we know
that he was built like the man his son would become: over six
feet tall and 230 pounds. Unlike his son, he was known for
a big, charming smile and having the gift of gab. Jim speaks
in measured sentences. Swinton Brown was garrulous, with,
as sportswriter Mike Freeman put it, the "persuasive demeanor
all good street hustlers possess." Jim Brown as a young man
was also handsome, but no one would ever think to call him
"cute." His facial features strongly resemble those of his mother,
Teresa. Swinton Brown was most definitely cute, and his ability to charm women was never an issue. Sweet Sue left only
weeks after his son's birth; time would pass before they again
saw each other. Upon his father's death decades later, the close-
lipped Brown would go out of his way to tell reporters that he
had not attended his funeral and held no regrets about the
decision.

St. Simons is one of a string of coastal barrier islands that
stretch from the Santee River in South Carolina to the St. Johns

River in Florida. Before the Civil War, it was dominated by mammoth cotton plantations where enslaved Africans vastly outnumbered white owners. The swampy environs were seen as unsuitable for wealthy white planters and slavers. Within ten years of the end of the war, this type of large-scale farming had been completely abandoned as the plantation economy collapsed and the' few whites on the island left. Former slaves remained and subsisted on food from small garden plots as well as the free-grazing livestock for approximately the next sixty years. The island was, for all practical purposes, theirs. Consequently, it was an area that, as bell hooks has written, "kept alive African cultural retentions that also offered a subculture distinct from the culture imposed by whiteness." The word "Gullah" is thought by some to derive from "Angola"—the departure point for many enslaved Africans.

Brown's grandmother worked the land, and the family ate what was farmed. It was not subsistence living. It was a life of abundance: perhaps not material abundance but an abundance of food, love, and affection. Games were not played under the watchful eye of male authority figures, but rather organized by the children of St. Simons themselves.

Brown remembers this time in his life with an infectious joy. These memories also dovetail neatly with Brown's politics of self-determination and black self-reliance. The natural, over-grown terrain of St. Simons was not an easy place for wealthy outsiders to conquer. It was rough living for some, but a place of lush, verdant beauty for those who lived in its wooded marsh-lands. Descriptions of the islands in the late nineteenth century sound like something out of magical realism. Sidney Lanier, a onetime Confederate soldier, wrote the poem cycle *Hymns of the Marshes* in tribute to St. Simons:

> *In my sleep I was fain of their fellowship, fain*
> *Of the live-oak, the marsh, and the main.*
> *The little green leaves would not let me alone in my sleep;*
> *Up-breathed from the marshes, a message of range and of sweep,*
> *Interwoven with waftures of wild sea-liberties, drifting,*
> *Came through the lapped leaves sifting, sifting,*
> *Came to the gates of sleep.*
> *Then my thoughts, in the dark of the dungeon-keep*
> *Of the Castle of Captives hid in the City of Sleep,*
> *Upstarted, by twos and by threes assembling:*
> *The gates of sleep fell a-trembling*
> *Like as the lips of a lady that forth falter "Yes,"*
> *Shaken with happiness:*
> *The gates of sleep stood wide.*

Yet "progress" would not be held back. Resort developers in the twentieth century saw these islands and envisioned a pot of gold. Fencing-in the black community was a literal process in the St. Simons of the 1920s with the passing of "fence laws." These laws effectively ended the raising of livestock in the black community of St. Simons and eroded independence, as the cows and hogs now had to be confined to pens so they would not graze on the luxury golf courses and country clubs being developed. These land restrictions, which undermined the decades-long tradition of collective subsistence farming, likewise created a large "free" labor pool to work in the burgeoning resort industry. The Brown family, against all odds, were holdouts, trying to live off the land and maintain their old ways.

The first big resort on the islands opened in 1928, which was the same year that the first Pentecostal proselytizers arrived to build a network of storefront churches. The Brown family attended these services, but no matter the passion of the preachers, they did not have a pull on young Jimmy Brown. As he said, "Most of the people in our church were Baptist and accordingly emotional. They'd faint and scream and cry and fan those fans. I'd grin when no one was looking."

Even as the landscape changed dramatically, the original African culture and rural life was maintained, which left an imprint on Brown. A 1931 article in the Topeka, Kansas, *Plaindealer* said of St. Simons, "Islanders have had only transient contact with the New World. They've continued to farm their little gardens, to fish, to haul lumber, on their own. They hold their church meetings and have their peculiar little separate villages; frequently they continue living in the old 'tabby' quarters of their ancestors. Some of them are still living in these 'tabby' buildings, which are solid as concrete of today although built a century and a half ago."

St. Simons is, in every respect, Jim Brown's "Rosebud." Like the boyhood sled that Charles Foster Kane saw as a symbol of his lost innocence and a parallel upbringing that could have brought humble fulfillment instead of legend status, St. Simons is Jim Brown's path not taken.

Emotional distance and pain have defined so many of

Brown's relationships, most centrally with his parents and the three children he raised with his first wife, Sue. To this day, he will discuss these relationships only in the most halting terms, saying, "I have my regrets . . . I could have been there more," and leaving you to read the shadow that flickers over his impassive face. Yet Brown's tone differs in the description he wrote of his boyhood home later in life: "I've never felt more love than I did as a child on St. Simons Island. The black folks on the island would watch out for their neighbors, share food. Someone would roast a bunch of oysters on a piece of tin roof, then pass the word to invite people by. . . . People would always save me some [food] even if I was out playing."

It's no mystery why Brown spent a lot of time outside, considering that where he lived was, as he wrote in *Off My Chest*, "an undiscovered thing of beauty. There were palm trees, fig trees, grapefruit trees, orange trees, pecan trees, and even banana trees—all worthy of climbing. There were moss-hung oak and cypress and cedar and longleaf pine and magnolia. . . . I could sit by the ocean and watch the porpoise roll in the surf and count the sandcrabs scurrying across the beach. Or I could run down the dirt roads into the dark woods and murky marshland and come upon crystal clear ponds for swimming and diving. In the ponds were alligator bones that enabled us kids to perpetuate—for our own excitement—the tales of alligators still roaming the island."

While his mother was Teresa Brown and his father "Sweet Sue," he was raised by Nora Peterson, his great-grandmother. The plan was for Teresa to someday send for her son, but she said that she wouldn't see "Man" until she was in a stable position and able to make it work. That took eight years.

Nora Peterson was, like her great-grandson, a physically imposing person. She was big on sweets and hugs and would wrap Jim in her pillowy arms. She made him feel safe, and though she called him "Man," he had his own nickname for her: "Mama." Of his own mother, he said, "I was never able to bring myself to call her mama. Mama was my great-grandmother, down on St. Simons. I didn't know what to call my mother. . . . This hurt her, I know. But in a way, I had two mothers, and mama had gotten there first. . . . She was all I had, and I was all she had."

Baby Jim Brown, "Mama," Aunt Bertha Powell, and his grandmother Myrtle Powell made a home. They lived together in a sturdy one-story house: three strong women and one little man. When Brown was forty-five, he spoke of his great-grandmother with heartbreaking affection. "She would say, 'I love you forever,'" he remembered, "and for as long as I was on St. Simons, there was always the ocean and the white sand, and there was never a question of belonging."

Brown may recall St. Simons romantically, but he takes pains to not romanticize the racialized poverty that marked his early years. In his autobiographies he wrote, "On St. Simons Island we weren't allowed to enter the only theater to see a movie. Our water fountains were trickly. . . . Our black school sat in the backwoods. It was basically a shack divided into two rooms. . . . I didn't use the word racism, but I knew when I didn't like something. . . . As a small boy I could throw a stone from the beach and hit Sea Island, the famous resort where millionaires go to golf and sunbathe. . . . When did I first feel racism? I felt it when I was a baby. I sensed the apprehension of the women in my family. By the way they held me, whispered to me, they seemed to be saying, Son, you have to be careful."

He also experienced what must have been an indelibly traumatic vision of violence, seeing a girl die in front of him. He said, "We used to swim in the goddamned marsh, you know. I don't know what was in there. We'd go out there and do that shit. And one day, one young girl got drowned, dealing with us in one spot. She started rafting and she fell off the raft; I was on the shore. And we couldn't save her, man. They dragged it, found her body. And when I go back, I go out there where that was, just to feel and see and whatever."

Even though he was raised by three generations of women, Brown asserts his manhood stubbornly when talking about St. Simons. He says repeatedly in interviews that he did "not miss having a father" and even admits how he did not miss not having his birth mother. He gives the impression of being entirely self-contained, so solitary that by the time he was seven years old, it wasn't just Mama who called him by his nickname. "The other kids, it's true. They also called me 'Man.'"

His greatest admiration of St. Simons is connected not to family or religion but to the fact that it was home to entire African tribes who, when enslaved, chose a watery grave over bondage. He wrote with awe in his second autobiography, *Out of Bounds*, cowritten with Steve Delsohn: "One of those tribes, the Ibo warriors, were kidnapped to St. Simons Island. Rather than live out their lives as slaves, the Ibo marched into the ocean to their deaths."

At the age of nine, much to Brown's torment, he was summoned by his mother to leave the idyllic all-black surroundings of St. Simons. His new home would be in Great Neck, Long Island, to live out a stormy relationship alongside Teresa Brown, with whom he was still angry for abandoning him—a mother he still refused to call "Mama."

Moving to Great Neck from St. Simons was an indescribable culture shock for young Jimmy Brown. Great Neck had long since made the transformation from farmland to elite Manhattan suburb before Brown's move north. Imagine the rural isolation, segregation, and self-sufficiency of his island. Now picture an area of such affluence that people like F. Scott Fitzgerald and families like the Vanderbilts called it home. He went from Gullah to Gatsby. The wealth, however, meant work for housekeeper Teresa Brown and cramped living quarters atop garages or in guesthouses.

The Browns lived primarily in the servant quarters in the home of the Brockmans, a family Brown remembers fondly. The Brockmans tried to provide a home for Teresa and Jim Brown, but outside that home, it was a difficult adjustment. Brown has spoken about how he was bullied upon arriving in Great Neck because he dressed like a "country boy." The bullying ceased after he beat up a child who said he looked "pretty." Up north, in a white community, "pretty" was almost certainly a homophobic taunt. Yet one has to wonder if Jim heard it differently: "Sweet Sue," he was told, was pretty. Not Jimmy Brown.

Great Neck may have been overwhelmingly white, but it was known for its liberal, civil rights–oriented values. As one local, Martin Sokol, wrote in his review of a book about the town: "Its citizens actively care for the poor and disadvantaged. [With its] reputation as a tolerant, progressive community [Great Neck] actively supported civil rights from the movement's earliest days. Wealthy residents have, through the years, attracted presidential aspirants seeking early financial and political support. . . . [It is] a very wealthy, unique, American town whose residents never stopped caring for those less privileged."

The Manhasset Secondary School was built by the Works Progress Administration under the New Deal, not long before Jim Brown entered its doors. It was a public school attended by children of wealth. While the Manhasset school system has been successful for decades in a variety of athletic pursuits, it's had the most glory, going back for almost a century, in lacrosse. If you go into Manhasset High School today, there are no footballs signed by Jim Brown on display, but there is a lacrosse ball bearing his signature.

Even with all its liberalism, Great Neck had pockets of deep poverty, and for the small black population, residential if not scholastic segregation. Yet it was also nurturing. For young Jimmy Brown, adrift in a new environment, dealing with an absent father and in a state of constant conflict with his young mother, he took intensely to the adults who quickly spotted his combination of quiet intelligence and otherworldly athletic ability. The men who became his substitute fathers were prominent and they were white: football coach Ed Walsh and a judge named Kenneth Molloy.

Walsh was seen as a leader in a Manhasset community that believed it had overcome many racial divisions through the healing powers of integrated, successful sports teams. White city leaders would often highlight how the athletic success of male African-American students united the region. However blind this may have been to the struggles of black students who weren't athletes as well as to the issues faced by black women, Brown was held up proudly as a prime example of their model student-athlete, winning thirteen letters in track and field, football, basketball, baseball, and lacrosse during three years of varsity competition, while also serving as chief judge in the school's honor's court. Despite dalliances with "gangs" that sound more like social clubs than the groups he would work with in later decades, Brown largely stayed on the straight and narrow. Several high school classmates described him as "arrogant," yet this arrogance was a by-product of being the surrogate son of some of the most prominent men in town: men like Ed Walsh.

Coach Walsh first met Brown when he was ten years old. Brown was playing basketball, and as Walsh remembered, "He was this pudgy kid, a fifth-grader, gliding around the court. And I said, 'You know what? He's going to be great.'" Walsh introduced himself to the young man with the idea that this could be someone who would make Manhasset football known across the country.

Walsh was ahead of his time in how he chose to relate to his young players. In this era, a coach's physically manhandling players and raining down verbal assaults to get them to "man up" was not only allowed but encouraged. Yet Walsh was by all accounts a kind and quiet leader. He was 145 pounds—probably less than what Jim Brown weighed in junior high school. His approach was built around "structure and discipline," with respect for his young players and without a bully coach's roar. For all Manhasset's wealth, the football team was where many of the students who lived in poverty congregated. And they loved Coach Walsh.

"The problem was many of the kids did not come from a structured background," Walsh said. "Some came from broken homes with no father, or they had a mother and father who both worked in New York City all day and did not see the kids that much. Some of these kids were practically raising themselves."

Brown needed Walsh in his life because his situation at home was stormy at best. Living in one room with a single mother was a constant source of strain. Fierce fights would break out when Teresa, who was still a young woman, just thirty years old, went out on the town. When Sweet Sue Brown would pop in at intervals, the normal nasty fights between mother and son were replaced by volcanic, even violent encounters between Sweet Sue and Teresa while, as Walsh remembered, "Jim would just sit there in another part of the room and not say a peep."

This stewing anger in young Jim Brown was released through football. On typical teams, the quarterback sets the lead in the huddle. In Manhasset, it was Jimmy Brown. Over three years on varsity, where he averaged more than ten yards every time he carried the ball, it was resolutely his team. One teammate remembered Brown looking at everyone in the huddle and saying, "If you guys don't start blocking for me, I'm going to kick all of your asses. I'm going to climb over your backs. Stop playing like fucking sissies. Start blocking."

Before Walsh, studying was an afterthought for Brown. It is not that he didn't possess the mental faculties to become a solid student—he had them in abundance; it is that Brown had no motivation to care about his own education. Walsh made grades and homework a prerequisite for staying on the team, and Brown, who had been straying back and forth between football and what was then called "juvenile delinquency" as a member of a street gang called the Gaylords (to be clear, "Gaylord" had a very different connotation in 1950), dedicated himself to the classroom and playing sports.

Once committed to athletics, Brown led an outwardly charmed life in Long Island, and people in the community still speak of him in admiring, glowing terms: as a favorite son. This affluent, largely white area showered the son of a housekeeper with love because he was athletically exceptional as well as a living example that they did not hold people back based on the color of their skin. Brown resists this analysis to a degree, saying, "It wasn't just love for me because I was a star athlete, but love for me because, collectively, people took pride in their children. I played basketball on Sundays with the school superintendent and his son. And it was normal."

People "took pride in their children" but that same familial affection was not found in the home of the teenage Jim Brown. Even though he was lavished with love by white coaches and administrators and teammates, as a teen he would "walk the streets at night." He had glory on the field and in the classroom, but not much of a home. He could not stand that his young mother was "messing around" and "dating a lot." He remembers that "gentlemen would come to the house and I wasn't very pleasant. I went to many lengths to see that they wouldn't come. My mother didn't like that. So she told me I could leave." Here Brown breaks into a small smile. "Mom was a swinger just like Dad."

Even though Brown rarely saw his father, he was driven by a sense of competitiveness to be a "better man" than Sweet Sue. He says, "I had all of the built-in excuses, and I told my father, 'You go your way, I'll go mine. You don't need to do nothing for me.' I said, 'Nobody's ever done nothing for me, I don't do nothing for you. I do for me.'"

Around this time, Jim and his mother were staying with a wealthy white family, and young Jim spent long hours alone. When asked if he has any memories of depression during this time, whether he was in deep mental distress, he thinks for a while before answering, rubbing the side of his stubbled face with one of his knotted hands. His face dips and his omnipresent scowl becomes something softer, approaching a frown. He says, "No, not depression. I always say to people that solitude is a treasure. To be able to utilize solitude properly is a great gift. Even today, I can come home and for two hours don't have to bother with the kids and don't have to hear nobody. I go in that bedroom all by myself.

"There's nothing that bothers me, no one trying to talk—so I love it. Solitude is a powerful thing. People who can't use solitude always have to find some kind of bullshit to do. I grew up very independently and even though I got into sports, solitude was my existence. So I grew to be pretty hard to deal with because I don't need much."

He gestures in the direction of his swimming pool and deck with its view of Los Angeles. "I don't need this pool. I don't eat a lot of food. I can be alone. And I understood the power of that a long time ago, to be able to just let something go. I'll tell you what was really interesting: this allowed me in football to shut out the pain, to absorb the pain without aggression, or without emotions—it's like you let somebody slap the shit out of you and you don't do nothing. Should you do that? No, but what I'm telling you is that through solitude, I could see my real existence, see what my mother had to try to do to survive, see where I was, and see the adjustments I had to make. So I made them. I pursued an education first, and loved only the people that really helped me."

Brown often found himself living in the home of his high school girlfriend, Henrietta Creech, where he would find refuge after the more explosive blowups with his mother. Henrietta was a beautiful black drum majorette at a rival high school. Brown remembers that he "fell for her hard." When in college, he conceived a child with her, a daughter named Karen. He will not discuss that even all these years later, but in *Out of Bounds*, he wrote, "I'm not a man prone to regret, but I should have married Henrietta. After she had Karen, I knew she wanted to marry me, but she was so strong, she never harped on it. Henrietta just started raising Karen by herself, with the help of her parents. I've felt guilty about that all my life. I made a choice— if I was going to finish college, have an athletic career, I felt I could not take on a wife and child. I'm not sure what I would do if I could go back, I might make the same choice. And yet, I've always felt what I did to Henrietta was terrible. If people are going to crucify me, crucify me for that."

Brown's priority was athletic glory, a goal fed and fostered by his male role models and the attendant warmth he received at a school that seemed to be in a state of awe over the athletic demigod in their midst.

"Long Island was not where racism was prevalent. It was the opposite," he remembers. "From living on top of another man's garage to going to Manhasset, to meeting my high school coach and the high-quality character of my classmates, really made me understand what people should be like. Somebody messed up when they let me meet these good people, because now I knew what goodness was. That other shit I was soon to see wasn't so good! But the system slipped up and allowed me to get around some good people, and Manhasset saved my life. It helped my self-confidence, my self-esteem, my work habits, my appreciation for education, my appreciation for sports, my ability to judge a person by their character, and my need to not be afraid. I couldn't have made it without them.

"On the one hand, racism is everywhere. On the other hand, I was lucky enough to go to a high school with these special people who cared about all of us. . . . Sometimes people don't want you to talk about the good things; they want to just knock all the bad stuff out there. I was lucky. I saw good. I saw that it doesn't have to be the way it so often is."

There was no sport in Manhasset at which Brown did not excel. On the football field as a junior, he—and this is not a misprint—averaged 15.1 yards per carry. When he was a senior, other teams geared their entire defenses toward stopping him, so his yards per carry "dipped" to 14.9. In basketball he set a Long Island high school record, scoring 53 points in one game.

From among the forty-two colleges that offered Brown athletic scholarships, he picked Syracuse University, the school of his mentor, Manhasset school superintendent and future New York State Supreme Court judge Kenneth Molloy. Brown was unaware, however, that the Syracuse football program had no interest in him. These were different times, with primitive levels of scouting, and while schools throughout the country were drooling over the prospect of signing Brown, Syracuse was not, simply because the program had a racial quota of zero and did not intend to sign a black player.

Molloy, a former Syracuse lacrosse star and chairman of a fund-raising committee to build a new field house at Syracuse, interceded with the chancellor so that his beloved "Jimmy" was finally admitted, albeit *without* an athletic scholarship. Brown, remarkable as it may seem, arrived on campus knowing that he was there to play football but not knowing that he did not have a scholarship. (Lacrosse was an afterthought at this point.) Molloy proceeded to surreptitiously raise the funds to pay his tuition. The judge penned a dramatic letter to community leaders that would forever alter Brown's life. It read:

> You were undoubtedly one of those who felt pretty proud of Jimmy Brown and his athletic record at Manhasset High School. . . . There was good reason for our pride in this fine young American—and there will be more. But

we need your help. That is, Jimmy Brown needs it. Here is the situation: Jimmy recently matriculated at Syracuse University. When he did this, he relied upon the assurance of certain residents of Manhasset that they would contribute toward his expenses there. Frankly, Jimmy and his family cannot handle that, for it will come to about $1,000 for this semester. Given this chance, however, Jimmy will, we are convinced, give us in Manhasset ample reason to continue our confidence in him as an athlete and as a representative of all that is fine in young American manhood. Several of us have joined to see what can be done to give Jimmy Brown his big chance. We think this will be one of Manhasset's soundest investments. We think, too, that you may feel the same way about this or you would not have gotten this letter. If you agree, please send us your check to the order of Arthur H. Wright—as generous as you can make it—in the enclosed envelope.

Sincerely yours,

*Kenneth D. Molloy*

There is a fib in this letter, of course. Molloy represented the idea that Brown was depending "upon the assurance of certain residents of Manhasset," but Brown actually had no idea that this was happening until he arrived on campus and started classes.

As Brown remembered in 1968, "Judge Kenny Molloy, one of the greatest men in my life, was a graduate of Syracuse, and he wanted me to go and made a deal with them behind my back that he would pay the first year if they gave me a tryout there. Didn't know I didn't have a scholarship, and didn't know it until I got up there. . . . And I knew something was funny 'cause they had me eating in a regular chow hall and all the football players were eating in a special chow hall. So I knew something was wrong, and found out later that he had made a deal."

Molloy's methods seem odd, but he loved Jim Brown and his school. He also hated the racism he saw in the Syracuse football program and believed that Brown could be a game changer. Molloy told the story in later years of making this personal plea to Syracuse head football coach Ben Schwartzwalder to take Brown on the team as a walk-on, non-scholarship player. Molloy remembered that Schwartzwalder told him, "I'm not prejudiced, but no more blacks on my team. But I'll consider it if you can get Jim to obey ten rules." The first rule was "No dating white girls."

The culture shock in coming from Long Island was shattering, even more so than the transition from St. Simons to Great Neck. Brown remembered, "When I came to Manhasset High School, I was never denied an opportunity. I was living among all these white people, receiving all this warmth and support. It lulled me to sleep. I believed everyone would be as good as the people of Manhasset. I came to Syracuse with my guard down. At eighteen I wasn't prepared for their venom."

It was a near unimaginable scenario: Brown was offered scholarships to every major school in the country but dreamed of being "an Orangeman" because his mentor—his father figure—had attended Syracuse. This mentor conspired behind his back so that Brown would think he had a scholarship. There were other NCAA programs that had much better integration histories than Syracuse, but Judge Molloy wanted the Manhasset phenom to bring glory to his alma mater, change the racial trajectory of the program, and stay relatively close to home. A price was paid for what must have seemed like a harmless duplicity; those early days at Syracuse were scarring for the teenage Brown.

Molloy later said with no small amount of pain, "At the time Syracuse didn't want any black athletes up there. . . . I put the kid in the mouth of a cannon." That "cannon" was Ben Schwartzwalder, but the adjustment issues cut deeper than one hard-ass coach.

Brown arrived on campus for fall football practice and found he wasn't staying in the athletic dorms with the rest of the team. He was alone and isolated, but the journey from Long Island to Syracuse would almost certainly have been a problem for him even if he had been welcomed with open arms. Syracuse is known for its freezing, blustery winters, making for an insular environment that could test the sturdiest of constitutions. Black novelist John A. Williams described Syracuse in the 1950s: "Syracuse is a city that traps people. You wait to make your move when the summer is over; summer is a dazzling thing here, with the hills and lawns and trees a lush velvet green. But then comes autumn and the city and the outer edges of it are a wild splash of color: bronze, flaming red, ochre, slowly dying green. No one moves during the winter when the Canadian winds, skirting the western edge of the Adirondacks, come roaring down upon the city. The winters are usually so hard that it takes until spring to get over them, and by then you are trapped again."

Feeling waves of resentment from Coach Schwartzwalder, Brown looked for some sort of support system. It took months to find. In the first half of the twentieth century, the black population in Syracuse had gone from almost nonexistent to roughly 5 percent by 1950. It was a rootless community that had grown by 120 percent over the previous decade. This was part of "the second great migration" after World War II, as African-Americans traveled north for industrial employment. In the Syracuse of that time, steel plants as well as General Electric were willing to employ blacks in industrial union jobs.

Syracuse University was even less diverse than the town. "During the 1920s," a historian of the school wrote, "black enrollment averaged a total of twenty-five students per year, and in 1942 only three blacks attended the university."

When Brown entered Syracuse in the fall of 1953, he had few African-American classmates. A study of the college yearbook, *The Onondagan*, for 1957 indicates that of the 1,627 who graduated with that class, fewer than ten, less than 0.5 percent, were black.

In a history of the school from the 1940s through the 1960s, John Robert Greene stated that Brown was "as well known for his volatility as for his ability. He threatened to quit the team many times; several times Molloy, or sometimes [lacrosse coach] Roy Simmons, talked him into staying.

"Brown often slept at practice and regularly skipped calisthenics," Greene wrote. On one occasion, Brown walked off the field after Coach Schwartzwalder berated him. "I was tired of him," Greene quoted Schwartzwalder. "But I was told by people that I had to take him back. They didn't care what concessions I had to make. Must have been a thousand people come to see me. So I talked to Jim."

Brown's college roommate and basketball teammate Vinnie Cohen, who is African-American, summarized conditions at the school: "For African-Americans, the America of the 1950s—and the Syracuse of the 1950s—was not a very nice place to live."

Brown was alienated and wanted to drop out, but he was developing a following of admirers on campus. When you are built like "a Greek god in African skin" at a nearly all-white institution in upstate New York, it is inevitable that you will be an object of attention. Professor Ralph Ketcham, who taught Brown's freshman citizenship class, later remembered: "Whenever he came into a room, he was a spectacle. He was perfectly quiet. It was a class that ordinarily encouraged discussion. I don't remember if he ever discussed at all. It was as though his mission was to do exactly what he had to do to pass his courses. He was by no means the worst student in class. It was clear this wasn't a class that excited him. I don't know that any of his classes did. He was intent on the athletic field. Even in his freshman year, he just moved right into that mold."

A review of Syracuse football programs from 1954 to 1956 shows that there were no black coaches on his sideline or the sidelines of his opponents; that Brown was the only African-American on the Syracuse team; that of the eight teams listed in the programs, only two—Pittsburgh and Penn State—fielded black players. Penn State had six black players. That was the apex of inclusion. Penn State was the only team to violate what was called "the rule of two"—no more than two black athletes on a team.

The "rule of two" in Syracuse basketball had a bit of a different meaning. It meant no more than two black players were permitted on the court at the same time, and it kept Jim Brown, despite his record-setting high school hoops ability, on the bench.

Vinnie Cohen remembered, "It's frustrating playing three years and demonstrating every day that you're better than three-fourths of the team and still not getting the opportunity. That can damage your pride."

One local black family, that of twenty-one-year-old Eddie Cowsert, provided a refuge for athletes as well as home-cooked southern-style meals. As John Carroll wrote in the College Football Historical Society newsletter, "Syracuse athletes like Brown, Cohen, Ernie Davis, John Mackey, Floyd Little, and many others were extremely grateful to Cowsert and his family. In the 1990s, Brown, Cohen, and Mackey prevailed upon the university to make a special award to Cowsert for his aid and support of African-American athletes in the 1950s and 60s."

Brown needed this support because the boy who was known as Man was being broken by someone who saw himself as unquestionably tougher than this "kid" who was forced on his team by a wealthy donor. That person was Ben Schwartzwalder. A grizzled World War II veteran who had won numerous medals at the Battle of the Bulge, he was a giant on a campus that was referred to as Schwartzwalder University because of the football team's success. He coached Syracuse from 1949 to 1973 and earned a 178-96-3 record and enshrinement in the College Football Hall of Fame. He is still revered on campus for leading the school to its sole national championship, the 11-0 team of 1959.

Schwartzwalder was also eventually driven from his job in 1973 when a series of losing seasons coincided with a full-scale revolt of his black players, who felt like they were being treated with racist contempt by the coaching staff. Most notoriously, this treatment was demonstrated in 1969 when eight black players, the "Syracuse Eight," boycotted spring practice after Schwartzwalder reneged on his promise to hire a black assistant coach. The school president had to intercede and insist that Schwartzwalder hire the assistant. The coach did so, but also kicked the nine protesting players off the team. At the start of the 1970 season, Syracuse had a black coach and, briefly, no black players.

Brown was just the second black student-athlete in Syracuse football history, and he had to negotiate the legacy of the first black player, Avatus Stone, who was described as "a new kind of negro in an old time," which is a euphemistic way of saying that he was not subservient, talked back to Coach Schwartzwalder, and dated white women.

In *Off My Chest*, Brown remembered, "[At Syracuse] I had to prove that I was interested in touchdowns, not white girls. Was this the open mind of higher education? Was this the academic world of the enlightened North? After a time, I proved that I not only had no interest in miscegenation but could score touchdowns as well, and then I was accepted."

He also heard again and again, like a hectoring catechism: "Don't be like Avatus Stone." As Brown recalled to Alex Haley in a 1968 *Playboy* interview, "When I arrived, the only black man on the team, the coaches had nothing to say to me except, 'Don't be like Avatus Stone!' My whole freshman year, I heard so many sermons about what I should be like, I got so many hang-ups, that my attitude became as bad as theirs. In practice, I was snubbed and ignored until I got to where I'd just sprawl out on my back during drills and nobody said a word to me. I was as sullen as they were, and the freshman season ended and the sophomore season began with me on the fifth string."

When Brown complained about his fifth-string status, his coaches suggested that if he wanted to get on the field, he'd better learn how to punt.

This experience has never left Brown. "There was a period when I was vicious on Syracuse," he remembered in 1995. "I totally resented that they saw me as the second coming of Avatus Stone. I resented the fact that they almost broke me, that they made me doubt my own abilities."

Brown wanted to quit, and for the first time in his life felt unwanted, even on a football field. He said to himself, "Maybe I can't play. I don't want to be here." All of his old Manhasset mentors encouraged him to stick it out. His high school coach Ed Walsh said, "You've got to go back and prove Syracuse is wrong." Kenneth Molloy also urged him not to give in. They would say, "You're not like Stone, and you've got a chance to show them you're not." They told him he could be "a credit to your race." Brown reflected on this idea of going back and not only playing hard but also being "a credit to his race." He wrote,

"I always felt like an animal who is being tolerated in the living room as long as he didn't shed here on the sofa."

This new advice from the people he respected the most to be "a credit to his race" was deeply jarring for Brown. He had journeyed in just a few weeks from a situation where he barely had to think about race, where he was a hero in a white community, to one where he was singled out and ostracized by coaches for the color of his skin, and he had been sent to this hell by the people he trusted most back home. But Brown is grateful to Molloy and Walsh for kicking him in the ass and compelling him to return. There are no criticisms of Ken Molloy or Ed Walsh allowed in his presence, even to this day. One can't help thinking that on some level, this had to feel like a betrayal, but rather than feeling bitter, he chose to interpret this as tough love, a rite of manhood.

As for Syracuse, he said, "Every day when you woke up, you had to think 'black' first. You had to think about discrimination, about how to conduct yourself, where you could go, if it's going to be fair. You had to make all of these considerations just because you were of a different color. I was the only black person playing and had to deal with that every day of my life up there."

Or, as he also said, with a rumbling bass in his voice, remembering the greatest of his freshman year indignities, "They wanted me to punt, man. Punt!"

Brown, suffice it to say, did not stay a fifth-string player or prospective punter. In the fourth game of his sophomore season, Brown cut loose. Playing Syracuse's upstate rival Colgate, Brown rushed for 101 yards on only 15 carries, including scoring runs of 41 and 17 yards. Syracuse won 31–12. For the season, in limited action, Brown rushed for 439 yards on just 75 carries, a gaudy 5.9 yards per attempt. In addition, during those days when players were expected to line up on offense and defense, Brown—again in limited action—led the team in interceptions.

These flashes of brilliance made him something of a folk hero on campus. Students would chant, "We want Brown!" as he sat on the sidelines. Despite his newfound status, Brown was sent back to the sidelines after one poor outing during his junior year. Coach Schwartzwalder was benching the best player the school had ever seen. But Brown, now twenty years old, was confident enough at this point to not slink back to despair. He "saw fire" and by his next practice, as he remembered, "left first-string tacklers lying out all over the field and [I] ran four touchdowns in five plays. After that, they left me on the first string. . . . Once the coaches made up their minds, they were men enough to realize they had been wrong and they became fair in dealing with me, and then I gave them all I had. I think maybe having to fight my way up the way I did taught *me* more about being a man, too."

This is an early lesson that Jim Brown processed in a manner that went unchallenged by those around him. He had equated the earning of manhood and respect with his ability to "see fire" and kick ass. That will garner respect in the sports world. In the real world, it gets more complicated.

Brown's dynamic junior year, when he ran for 666 yards on 128 carries, a 5.2 yards-per-carry average, was a prelude of what was to come. As a senior, he rushed for 986 yards at 6.2 yards per carry and scored 13 touchdowns. He also set an NCAA single-game record by scoring 43 points against Colgate. Favored to win the Heisman Trophy after that senior season, which would have made him the first black winner of college football's most prestigious award, Brown finished fifth. This baldly racist result led sportswriter Dick Schaap to boycott the Heisman for decades, annually sending in a blank ballot. The winner that year, almost as if the voters had an ironic sense of humor, was Paul Hornung, the Notre Dame star nicknamed "The Golden Boy," who had quarterbacked his team to a 2-8 record, throwing three touchdowns to go against thirteen interceptions. Syracuse went 8-2. In Brown's last three years, the team went 20-7-1.

But it wasn't just Hornung. Brown also finished behind Johnny Majors of Tennessee, in second place, who rushed for slightly more than half the number of yards as Brown, with a lower average per carry and fewer touchdowns. Third-place finisher Tommy McDonald of Oklahoma also had fewer yards and touchdowns than Brown.

The Heisman would not be awarded to a black player until Brown's replacement as running back at Syracuse, Ernie Davis, claimed the honor five years later.

Brown summed up his college football experience thus: "From the beginning, I saw they liked black players who didn't talk, so I didn't talk. I gave myself to them physically, never drank or smoked, all the clean-living stuff you were supposed to do. As I became a star, they wanted more. They wanted me to endorse the system. Again, I am not a house nigger."

In Ben Schwartzwalder's world, Brown's talent did not allow

him to "transcend race." If anything, it made the old coach resent Brown all the more. He couldn't keep him on the sidelines, but he also did not want him on the field, in the practice facility, or at *his* university. He made Brown pay a price every day for his talent, a situation that could not have been more at odds with what the seventeen-year-old had experienced in high school, where his skills brought him deliverance from a difficult, isolated home life. At Syracuse they brought only more isolation.

If Brown had been a one-sport athlete, the situation on the football team might have broken him. But he was also an All-American in lacrosse, astounded onlookers in track and field, and even played varsity basketball for a brief time. He was the best amateur athlete in the country, with that classic Long Island sport, lacrosse, keeping him sane amid the "racial bullshit" on the football team.

Roy Simmons, Sr., was a godsend as the head lacrosse coach. Roy Simmons, Jr., Brown's lacrosse teammate and friend, says of his father, "He was a kind and gentle person. He knew the trials and tribulations it took to get Jim to Syracuse.

"Jim was the only black football player on the team. He heard a lot of racial slurs, and my dad always was there for him when Jim wanted to quit, or was down, [when] he had nowhere to turn to. There were no other black players, the head coach was not compassionate, and he was trying to earn a scholarship in football, so he had to prove himself. And so the only place he'd turn was to somebody that had sympathy for him, and that was my father. He was a very sympathetic guy, and he knew Jim's beginnings, and he was always there in Jim's corner."

Simmons Jr. remembers a Jim Brown in college who still lived a largely solitary and apolitical life. Simmons says, "I don't think I ever heard him mention anything politically. Although in his heart, I know he wanted equality. He struggled along the way, he heard words that he shouldn't have to hear, he probably wouldn't hear today, and he rebelled against racism on a personal level."

He was also a target in a different way. "He was always called racial slurs by opponents," according to Simmons. "It was constant, every game": opponents never hesitated to call him "nigger" as they entered scrums to grab loose balls in the high-contact sport. But it didn't slow him down. "The more someone called him a disgusting racial name," says Simmons, "the more he scored. He punished teams that used that stuff by embarrassing them on the field."

When asked about Roy Simmons, Jr., Brown grins with something approaching delight: "Yeah, Roy was fast as hell, good lacrosse stick-handler, great lacrosse player, and basically, an All-American, of course. And could really run. And a very nice guy. Feels good to talk about him."

While Brown was getting a crash course about racism on the Syracuse campus, he experienced it at the hands of the police as well. Years later he told Alex Haley the story of driving in the South with teammates:

After passing through a small town, they saw a police car suddenly appear from behind, speed past them, and cut them off, forcing the players' car to a stop. A stunned Brown watched as a cop got out of the car with his gun drawn.

"Get out, niggers!" the policeman shouted. Jim's group

exited the vehicle. "What are you making dust all over white people for?"

At that moment, another police car pulled up to the scene. The white driver of that car got out and approached.

"You hear me, nigger?" the first cop yelled. Brown, overwhelmed with emotion, didn't trust his response, but he knew he had to say something.

"I don't know what a nigger is!" he said.

Then the cop jammed the pistol right in Brown's stomach. "Nigger, don't you know how to talk to white folks?"

One of Brown's teammates spoke up. "He's not from down here, he's from up North."

"Nigger, I don't care where you're from," the cop persisted. "I'll blow you apart! Where did you get this car, anyway?"

"It was given to me," Brown said.

"*Given* to you! Who gave you a *car*?"

"It was given to me at school."

"*What* school?"

"Syracuse University."

The other cop intervened. "That's right. I recognize this boy. He plays football up there."

That seemed to be enough for the first cop to back down. He took his gun out of Brown's belly. "I'm going to let you go, but you better drive slow and you better learn how to act down here, nigger!"

The brush with the police would haunt Brown for years thereafter.

"I don't know why I even told you that," he said to Haley. "It's not good to dredge that stuff up in your mind again. But you see, you don't forget a thing like that, not if somebody handed you every trophy in football and fifteen Academy Awards. That's why a black man, if he's got any sense at all, will never get swept away with special treatment if he happens to be famous, because he knows that the minute he isn't where somebody *recognizes* who he is, then he's just another *nigger*.

"That's what the Negro struggle is all about; that's why we black people have to keep fighting for freedom in this country. We demand only to live—and let live—like any ordinary American. We don't want to have to be somebody special to be treated with respect. I can't understand why white people find it so hard to understand that."

It was a violent world that treated him with psychological and physical violence, and football was his ultimate refuge. He later wrote: "I always played for myself, and for my team and because I loved the game. To ensure I never lost that spirit, I vowed there were certain things I would never do, certain feelings dredged up by racism, I would have to avoid. I knew I could never play football with a broken heart. . . . When I went from fifth string to All-American, earned my degree, I made myself a promise: for the rest of my life, I will never let anyone tell me what I can and cannot accomplish. As a black man in America, I would draw on that credo again and again."

After four years in the "Black Forest" of Schwartzwalder's Syracuse football program, Jim Brown was ready to enter the NFL, with a massive chip on his shoulder and an equally strong sense of mission: to never have his excellence or manhood doubted again, either on or off the field. After the Cleveland Browns drafted him in the first round with the sixth pick in

1957, he swore to never allow himself to feel small, in the way Ben Schwartzwalder so often attempted to make him feel. Jim Brown was someone with untreated psychological wounds and someone who believed that acknowledging those wounds would cripple his sense of manhood, right when he needed it most.

# THREE

# MAN AMONG BROWNS

—

*You are Art Modell. It's the summer of 1966 and, to use the parlance of the day, you have the world by the balls. You're forty-one years old and you own the Cleveland Browns. You aren't some sort of boss-aristocrat, handed the team by your rich daddy, but a Brooklyn kid who dropped out of school at fourteen to support your family. You grew up poor as a pauper. Your father lost everything in the 1929 stock market crash and died when you were just a kid. You took work where you could find it, eventually landing a job on the Brooklyn shipyards scraping rust and barnacles off the hulls of the massive destroyers and vessels that would win World War II. After serving in the military yourself and helping take out those Nazi bastards, you parlayed your success in advertising to buy the Browns in 1961, plunking down just $250,000 of your own money.*

*You know what poverty smells like. You know what it looks like, what it tastes like. Never again. Now you own an NFL franchise and are kicking ass on a daily basis. You force out the head coach that the team is named after, local legend Paul Brown. Of course, you chose to do it during a Cleveland newspaper strike, so the backlash was minimal, but your "Browns without Paul Brown" won it all in 1964, vindicating your decision, and there are nothing but blue skies ahead. This is Cleveland, and you give generously to local charities, the symphony, the ballet. You stand astride a midwestern city "on the grow," and it is going to be all yours. Sinatra will one day sing of your old hometown, "If I can make it there, I'll make it anywhere." Bullshit. Tons of people "make it" in New York City. Try making it in Cleveland. Now, that takes some sand. You're making it, baby, and everyone in Brooklyn— especially the Irish and Italians who smacked you around on the way to school—can kiss your Jewish ass.*

*Your brash demeanor doesn't come just from the self-confidence of being a self-made man or your uncanny ability to charm NFL owners and the stadium janitorial staff with the same quips and patter. It comes from having the greatest runner in football history on your roster: Jim Brown. He's in his prime, coming off an MVP season, his third in the past eight years. He's charismatic. He's a "lady killer," you like to say to people with gossipy glee and a wink, knowing that Jim is a smooth operator with the women around town and, alas, can be a bit rough with the gentler sex. He's even in the movies trying to be a black John Wayne. His latest is going to be a blockbuster, some World War II film with Lee Marvin called* The Dirty Dozen. *But production has slowed. Rain in England, they tell you. Your stud running back contacts you and says he's going to be a few days late to training camp. Because of some drizzle? Oh, hell no. He may be the star, but it's your team, your city, and he's your runner. So that's not going to happen. You're Art*

*Modell! Master of the universe! He's coming home. You will fine him*
*every day until his ass is in training camp. He'll come running. Just you*
*watch. What could possibly go wrong?*

JIM BROWN MOVED TO CLEVELAND IN 1957, READY TO
make his mark on and off the field. By the following year,
during his second season and at the tender age of twenty-two,
he married Sue Jones and set about having a family. He portrayed himself to local reporters as a doting young husband and
father of three children. There were the twins, Kim and Kevin,
born in 1960, and James Jr., born in 1962. But the scenes of
domestic tranquillity and patriarchal strength were more media
fantasy than reality. Brown's attention was not on hearth and
home. It was focused on kicking ass on the field, partying off it,
and laying the political groundwork for his unique place amid
the black freedom struggle. He spoke of his absences from home
with great regret in the decades to come, saying he was never
the father he should have been. Kim opened up in Spike Lee's
documentary about Brown, saying, "Initially for the kids, I
don't think it really affected us. But later on when we really
wanted a dad, needed a dad, somebody to talk to, you know, it
kind of started messing with our heads. I wanted to be Daddy's
little girl. I wanted to be held, touched . . . taken places. I
wanted him to come to some of my ballet recitals, things like
that. And, you know, he wasn't there." Kevin remarked years
later that he could remember being hugged by his father only
once in his life.

Proving his manhood through fatherhood was not nearly as enticing as doing it through sexual conquest. Many women found Brown to be irresistible, and as a football star both on the road and in Cleveland, he had constant opportunities for sex outside his marriage. Brown was not one to let those moments slip through his fingers, and Sue was not one to bring it up on the precious few days her husband made his way home.

Almost a decade after their 1972 divorce, Sue recalled, "Before we got married he said there was always going to be other women. He said, 'You're never going to have a little picket fence. I'm Jim Brown, I can marry anybody in the world, and there are always going to be other women. Can you deal with that?' I said I could, and I did."

Painting this false portrait of his family life was not difficult. This was an era when the truth about a player's personal business was hidden from prying eyes. The media did not write about it, and there was little appetite among sports fans to know the hidden secrets of what happened when the cameras were turned off. The dominant opinion of Brown was therefore shaped by his bearing, his politics, and, above all else, his play.

Jim Brown's nine-year football career in Cleveland was marked by feats that still make grown men shudder with joy. The numbers and stories are so Homeric they can obscure how he turned the conservative, top-down sport of football into a political battleground: a battleground where he rarely lost. It also overshadows how he extended that battleground from the field to the locker room to the front office. Today there is much discussion about how another physically blessed, deeply intelligent Cleveland athlete, LeBron James, has changed the relationship between players and management, effectively acting with more agency than the jocks of generations past. Yet decades before LeBron, with only a fraction of the salary, labor protections, and power, Brown was blazing the trail. He was able to enforce his will on a franchise until they tried to finally put him in his place. Then he walked away at the height of his powers, deciding that his "place" would not be with people who would treat him as "something less than a man."

Before Jim Brown was identified with any kind of political black consciousness, he represented the seedlings of "Black Power" a decade before the phrase was popularly known.

The roots of the 1960s Black Power movement, as Peniel Joseph argues in his book *Waiting 'til the Midnight Hour*, did not develop, as it is often taught, out of frustrated 1950s civil rights marches or as members of the nonviolent army of Martin Luther King, Jr., looked for a more militant road when the movement spread north. Instead it was in the flowering of debates, discussions, and grassroots organizing that was taking place in black artistic circles, barbershops, and street corners, and in people influenced by the gospel of self-reliance and independence preached by the Nation of Islam. It was also interpreted by onlookers in the style of play Jim Brown brought to the field and how he carried himself when the play was done. Brown would show, before a mass audience starting to tune into football on their new televisions, that he was tougher and smarter than anyone or anything in his path. He was the future, and people either had to get with it or get out of the way.

Every Sunday was a showcase not only of excellence, but of *black* excellence, as Jim Brown ran through the toughest white linebackers like they were made of cheesecloth. A normal run by Brown could be transformed into a political act: Black Power before it had a name.

In the context of the civil rights movement's early days, white sportswriters sympathetic to Dr. King found such easy symbolism irresistible. When "Brown's Browns" manhandled the all-white Washington football team, owned by segregationist George Preston Marshall, *Washington Post* columnist Shirley Povich described a routine run this way: "From 25 yards out, Brown was served the ball . . . on a pitch-out, and he integrated the Redskins' goal line with more than deliberate speed, perhaps exceeding the famous Supreme Court decree . . . and the Redskins' goal line, at least, became interracial."

Brown likewise became a classic example of what Richard Majors and Janet Mancini Billson have described in *Cool Pose: The Dilemma of Black Manhood in America*: "The African-American male's relative impotence in the political and corporate worlds is countered with a potency and verve that borders on the spectacular, especially in athletic competition, entertainment, and the pulpit. Through the virtuosity of a performance, he tips socially imbalanced scales in his favor. 'See me, touch me, hear me, but white man, you can't copy me' is his subliminally assertive message."

References to Jim Brown as someone who chipped away at this societal "impotence" with every bruising run were peppered throughout the black newspapers of the time. Marion Jackson of the *Los Angeles Free Press* wrote, "The brilliance of Jim Brown has exploded the myth of Negro inferiority."

The black newspaper *Atlanta Daily World* listed Brown at

number two on its "top personalities of 1963," right behind Jomo Kenyatta, the newly elected prime minister of Kenya, and ahead of labor and civil rights leaders A. Philip Randolph and Dr. Benjamin Mays, and even Dr. King himself. And it wasn't just because of the way Brown carried himself on the field. It was the sharp, perfectly tailored suits he insisted on wearing when talking to the press after emerging from the locker room. It was his soft but commanding voice and steely stare projected through his rugged movie-star face. He was starting to use his cultural cachet to speak out, initially on the social responsibility of black athletes. In a speech he gave while on a speaking tour of historically black colleges and universities in 1961, when he was only twenty-five, he said, "The image of the Negro is changing. He is first educated, he is well-informed, he is alert, and he is changing with the times because of necessity. The Negro athletes are well behind the progress that Negroes in general are making today. We fight just as hard for equal rights as we fight to win games for our respective clubs. Our professional athletes are thinking that [achieving] progress is a part of our civic and moral responsibility."

This has been a common theme throughout his life, one he holds to this day. "I'm not inferior, man," he says. "They're like, 'Yeah, but you should just be glad that we accept you, and we're going to give you this medal and you should be happy with that.' I say, 'No, I'm not happy with that bullshit. I'm not looking for your trophies or your acceptance, or your validation.'"

The backdrop for this assertive expression of political and racial power was the Cleveland of the 1960s. According to journalist Scott Raab, who was raised in the city, Cleveland in that decade "was very tribal, very clearly defined by the Cuyahoga River, but the guy who stood astride the whole city and everyone's consciousness was this colossus, Jim Brown."

The city where Brown moved in 1957 was a place of strength and pride, with the sense that the postwar economic boom—fueled by heavy machinery industrial production—would be a permanent way of life. But by the end of the 1960s, Cleveland was on fire, literally. The great Cuyahoga River burst into flames in 1969, spurring the modern environmental movement and remaining an enduring symbol of a city so dysfunctional that even its water could not be trusted to extinguish flames. *Time* magazine turned the blaze into a national story, describing the Cuyahoga as a river that "oozes rather than flows" and where someone "does not drown but decays."

The symbol was profoundly potent for a city on the skids. Michael D. Roberts, a reporter for the *Plain Dealer* at the time, wrote in a retrospective of the decade, "No one predicted that . . . the 1960s would be as tumultuous and trying as any [Cleveland], or the country, for that matter, would endure."

After the end of Brown's football career, Cleveland's sports fortunes mirrored that narrative: the city had been parched for a victory parade since Brown led the team to that championship in 1964. This explains why the 2016 NBA champion Cleveland Cavaliers drew 1.3 million for their citywide celebration, with people rappelling down the sides of buildings to garner a closer look at glory. The hope was and is that the return of a title to the city will mean a return of the city's fortunes.

This sense of decline was not the Cleveland way, in either

the sports world or the real world, during Jim Brown's years there.

Raab, who still has his ticket stub from the 1964 NFL Browns title game, remembers, "This wasn't a city that anyone made fun of. It wasn't 'the Mistake by the Lake.' It was a pretty powerful steel town. Heavy union. People with families and womb-to-tomb-type jobs, mostly tool-and-die and auto industry jobs, lived in the city."

When Brown left football in 1966, Cleveland was on its way to becoming a husk of its former self. It was a place that he chose to leave, and then a generation of people followed, the city's population falling dramatically. As Raab puts it, "Jim Brown represented Cleveland before the fall."

Before "the fall" that began in the late 1960s, Cleveland was the sixth-largest city in the United States. Today it is the forty-eighth. Its sports teams—particularly the Cleveland Browns—have for decades symbolized with brutal clarity that this city's best days have passed. This has become so accepted that it is difficult to even remember that there was this other Cleveland—the Cleveland that earned the nickname "City of Champions."

The basis for this pride was nearly full employment among working-class men, although white men almost exclusively got the best union jobs. Cleveland was connected to Detroit's auto industry and Pittsburgh's steel industry, with its own auto and steel plants. It also employed and created an entire white middle class of designers and researchers in those industries. Yet the city was defined by its blue-collar strength. It was a place that burned coal to make steel; the air was acrid and, in neighborhoods like the Flats, thick with soot. David Whitehouse, who grew up in

Cleveland in the 1950s, remembered, "In the Flats, you could wipe your face with a rag and the rag would be coated with the blackest possible grime."

Jim Brown's Cleveland may have been booming industrially, but it was also highly segregated, racially and economically, with black folks living on "the poor side of town." Brown's belief that there needs to be an economic—not merely a political—civil rights response to racism was clearly seeded and nurtured by what he witnessed in Cleveland. He saw a city generating capital, with the black side of town employed in many of these industries but shut out of ownership or prominent positions in the powerful unions. (The latter may be the basis for his general antipathy toward his own union, the NFL Players Association.) Cleveland would have been an ideal city to match Brown's belief that "the black side of town" could stay black but also develop economically. That is why he would speak at great length about why the path of self-determination and community development was preferable to forced integration in housing, schools, or unions. He would say that he wanted to teach people how to "work the system."

Lured by industrial jobs and the imperative to escape the Jim Crow South, the black population of Cleveland exploded during the postwar era. In 1940, the number of black residents was 85,000. By 1960, it was 250,000, and they lived almost entirely on the city's East Side. There was fear among white people about going through the black side of town. Journalist Alan Wieder says, "I'll never forget talking to Lou Hunt, one of the original people from the Student Nonviolent Coordinating Committee in Cleveland, who told me, 'Well, you think you were scared to come to our neighborhood, we wouldn't even think of going to Little Italy.'"

Racial segregation was complete. There was no difficulty in racial profiling because there were whole sections of the city and suburbs that were a no-go area for African-Americans. And that applied to Jim Brown, even with his fame and recognition. He was black first, before he was any kind of celebrity.

This migration and segregation were accompanied by an urban planning policy that herded poor and primarily black residents, including those who had been in Cleveland for decades, into the overcrowded Hough neighborhood. Later in the decade, Hough would become known nationally less as a neighborhood and more for the namesake Hough riots.

The black freedom struggle, not surprisingly, found purchase in Cleveland, as there was widespread community pushback against the redlining and overcrowding on the East Side. Martin Luther King, Jr., made regular visits to Cleveland and was met with audiences wanting to talk not in terms of soaring rhetoric, but about what they could do concretely to improve local conditions. King's speeches usually ended less in cheers and more in breakout sessions, with Dr. King as participant, to talk strategy. Brown was not a part of these efforts because he found King's approach to black liberation to be a tactical dead-end. As he said in 1963, "I heard Martin Luther King say, 'Smite me on my left cheek and I shall turn my right and I shall still love you.' Personally I cannot believe that freedom will be won through love. . . . Dr. King is a great man because he has courage and because he has the ability to draw the masses together and move them and therefore make a tremendous contribution to the Negro restlessness, but he is a preacher and a speech-maker. I for one will not march down the street and kneel and pray for my rights. That is just not my shit."

On April 7, 1964, to protest the construction of what would be a segregated elementary school on the East Side, the Reverend Bruce Klunder lay down behind a bulldozer and was crushed to death when the unwitting driver backed up. The photos of Klunder's body were published widely; they tormented a community that saw their aspirations in the beloved reverend's mangled corpse. Eight months later, Jim Brown's team won the NFL championship. This served to put a Band-Aid on the unrest. But tension still seethed.

Three years later, at a local white-owned bar on the East Side, a black man was refused a glass of water after purchasing a bottle of wine. He said the two men who owned the joint, brothers Abe and Dave Feigenbaum, called him a "nigger." A crowd gathered outside. "All the frustration and conflict of the past welled up in one wild rampage that swept through the Hough area in a violent torrent," Michael D. Roberts wrote. "Shops were looted, fires set, the sound of gunfire resounded through the neighborhood. The scene resembled street fighting on the television news in some far-off land."

People in Little Italy, fearful that they would be under siege from "rioters" in Hough, armed themselves and killed a black person during the uprising.

Cleveland mayor Ralph Locher, who won a close election in 1965 over future mayor Carl Stokes, called in the Ohio National Guard.

Over the next six days, heavy military weaponry and assault

vehicles—the kind being used in Vietnam—patrolled the streets of Cleveland. Snipers were perched on rooftops, and armed National Guardsmen were ready for combat. Police and guardsman killed four residents over the next week, and more than two hundred fires were set. In the aftermath, people spoke less about lawless residents or racist bars and more about the overcrowding and the failure of urban renewal programs to provide relief from the terrible conditions in Hough. Yet a county grand jury, led by prominent city leaders—people with no connection to Hough—said that the riot was the result of "outside agitators, maybe even Communists."

The tensions were further exacerbated when Cleveland police officers—from the same city swooning over Jim Brown—testified in front of a state legislative committee that black nationalist organizers should receive the death penalty. The cognitive dissonance was dizzying.

Brown, his friend and teammate John Wooten, and the Black Economic Union of Cleveland were not bystanders after the Hough riots. They were part of a group working on a shoestring budget to build a community center as well as employment referral and summer jobs programs. Brown wanted organizations that did not have to wait for the government to try to aid urban communities. He lobbied for grants and for the private sector to do it instead.

That same group also supported the mayoral run of Carl Stokes, who in 1967 would become the first African-American mayor of a major U.S. city. His election was absolutely a by-product of the Hough riots, but "Keep It Cool" Carl was unable to quell the tensions. In 1968, in what are known as the

Glenville riots, there was a four-day shootout between police and an organization called the Black Nationalists of New Libya. When African-American leaders, including those connected to the city's Black Economic Union, were unable to keep things calm, Stokes, like his predecessor, called in the Ohio National Guard. (The Guard would become infamous two years later when members took the lives of four people at Kent State University.)

By the time Stokes became mayor, Brown had moved to the West Hollywood Hills of Los Angeles. Before that move, he had lived in Shaker Heights with his wife Sue and his three children. Shaker Heights was "an inner-ring suburb," sharing a border with Cleveland but also distinct and affluent and not particularly integrated.

In this deeply divided city, Jim Brown's play was a point of unity, a source of pride and awe for both black and white Cleveland. This was a pre-cynical age when it came to sports heroes. These fans loved Jim Brown and he loved them back. Black fans and white fans, especially those in the cheap seats, mingled freely at Cleveland Stadium without tension. For a very short period, Brown had a column in the Cleveland *Plain Dealer*. In the March 15, 1964, edition he wrote, "How about Cleveland football fans? Compared to most other cities they're great. They support the team and basically have the right attitude. Loyalty is the thing players like above everything else. Mentioning loyalty reminds me that the young fans are the finest example of this. They live and die with you and are completely sincere. It's not the Hollywood stars or other celebrities the players appreciate most. It's the regular Joe, the average guy who comes out rain snow or cold to support his team. They are the ones who enable the Browns to have the largest attendance in the National Football League."

Brown never hesitated to distinguish between the racism he observed in the city and his love for fans both black and white. After leaving the team, he told the *Plain Dealer*, "The only thing I miss about Cleveland is the fans as they related to me on and off the field. I never got booed. They treated me very nicely on an individual level. Other than that, Cleveland reminds me of a bombed-out racist city that needs revamping. It's the only city I've been in where I feel totally separated on a racial level—the whites on the West Side, the blacks on the East Side."

Yet no matter how many people cheered for him on the field, he suffered in Cleveland when the uniform was off, feeling at the time a strong sense of alienation from the community as a whole. Brown had sixty thousand fans screaming his name, but when the uniform came off, he was told to enter country clubs and fancy homes through the back door.

Brown was stoic in the face of this sort of abuse. The way he carried himself was so powerful, so imbued with this sense of manhood, that it painted a false picture of who he actually was. Jim Brown was not a present father for his own children, but his image was so proudly patriarchal that it created a symbol stronger than truth. Radio host and cultural studies professor Dr. Jared Ball has observed, "His image was what a black man and a black father was supposed to be. He was so strong he seemed to be unbreakable and he seemed to live on his own terms. Looking back, it's easy for me to say it's got everything to do with the absence of media wanting to tell the stories of black families and black fathers in particular. At the time it was just a simple thing. My father wasn't there. And here Jim Brown was, so naturally I just started to look for 'Who's going to tell me how to do this?'"

Brown's time in the NFL also left a mark on his contemporaries, particularly black players who were looking for a way to use their platform to make a social impact.

On January 11, 1965, Hall of Fame running back Cookie Gilchrist organized a black boycott of the AFL All-Star game, to be played in New Orleans. In the Jim Crow city, players would have to endure separate and unequal accommodations in hotels and restaurants. AFL commissioner Joe Foss was confronted by all twenty-one of the black All-Stars, who informed him they wouldn't be taking the field unless the game was moved. They had full support in this stance from their white teammates. Foss immediately buckled and the game was played in Houston.

Gilchrist was inspired by Jim Brown's strength and the example of someone who demanded to be seen on equal footing. Even though Brown did not believe in protest himself, he inspired protest. Gilchrist said, "White folks will let you do anything you please as long as you show gratitude. You can make bread and play and party and have your name plastered all over but you better be a thankful boy and you better let [white folk] know you're thankful. Jim's attitude has always been he's got coming what he's worked for same as anyone. . . . He don't hide a thing. He ain't ashamed. He's one black man not about to be cowed by nobody."

This image of a great black father who was "not about to be

cowed by nobody" was built in part by the way Brown stood up for his teammates and organized resistance in one of the most autocratic locker rooms in sports, a locker room overseen by the man who gave the franchise its name: Paul Brown.

Paul Brown was an accomplished coach and essentially founded the franchise, leading Cleveland to three NFL championships in the decade preceding Jim Brown's arrival. Coach Brown's approach to football was ahead of his time, earning him plaudits as a "visionary" and "genius." But to Jim Brown and many other Cleveland players, Paul Brown was a visionary second and a flinty authoritarian first.

In *Off My Chest*, Jim Brown remembered these early days in his career: "I called him a Little Caesar. Silently, of course. As the other Brown in this opulently Brown little world, I kept my mouth shut."

Even though Jim Brown played the role of the quiet rookie, there was an early sign that he would be doing things his own way. He showed up to training camp as the first player in professional football to use an agent—an extremely controversial decision at the time. It was normal in those years for owners to simply refuse to talk to agents or lawyers; players had little recourse but to agree to not have legal representation. Jim Brown, however, insisted on being repped by his mentor, Judge Ken Molloy, and Paul Brown had little choice but to abide.

Jim saw in Paul Brown a style very similar to the "my way or the highway" military approach of Ben Schwartzwalder, albeit with a great deal more innovation and creativity in regard to the game and a lot less—in Jim's eyes—overt racism. Paul treated everyone the same: like pieces of equipment. "He was an original thinker, a man with ideas," Jim Brown wrote in *Off My Chest*. "But more than that, he was a painstaking organizer. He manipulated football players as he would chessmen (while encouraging little more self-expression than he would expect from chessmen). Doubling as general manager, he ran the front office as completely and sternly as he ran the ball game itself, attending to trivial details that could have been safely left to an office boy. . . . Players became extensions of his personality, not only while on the field but in some ways while off it. They dressed as he would have them dress, and if they were prone to habits that he considered to be vices (smoking, drinking, cursing, women . . .) they pursued them with the furtiveness of CIA agents."

The media line on the early years of Jim Brown was, "This guy is lousy copy." Brown's response to this view was, "For a considerable time [as a young player] I played the part of the big dumb fullback as well as I could, which is to say with a maximum of physical effort and a minimum of dialogue."

Brown may have kept quiet, careful to "show no attitude," but as he said, "what happened on Sunday was my attitude."

When Brown did speak in these early years, he took great pains to be as uncontroversial as possible. In 1958, he was asked by the black newspaper *Atlanta Daily World* to speak about racism in the NFL. All he would say was, "It doesn't matter who carries the ball. Every guy wants to win or at least get into the playoffs to share some of the extra money."

In this same article, Paul Brown gushed about his star runner, saying, "I know you're going to ask what I think of Jim Brown. Jim is terrific. . . . We are tickled with Jimmy. . . .

There's one thing others have missed about Jim Brown. He is a stabilizing factor. He gives confidence to others. My club looks to Jim Brown."

On the field, Jim Brown was, in his own words, "Paul Brown's big brute," and Paul Brown treated him like a brute; a plow horse, to drag his squad toward victory. This was the way football was played. As is not the case today, no one at that time was thinking about the physical toll on the athletes. The financial investment in players was minimal and they were often overused into physical oblivion, worn down to a nub and then discarded. Nowadays, many in the NFL lionize all the "tough guys" and "iron men" from that early era and shake their heads at current players as if they don't measure up, without remembering the acres of athletes who were simply run into the ground. But Jim Brown truly was that one in a million who was stronger than the ground itself, to the amazement not only of teammates but of opponents as well.

In one game against the brutal New York Giants, Brown was kicked in the side of his helmet (helmets then were about as thick as a piece of canvas). In *Off My Chest*, he recounted, "I played the second half. I had regained my senses somewhat, but I was still in a sort of a mental no-man's-land. I was dreamy out there. Sam Huff, the New York middle linebacker, who year after year has keyed on me with such slam-bang tackles that fans imagine we have a personal grudge against one another, was shocked to see me in the game. '[Paul Brown] is crazy,' said Huff. 'He should get you out of here.'"

The Giants even helped Brown to his feet after tackling him, and Paul Brown was actually criticized by the press for "overusing" his fullback, a critique seldom raised against any coach then, let alone a legendary team patriarch. But the stark fact was that Jim Brown was carrying the ball on roughly 60 percent of all offensive plays. "Overuse" was barely in the football lexicon but the running of Jim Brown provoked it. Paul Brown's stock response when faced with this charge was, "When you've got a big gun, you shoot it."

The concern was so severe that public criticism was even levied from other coaches, something that just didn't happen in those days and rarely, if ever, happens now. But Sid Gillman, head coach of the Los Angeles Rams, said of Jim Brown, "If he carries the ball that much . . . he's got to wind up either punch drunk or a basket case."

"I have never seen an athlete be as physically abused, and still play at such high level, as Jim Brown," team owner Art Modell commented. "Things were done to Jim that today would lead to players getting arrested."

In an odd way, after the experience at Syracuse, Jim Brown initially appreciated Paul Brown's no-nonsense, treat-everyone-like-a-piece-of-a-machine approach: "In the 1950s there was widespread racism, in the nation and in professional football," the player wrote in *Out of Bounds*. "Paul's dictatorship discouraged cliques and that discouraged racial prejudice. His rules were not to be questioned, by anyone. We all had to abide by them equally. That was very pleasing to me."

Paul Brown was indeed an equal-opportunity general. He wanted only the opportunity to coach the best players and treat them all the same: very poorly. It meant that he, with far less fanfare, was the Branch Rickey of his sport, helping break the

NFL's color line by signing guard Bill Willis and fullback Marion Motley in the fall of 1946, seven months before the debut of Jackie Robinson. (The color line had existed only since 1932, and football was far less culturally important than baseball at the time, which explains why Paul Brown has been such a footnote in the history of sports and integration.)

As Paul Brown said, "I never considered football players black or white, nor did I keep or cut a player just because of his color. In our first meeting before training camp every year, I told the players that they made our teams only if they were good enough. I didn't care about a man's color or his ancestry; I just wanted to win football games with the best people possible."

This connected with young Jim Brown after the Syracuse experience. It also got old mighty fast. The 1962 season was Jim Brown's sixth in the league and his worst statistical campaign since his rookie year, rushing for 996 yards and only 4.3 yards per carry. It was the only year of his career that Brown did not lead the league in rushing and the first time since his rookie campaign that he did not break the 1,000-yard mark. In the aftermath, Paul Brown, despite 158 career victories and seven championships as a head coach over seventeen seasons, was finally dismissed from the team branded with his name.

The beginning of the end for Paul Brown was when his "big brute" of a fullback finally spoke publicly about his problems with how the team was being run, namely that there was no input from players about strategy and tactics on a week-to-week basis. Today such high-profile pushback against a head coach is not necessarily common, but it does happen. In the past, it simply was not done. Jim Brown made clear that his decision to speak out was not just about calling plays, which he believed was growing stale. It was about manhood. It was about control. It was about asserting his humanity in the face of a coach and an owner who saw him as a "gun to be fired." Given the social context in both segregated Cleveland and the nation, his statements had enormous power.

"I've always wanted to play for a coach I feel like going out and dying for. Paul Brown is not that coach," said Jim Brown. "Morale-wise, I think things will improve [when he leaves]. Football players don't like being treated as inferiors."

In the March 1963 issue of *Sport* magazine, Brown said, "I'm the kind of player who must perform freely, be relaxed. After so many years it's an established fact that a player should know a little about the game. When this isn't recognized, it's hopeless. . . . I have to express myself and if I can't have this understanding with the coach it's his prerogative to trade me. . . . Personally, I have been treated well, but I'm definitely not happy because as a team I don't feel we accomplished what we should have."

That fall, Brown told Joe Williams of the *New York World-Telegram*, "It was the coach's lack of compassion for a human being that kept him from being a great man."

The toppling of Paul Brown did not happen by accident. It was organized collectively inside that locker room. After retirement, in 1968, Jim Brown revealed to Alex Haley, "Our professional lives, our careers, were involved. We happened not to be the brainless automatons he wanted his players to act like. So we did what we had to do—in what we saw as the best interests of the players, the owner and the fans. And later events [winning the 1964 championship] proved us right. That's really all there was to it. . . . Some other players and I finally told [owner] Art Modell that unless the coaching methods changed, we'd either insist on being traded or quit."

Paul Brown was gone, and the young, brash Modell, all Brooklyn attitude, was in charge and unchallenged. Or so he thought.

Modell's first move was to hire Blanton Collier, a former assistant to Paul Brown, as the new coach in 1963. The phrase was not used at the time, but Collier was a "player's coach," the antithesis of hard-ass Paul Brown. And—true to the form of a player's coach—Collier made a point to ensure that his star player was as comfortable as possible. He let Jim Brown practice how he wanted to practice and give input into the strategy of offensive game plans. Brown in return told the media that he had the "highest respect in the world" for Collier. Sure enough, in 1963, Brown had his best year as a pro, rushing for a then unheard-of total of 1,863 yards over a fourteen-game season. If this had taken place during today's sixteen-game schedule, that would project to a record 2,131 yards. To give another sense of Brown's dominance, the number-two rusher that year was the Packers' Jim Taylor, who amassed 1,018 yards. As in other seasons of Brown's career, you would have to go back to Babe Ruth in the segregated era of Major League Baseball to find a player able to statistically lap his closest competition to such a towering degree.

At the time, in a dig at Paul Brown, Jim Brown said, "Collier gives us personal responsibility and a voice. He is not autocratic. He leaves it up to me to work the way I want to work."

Paul returned fire later with a political attack on Jim, saying that there were never "racial problems" in the Cleveland locker room until Jim came to play there. But as Jim Brown said in response, "One man's racial problem is another man's equal rights."

In the last days of playing for Paul Brown and for the rest of his football career, Jim Brown became vocal, taking the leadership he had earned on the field to create the kind of locker room that the old Cleveland players still discuss with awe. With his quiet voice and penetrating stare, he organized his teammates—particularly his black teammates—to take absolutely no shit. It is all the more stunning that he was able to do this not with a union or any kind of protection but just by, as cornerback Walter "Doc" Beach said, "asserting his African maleness."

Bobby Mitchell, Brown's backfield partner in Cleveland and a future Hall of Famer, recalled, "He was going to test you as a person and test you as a man immediately." His message, in Mitchell's words, was, "You are responsible for you. I'm responsible for me. But we are responsible for us. A black unit."

Brown fostered this leadership not only by talking football but by mentoring his black teammates about fiscal responsibility, the importance of having a lawyer or an agent negotiate their contracts, and the value of wearing coats and ties on the road, presenting themselves as businessmen who happened to play football. He would drive them into Cleveland's most impoverished black neighborhoods to walk among residents, loan money to new businesses, and also party in urban corners where the media did not dare tread. As they shared these experiences,

Brown began to plant seeds in the minds of his teammates about forming what he called a "National Negro Economic Union." He told them, "Imagine if we could take this financial power and recognizability and build up our own communities. King's way of pleading for equality won't cut it."

But the most significant stance he took was to tell the other Browns players to protect their dignity in a dehumanizing sport. He carried a briefcase to work, wore a suit on the road, and encouraged his teammates to do the same. This very act was seen as somehow politically aggressive, which says a great deal about how infantilized these men playing a "boys' game" could be in the eyes of management, media, and the public. When Brown responded to the jeers by saying simply, "I dress for work because this is my business and I demand to be taken seriously," it inspired his black teammates to follow. Brown promised them that if they stuck together, he would use his stardom to have their backs.

Walter Beach tells a story of finding out that he was cut from the team, until Jim Brown said otherwise.

"Eddie Linsky was the linebacker coach. We called him 'the Turk,'" Beach remembers. "Every time somebody got cut he would be the one that would notify us. So Eddie said, 'Walter, Blanton wants to see you . . . and bring your playbook.'

"Now, in the National Football League you know what that means. They talked to me and said they were gonna go with some other player. I thought I'd been doing well, been having a good camp. But what could I do? I thought, 'Okay. Well, I can work at my father's store, I guess.'

"So I went back upstairs and I started packing and Jim comes around and he says, 'Doc, c'mon, let's go to practice.' I said, 'No, man, they just placed me on waivers.' He said, 'You serious?' I said, 'Yeah I'm serious, they just put me on waivers.' He said, 'Aw, man . . . wait, wait, wait. Just stay here. I'll be right back.' It took about thirty, forty minutes. Jim then showed up and just said, 'Let's go to practice.' I said, 'What do you mean, let's go to practice? I told you that they placed me on waivers and they wasn't going with me.' He says again, 'Let's go to practice.' And he grabbed me by my arm and you could say he literally dragged me down to the training field.

"When I get to the locker room they're putting all of my equipment *back in my little cubicle*. So I get dressed, and it was one of the most difficult moments in my life because I don't know what to do. I'm kinda in limbo. We go through the calisthenics and I pause, and then not knowing what else to do, did the calisthenics.

"So I played professional football with Cleveland from that point on and never had a discussion with the coaches or management or anything—I just played. . . . I think it was thirty or forty years later, one evening Jim and I were talking and I said, 'I've always been curious. What did you say to the Cleveland Browns management that day?'

"He said, 'I knew what that was about. It was about racism. But I never mentioned race. All I said to them was, 'If you want me to do the things so that we can make this a championship team, then y'all got to keep the people who are going to make this a championship team. Y'all know Doc can play. So why would you be sending him away if you know he can play?' I said, 'Man, I really appreciate you being my friend.' Jim said,

'Doc, I got a lot of friends. I did it because you could play foot-ball. I didn't do it for you because you were my friend. I've seen a lot of friends get cut.'"

Jim Brown also started to speak out while in uniform. When asked whether he had ever been subject to racial slurs on the field, his response was not the placid "Everyone loves you as long as you can play" line that he gave the black press earlier in his career. Instead it was as heavy as his stare. "The fact that I have so seldom been a target for slurs on the field neither pleases nor displeases me," he wrote in *Off My Chest*. "It is a matter of little consequence. I do not crave the white man's approval; I crave only the rights I'm entitled to as a human being. The ac-ceptance of the Negro in sports is really an insignificant devel-opment that warms the heart of the Negro less than it does that of the white man who salves his troubled conscience by telling himself, 'Isn't it wonderful that Negroes and whites are out there playing together?'"

A Cleveland sportscaster, John Fitzgerald, told Brown, on television, to quiet down and concentrate on football. Fitzger-ald later explained himself to Brown more privately: "I've al-ways admired you as a football player, Jim. I've never looked on you as a Negro." "That's ridiculous!" Brown replied. "You have to look at me as a Negro. Look at me, man! I'm black!"

This was a political moment when black athletes were saying for the first time, "If you respect me on the field, then you need to respect me when the pads come off." As Brown wrote in *Out of Bounds*, "On the football field they wanted me to be brave. Wanted me to take the ball when we were all backed up, our own one-yard-line, carry us out of there, where we could be safe. Away from football, they wanted me to be another guy. They wanted me to be docile. How could I have the courage to run that hard, then be so weak off the field that I'd succumb to inequity? . . . The message got around: If you were black and you played for Cleveland, you had support. We took every rookie in, explained how we did things on the Browns. . . . The Cleveland Browns had the best organized blacks in all of sports. We partied, chased women, but we also discussed economics, and talked about life after football."

Or as Brown also said, as quoted by Mike Freeman in his book *Jim Brown: The Fierce Life of an American Hero*, "When you came to the Cleveland Browns, if you were black, you had to come a certain way. That meant being responsible off the field and being serious about playing on the field. We had to be about something."

As Brown organized his Cleveland teammates, the media branded him, in highly disparaging terms, as a "locker room lawyer." When asked today about that phrase, Brown emits a low and mirthless laugh. "'Locker room lawyer' . . . I laugh because you got to understand, they didn't get us, which means that you never gave up your manhood for the bullshit, and that seemed to be what the system wanted you to do. 'Give up your manhood and be grateful for what we give you, and if you do the right things, we'll take care of you.' What drove people crazy is that we didn't put our sport before our manhood. That's what the deal was. And in this day and age, it's still the deal."

The team under Blanton Collier won the 1964 championship and worked together seamlessly on the field, but when practices and games ended, the players often self-segregated. As

Brown said, "We'd come out of the stadium and there'd be two buses. And if I were the first black ball player, and I got on the first bus, when all the other black players came out, we'd all be on that same bus."

This self-segregation itself was an act of protest that grew from the Paul Brown days. Back then, the team wanted the players to all sit together at banquets and other public team functions, but behind the scenes and on the road, they assigned roommates on a racialized basis. This was some of "the bull-shit" that Jim Brown would not abide. "I have no bones, no muscles that the white man doesn't have," he wrote in *Off My Chest*. "But I do have as much dignity as any white man, and if this is not recognized in Mississippi I at least expect it to be recognized by my teammates and employers. In 1960 Paul Brown came to me and asked why all of our Negro players hung together . . . at football luncheons and banquets. . . . I replied that we were not going to make a show of looking chummy as long as the club's business manager assigned us hotel rooms in a manner that suggested we [black players] had leprosy."

By 1964, when Jim Brown was the highest-paid player in football, he would refuse to go to parties thrown by the Cleveland Browns organization. He later explained that "they'd have one party for everybody, then one for just the whites. You can't ask me to come to your house, then say I can only hang in the kitchen. If I've got to be a nigger, I still don't have to be a house nigger."

Brown speaks about how this type of self-segregation was fine when it came from the players but unacceptable when it came from management. Once he confronted Art Modell about how he was handling the players' hotel room arrangements. "There was an odd number of blacks," Brown explains. "And he was going to buy us separate rooms, because he didn't have two blacks to put in the same room. So instead of putting a white in a black player's room, he was going to buy an extra room. That shit you cannot do. That's something else. We love being together, no problem with that shit, but you're saying something else now. And we can't allow you to say that. Modell was outraged that I said he couldn't do that. I'll never forget, he said to me, 'I give more money to the NAACP than you!' I said, 'Oh, you must have immunity on your hands! How can I question you, then?'—Oh, I'm laughing—'I do more for black folks than you do!' . . . We weren't an easy group for white folks to deal with. Everyone said, 'Look, man, they're just different cats over there in Cleveland.'"

For Brown this has to do with the question of "leadership": how it is earned and how it is expressed in the company of men in a violent profession. He said, "One of those sports shows was talking about that term 'leadership,' and there is a lack of leadership in football. Look at that cornerback for Seattle. [Richard Sherman] makes comments to the press and we're all supposed to think that this is the leader, but that's not leadership. That's confusion. Our experiences were that we knew who the leaders were, and we always knew who we were. We played all season, and then if you spoke to the entire team, everybody knew that you were a leader. So when you spoke, everyone knew it mattered."

This leadership led the Cleveland Browns back from a losing

record in 1962 to the NFL championship in 1964, in just the second season after Jim Brown helped jettison Paul Brown for Blanton Collier. The Browns beat the storied—and heavily favored—Baltimore Colts, led by quarterback legend Johnny Unitas, 27–0. It was a stunning upset that shocked the NFL world. The Colts were stacked with future of Hall of Fame players including Lenny Moore, Raymond Berry, and John Mackey, as well as a young genius head coach in Don Shula. Not only was it an upset; it has proven to be historic. There has never been a shutout in an NFL championship game since. They won because a fevered Cleveland crowd turned the atmosphere into something electric. (This was before the days of neutral Super Bowl sites.) The crowd buzzed quietly when quarterback Frank Ryan was under center, roaring with every completed pass. When it was Johnny Unitas's turn to take the ball for the Colts, there was a jarring cacophony. The Colts were completely stymied. Meanwhile, the entire Hall of Fame–stacked Colts defense geared up to stop Jim Brown, which opened the door for Ryan to throw three touchdown passes to Gary Collins. Despite this, Brown still ran for 114 yards on 27 carries.

But it was the Browns' D on this day that made history. Johnny Unitas was to quarterbacks what Jim Brown was to runners: the standard for all who would follow. Johnny U finished his career as a four-time MVP and effectively created the quarterback position as we know it today. The ten-time Pro Bowler threw the ball downfield with a range and accuracy that would not be matched until a completely new generation of quarterbacks entered the sport. The idea that the Browns would hold Johnny U scoreless in a championship game was the equivalent of shutting down Michael Jordan in a decisive playoff series. The Browns defense deserves far more credit for this than they have received. One person who always gives them that praise is Jim Brown.

When Brown is told, "It's amazing you did not allow that Colts team to score a single point," he says only, "Don't say 'you.' I didn't shut out anybody. I wasn't playing defense."

According to Jamil Smith, a journalist at MTV News who was raised in Cleveland two decades after the championship season, this game loomed larger every year. "At least in the consciousness of Clevelanders, it was never like, 'Oh, that's Jim Brown the movie star or activist.' It was always, 'a Cleveland Brown, period.' And no matter what he does, no matter what he is associated with, whether it's [work to keep kids out of gangs], movies, or off-field controversies, it's always, 'Jim Brown is the best running back that ever lived, and dammit, he's ours.' And there's a sense of real pride in knowing that the best running back that ever walked the earth was in our uniform. No matter how many disappointments we have suffered since—and there have been many—it was empowering to know that we had this standard in our past."

In his autobiographies, Jim Brown observed: "I guess it's no surprise that what I [love] most about playing football [is] playing football," and "I can only say that football . . . is fun. At twenty-eight, I have a lot more fun ahead of me."

Yet after the 1964 championship, the love and fun would be challenged by the first of many high-profile controversies involving violence against women. In 1965, an eighteen-year-old black woman from Cleveland named Brenda Ayres accused Brown of assault and then filed a paternity suit against him. It pressed his young fans to do something that was unfamiliar at the time, but very much a part of our present-day sports world: judge their hero by his personal behavior. Once again, Jim Brown was blazing a trail for the twenty-first-century athlete.

Unlike other male athletes with various children born out of wedlock and whose brawls, affairs, and other crimes and misdemeanors were covered up by a dutiful press, Jim Brown had a wide-open trail in the Brenda Ayres case. Brown's defenders have described this as a racial double standard, and true or not, conscious or not, there was no doubting the salaciousness of the trial that captured Cleveland's attention. It also must be noted that if Brown's supporters thought he was getting a raw deal, the treatment of young Ayres in the press was vicious. She was described in newspapers as "a Cleveland dropout" and was dissected by cruel media in every possible way, including assessments of her height, weight, and attractiveness. Ayres had accused the twenty-nine-year-old Brown of assault and battery and, as the papers put it at the time, "forcing an unnatural sex act," leaving just what that act was to the imagination. Brown's lawyers accused Ayres of being a part of a "shakedown." As reported through such headlines as "Girl Breaks Down During Testimony," Ayres, testifying through her tears, said they had met in a hotel room several times in the past. Brown's wife Sue, according to reports, was in the courtroom that morning but did not return for the afternoon. The strain Brown's infidelity caused in their marriage was something she could suffer privately but not in the public eye.

If the white press seized on this case as a chance to bury Brown, the black press took a far more lascivious approach, attacking Ayres but also keeping a close eye on the facts of the trial. Here is how *Jet* magazine reported on what was happening in the courtroom: "In the intimate art of love making, James Nathaniel (Jim) Brown was accused by a Cleveland teen-ager of bringing gridiron tactics into the bedroom. Attractive high school dropout Brenda Ayres charged that the powerful football hero hit, kicked, and made attempts to force her into a repugnant love-making act after having normal sexual intercourse. . . . In the end, the jury believed Brown [and] found him innocent of the slanderous charges."

The Cleveland Browns organization and Art Modell had no official response to any of this. There is no record of Jim Brown losing any of the corporate or Hollywood friends he was attempting to cultivate. This was a different era, when such a scandal could be endured and survived as long as juries declared verdicts in Brown's favor. It also speaks to how black women were treated as dispensable and untrustworthy, at a lower social rung than Jim Brown, both in the white press that ignored them and in the black press that treated Ayres like she was bringing down a hero for a payday.

The following year Brown was back in court, again facing off against Ayres, who accused him of fathering her child. Brown publicly mocked this claim as "ridiculous" and fought back ferociously, hiring a team of top attorneys that Ayres could not hope to match. Ayres lost her paternity suit. Several years later, Ayres called Brown and asked him to meet his daughter. He knew at first glance that the child was his, but it was not until 1989 that Brown publicly acknowledged his daughter Shellee. It is a reminder that trusting Jim Brown's public statements about allegations levied against him by women is fraught with peril.

As for Brown's young fans, especially those in Cleveland, they followed the Ayres trial closely, siding with their hero and convinced that he was being railroaded. The jury's decision backed their belief that Brown was, if not pure, at least intact as a role model. Fan David Whitehouse remembered, "Our disbelief was rooted in love."

Brown's broader status as an NFL god was not altered a bit by the trials. At that time there was only one person who could stop Jim Brown from carrying a football to glory, and it wasn't Sam Huff or Alex Karras or the attorneys of Brenda Ayres. It was Browns owner Art Modell. The problems started when handsome, charismatic Brown started to take movie roles in the off-season. His big break was clearly imminent when he was hired—alongside an all-star cast that included Lee Marvin and Charles Bronson—for the Robert Aldrich film *The Dirty Dozen*. Brown was unable to report to training camp on time in the summer of 1966 because heavy rains had hammered the set and repeatedly delayed the filming in England. Modell's response was to issue a pugnacious public statement, vowing to fine Brown for every missed day of training camp, and bench him upon his return. As had happened with Schwartzwalder and Paul Brown, Jim Brown was simply not going to be, as he said, "punked." Instead, suddenly and without warning, he retired from football in his prime rather than suffer a public rebuke.

This decision to walk away, he said, was easy, and he set out to make his case for early retirement as public as possible. Brown wrote an open letter to Modell and read it to reporters on the *Dirty Dozen* set for maximum effect. It read, in part, "I honestly like you and will be willing to help you in any way I can, but I feel you must realize that both of us are men and that my manhood is just as important to me as yours is to you."

On November 26 of the previous year, Jim Brown had been on the cover of *Time* magazine, clean-shaven in his football uniform. Eight months later *Time* led an article on him with the following description: "Dressed in Army fatigues and sporting a ten-day growth of beard, he looked more like a Cuban revolutionary than the best running back in pro football. He sounded pretty revolutionary too. 'I want,' said James Nathaniel Brown, 30, 'to have a hand in the struggle that is going on in our country.' Thus Jim Brown, fullback of the National Football League's Cleveland Browns and the biggest ground gainer (12,312 yards over nine seasons) in the history of pro football, announced his retirement from the sport that made him famous."

He told *Sports Illustrated*, "I quit with regret but no sorrow. I've been able to do all the things I wanted to do, and now I want to devote my time to other things. And I wanted more mental stimulation than I would have had playing football. . . . All through my career I was always looking to not stay too long. For all the guys who stayed too long . . . I thought it was embarrassing. People had sympathy for them, and you should never have sympathy for a champion."

Later in life, he revealed what he thought the moment he heard that Art Modell wanted to bench him for not reporting to camp: "My first year in the NFL I led the league in rushing. My last year I was MVP. Bench THAT, motherfucker."

*New York Times* sports columnist Robert Lipsyte was in London to do a story on the filming of *The Dirty Dozen*. "It was very obvious at the time that he had not made any kind of a decision about whether or not he was going back to football," Lipsyte remembered. "I think he wanted to. He wasn't over yet, and still loved the game.

"It was apparent that he was being forced into a decision, because the movie was running late. He obviously couldn't just pick up and leave. I had the feeling that the great Jim Brown was never going to admit that he was forced into a situation where he had to make a decision. Because he could have said, 'Hey, the movie is running late, I'll see you when I see you.' Jim Brown could come back to Cleveland with his head on backwards and they would still suit him up for the game, right? He could do anything he fucking wanted.

"But I think that he really needed to show that he had control. So instead he made this big statement that he had decided that movies were going to be his career. And when Modell said he was going to fine him, Jim saw it as an affront to his manhood. . . . Everything comes back to his manhood. Every opponent in the world, in his mind, is challenging his dick. Although, you know, it's so obvious that he made the right decision. It added to his legend, and besides, how much longer could he play?"

It speaks to the stature of Jim Brown that the blame for this decision fell upon Art Modell. The forty-one-year-old owner had previously taken heat for exiling the legendary Paul

Brown—which was met in Cleveland initially with skepticism, followed by acclaim after the 1964 championship. But now Jim Brown was seen as being pushed out as well, and the sports life of the city was never the same, with the idea of the "curse of the Browns" gaining traction and "God hates Cleveland" becoming a mantra among local sports fans. Over the next thirty years, this team would make the AFC Championship Game, one step removed from the Super Bowl, seven times and lose every contest. Cleveland's pugnaciously die-hard fans saw Modell as the one constant in this era of frustration. After the 1995 season, Modell moved the team to Baltimore, consecrating his place as one of the most infamous franchise owners in the history of sports. Despite Modell's historic role in forming the modern NFL, he has never been elected to the Pro Football Hall of Fame, partly because the hall's locale, in Canton, Ohio, is so close to Cleveland that, it is feared—even after Modell's death—protesting Browns fans would mar the proceedings.

Later in life, Art Modell was calling Brown "the greatest player who ever lived"; he even invited Brown to speak to his Baltimore Ravens before their dominant 2001 Super Bowl victory over the New York Giants. Brown was like Gary Cooper's character in *High Noon*, finally, after thirty-five years, winning the showdown. He said, "I feel very satisfied that I got out when I did. Because at the end of the game, after nine years, something's going to pop and that's the end of that. I got to walk away."

Jim Brown entered and left the sport with his "manhood" intact. He also created an example almost impossible to replicate: the player who never missed a game, the player who left on his own terms, the player who—although this was more legend than fact—was indestructible. The Jim Brown narrative helped forge a "man code" that defines the league: the idea that your manhood depends on your ability to inflict violence on others and deny the presence of pain—both physical and psychological—in yourself. This "man code" is also, of course, loudly, proudly, and aggressively heterosexual, with women existing only as extensions of desire for either sex or violence. It is a man code that has wrecked generations of players attempting to follow its path.

The value system of football exacts this price because at root it is the valorization of brutality. Ralph Wiley, the great sportswriter, said it with a wry grin on his face: "We're all drawn to the spectacle, the violence. Who will live and who will die?"

Jim Brown has always celebrated his own place at the top of this pyramid of scar tissue and painkillers: the toughest man in the toughest sport. In his middle-aged memoir *Out of Bounds*, he wrote, "Football is not about tricky plays. It's about dominance. Physical and mental dominance. And the best way to dominate is to run the football. If you can run on a team, shove it up and down the field, it means you're kicking ass (that's physical) and both of you know (that's mental). Running is power. Give me a team that can run and play tough defense, *I* can take them to the Super Bowl. . . . I didn't want to be hanging out in the training room, screwing around with doctors. I didn't want to be weak. I wanted to be a bad motherfucker. . . . During games, for instance, I almost never drank water. . . . I'd look at water, not drinking it, as a test. Three hours of football. I will not deviate. I will not acquiesce. I am a warrior."

Brown also said, "The key in the NFL is to hit a man so hard so often he doesn't want to play anymore. You let the defense know you're hurt, next play they'll be twice as motivated to finish the job. By getting up with leisure every play, every game, every season they never knew if I was hurt or if I wasn't, I was screwing with their heads and trying to save my own."

Syracuse football star Don McPherson responded with no small amount of exasperation when he heard these sentiments. "We need to stop making manhood about tearing ourselves apart. Forget about more players retiring early, fixing tackling form, or the labor pool shrinking. If the NFL doesn't cut out this macho crap, it'll still be the same game—profitable, yes, but forever grinding up men like pieces of meat."

These kinds of masculine ideals carried over into Brown's personal life, as they do for so many players and fans. His first wife, Sue, from whom he was divorced in 1972, told Pete Dexter for *Inside Sports* magazine, "When I divorced him it wasn't his temper or the mood changes. It wasn't other women." Rather, she explained, it was the neglect.

"When we were out in public, we were always hugged up. At home, he was someplace you couldn't touch. . . . Listen. Jim is not a normal person. The dentist couldn't numb this man's gums. He could drink champagne—bottles of it—and never get drunk. It never fazed him. He played football with broken ribs and some nights he'd come home and I'd have to take his clothes off for him. Some nights I'd bathe him. But he could play like that. I never knew how."

The sport's endless violence and aftereffects—as well as the lies that spill out of the mouths of NFL executives—are often compared to those of the tobacco industry. It makes sense on multiple levels: The exhilarating violence of the sport can certainly feel as addictive as smoking. In addition, despite all the public relations campaigns to make us believe that the game is now safer, it can never actually be safe; just as a cigarette can be advertised to have less tar or a bigger filter, yet there is no such thing as a cancer-free smoke.

But there is one rather profound difference: if you meet people suffering from lung cancer, they invariably wish they had never reached for that first cigarette, and if they have kids, they pray their children don't pick up the habit. It's an experience defined by utter regret. Many ex–football players don't want their own kids to put their bodies through what they have gone through, but very few will ever say, "I wish I'd never played." In a society that can be incredibly alienating and where men have little common space to bond with other men, football provides a sense of fraternity many cannot imagine their lives without. That it's a fraternity born in violence and brain injury, a fraternity that leaves most players bankrupt, a fraternity that leads to insanely high divorce rates, and a fraternity you would never want your own children to join rarely enters the mental calculus of the sport. As noxious as comparing sports to actual war can be, it's a disconnect you really hear only when men speak about their experiences in combat: difficult to endure and yet, at least by some participants, remembered with pride.

Today Jim Brown says that he is happiest when he gets to "go back and deal with the Browns, deal with the young guys, and see how anxious the young running backs are to relate. . . . It's like caring, love, and respect, and all those things are stepping up and taking their rightful place in my mind. All the rest of it is shit."

He may have walked away from football, but, as with an ex-smoker picking up a half-lit butt someone threw on the street, a part of him never really left.

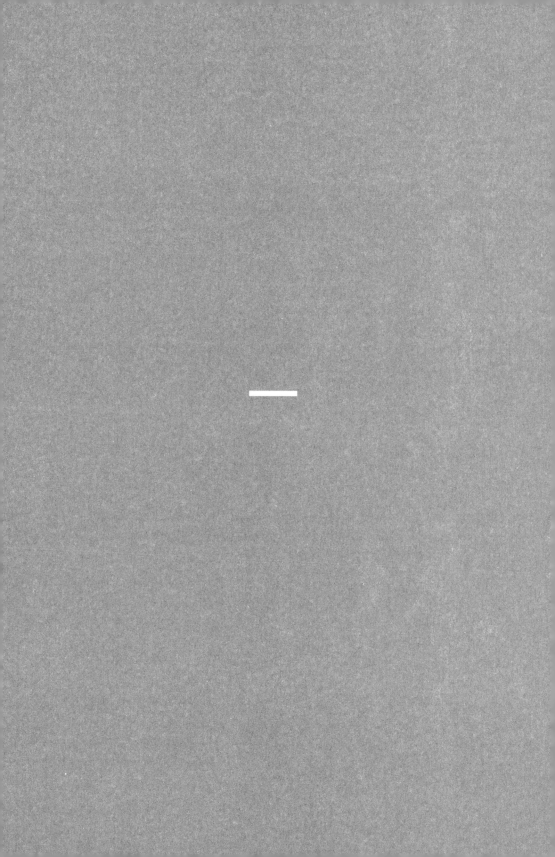

# FOUR

# JIM BROWN'S BLACK POWER: "IF I EVER MARCH, I'LL MARCH ALONE"

—

I will fight for my right to be free. . . . I will die for that right. People say, Yes, the white man has his foot up your ass. Be patient. . . . He must adjust to not having his foot up your ass. Give him another two hundred years. Let him ease it out.

I say, No. Take it out. Now.

—*Jim Brown*

*You are Huey Newton. You founded the Black Panther Party for Self-Defense, an organization that fused the politics of socialism with black nationalism, in Oakland, California. You rapidly become a national celebrity after you are shot in the stomach during a confrontation with the Oakland police—a confrontation that left Officer John Frey dead. You are sentenced to fifteen years in prison and the phrase "Free Huey" becomes a slogan of the times. The Black Panther Party grows dramatically while you are behind bars, and after several mis-trials you beat the rap. One Oakland politician says, "Huey could take street-gang types and give them a social consciousness." That's real power.*

*You have no love for big business. You have no love for those who want to work "inside the system" and you sure as hell have no love for President Richard Nixon. And yet . . . when Jim Brown calls you and asks you to hang out, you say yes. You spend countless hours talking in his house overlooking Los Angeles. You know that Jim Brown supported Tricky Dick. You know that he is trying to aid the development of businesses in the black community, more than he stands for any kind of revolutionary consciousness. You know this, yet you need to hang out with Jim Brown. "It's a manhood thing," you say. "We need to be men to achieve our liberation, and Jim Brown is 'the man.'" You recognize that if Jim Brown is doing it, then it is on some level for the greater good. You might not agree with his strategy and tactics, but hey, he's Jim Brown. He is a symbol of resistance, and that symbolism is more important than any words he could utter or political candidate he might endorse. You connect because you rec-ognize in each other that willingness to die for what you believe in. You eventually do die by the bullet in 1989, but not in an instance of "revolutionary suicide," fighting an oppressive state. You are killed trying to buy crack, after years of addiction. The shine is off your celebrity and your funeral is not the national remembrance—the polit-ical statement—you imagined during the glory years of the Panthers. But Jim Brown is in attendance and gives one of the eulogies. He speaks. He shows respect. Your life wasn't anything close to what it could have been. But having Jim Brown show love over your fallen body? It could have been a hell of a lot worse.*

ON FEBRUARY 1, 1960, FOUR COLLEGE STUDENTS IN Greensboro, North Carolina, sat at the whites-only lunch counter at the local Woolworth's. They were refused service, yet rather than leave, they chose to remain in their seats. The managers at that Woolworth's also made a choice: instead of serving the students, they shut the lunch counter down. The students repeatedly returned. They were cursed, beaten, and threatened. Lit cigarettes were flicked at their faces, but they would not be moved.

Their courage sparked a new phase in the black freedom struggle. Over the next year, more than fifty thousand people—mostly black, some white, most of them young—participated in demonstrations of one kind or another in over one hundred cities. More than five thousand people were jailed in acts of civil disobedience, an assertion of power enacted by women and men working side by side. As bell hooks wrote, it was a moment where there was a possibility for a "historical movement for racial uplift rooted in nonviolence and gender equality."

It was also a moment when you did not have to be some kind of star athlete to prove your worth. Instead you could be the kind of person whose courage was earned by facing fearsome obstacles that most football players couldn't comprehend. Instead of confronting a linebacker who wanted to tear your head off because of the color of your uniform, you could have the mettle to sit in a restaurant and face dozens of people who wanted to literally tear your head off because of the color of your skin. If you could endure the cigarette embers flicked at your face, the saliva spit in your eyes, and the threats to your life, you could be a different kind of hero rooted in the American imagination. You could be a freedom fighter.

By the end of 1960, lunch counters were open for business to those with black skin in Greensboro, as well as in many other places across the South. Protest was legitimized and people believed that what they did truly mattered. The moment would be animated by the words of Dr. King, who spoke of "the fierce urgency of now" and said, "Three hundred years of humiliation, abuse and deprivation cannot be expected to find voice in a whisper."

As Jim Brown was busting through defensive lines and starting to find his voice, the black freedom struggle started to roll from the South to the North. During the summer of 1964, the year Brown won his only NFL championship, there were one thousand arrests of civil rights activists, thirty buildings bombed, and thirty-six churches burned by the Ku Klux Klan and their sympathizers. That same year, the first of the urban uprisings and riots in the northern ghettos took place. The Black Power movement may have found its roots in the North throughout the 1940s and 1950s, but it exploded into the national consciousness and as a slogan in the 1960s. This phrase meant many different things to different people. That was its strength as a slogan, and also its weakness. To some, like the Black Panther Party for Self-Defense, it meant revolution. To bell hooks, it conjured something negative: the complete "embrace of patriarchal masculinity" and a shift from a movement for uplift that could link a fight against sexism with the push against racism.

To other forces, it meant a patriotic assertion of black capitalism: the idea that Black America needed to build up its own economic institutions and enrich itself as a path to liberation. Only that path, not the path of protest, could bring power in a society that valued—the argument went—wealth even more than maintaining white supremacy. The first major Black Power conference held in the United States was in 1967, and it wasn't put together by the Black Panthers. It was organized by a Republican businessman named Nathan Wright, Jr., with the message that black Americans needed to organize for their "fair share of the pie."

Most have placed Brown firmly in that latter camp: they thought that he was an advocate for Black Power because he stood for economic self-determination and wielding capitalism as a weapon to fight racism. The reality however was more complicated. Brown's athletic legacy of physical prowess as well as his fame, charisma, and intellectual curiosity meant he was sought out by forces as disparate as Malcolm X, Huey Newton, Louis Farrakhan, and Richard Nixon. They all wanted to be able to count Brown among the allies for their particular agendas and movements. Yet Brown was not looking for a movement or to attach himself to anyone else's agenda. He once said, "If I ever march, I'll march alone." He was an organizer but not a movement builder. He was someone who worked to see the black community assert its economic independence and fight racism, but also someone who looked at the existing manifestations of the "fight against racism"—marching, demonstrating, even arming yourself for revolutionary ends, as the Panthers did—and saw a waste of everyone's time. Although Brown was also quick to say that if the economic opportunities he craved for the black community were cut off, maybe he'd change his views.

He said during these tumultuous days, "I hate to think what would happen if white society refuses to let us bring economic power to blacks. First the black guerrilla network will spring up all over the country and I'd be there with them. Just because I'm making money as an actor that doesn't make me satisfied."

This recalls a scene in the 2009 blaxploitation satire film *Black Dynamite*. A stock Pantheresque revolutionary calls the titular hero an "Uncle Tom," and Dynamite—who sports a *very* "Jim Brown" mustache and fashion sense—says, "Listen, sucka, I'm blacker than the ace of spades and more militant than you and your whole damn army put together. So I tell you what: When your so-called revolution starts, you call me, and I'll be right down front showing you how it's done. But until then, you need to shut the fuck up when grown folks is talking."

That's Jim Brown. He would not be down with mass struggle in the streets because he did not think mass struggle was an avenue to change, but if things got real, he said he'd be on the front lines. No one doubted him.

When asked at what moment he was first aware that there was even such a thing as a civil rights movement, he said, "As soon as there was one, I was conscious of it. If you were black and you were dealing with anything, then you had to deal with being black. Shit, if you wanted anything, you were going to face the bullshit. So, I was very conscientious of everything that I could be conscientious of. I wanted to know Paul Robeson— he was my number-one guy, a great man. I was able to express my appreciation for his contributions and let him know that I had great respect for him and everything he did. And Robeson was doing it, fighting, for decades before anyone knew Dr. King."

Brown's analysis of Martin Luther King, Jr., and the non-violent wing of the civil rights movement has been remarkably consistent over the course of the last sixty years. He may have been aware of King's civil rights movement from its inception, but he did not believe in its tactics or goals. He said in the mid-1960s, "I don't ask for integration. I just don't want to be segregated. I have no desire to live in a white neighborhood but if the house that best suits my fancy happens to be in a white neighborhood, then I want that house. The hell with integration. Just don't segregate me."

That belief was earned through experience. He told Alex Haley, "I never will forget being bluntly refused an apartment in Cleveland soon after I moved there. The landlady looked me in the face and said, 'We only take whites.' I wound up buying the home we have now, in a nice, modest, predominantly Negro neighborhood. At the other place, I hadn't been eager to live around white people; I had just wanted a place near where the Browns practiced. It wasn't integration I was after; I just was bitter about being *segregated*, you understand?"

Brown, greatly influenced by Malcolm X's speeches about economic self-determination, did not believe in nonviolence as a guiding philosophy. It didn't fit with who he was or how he thought respect from white America would be earned.

This position has not changed even with the subsequent deification of Dr. King over the last fifty years into something approaching American sainthood. Brown says today, "I didn't think much of Dr. King. I mean, I am not trying to put him down, but if you think about the majority of the rhetoric, it's about what's being done to us. It doesn't have damn near anything that says what we're going to do for ourselves."

Whatever one thinks about Brown's politics, they are a reminder that he, Muhammad Ali, and Malcolm X are often described in a lazy fashion as "civil rights activists," when all three explicitly either criticized or even opposed the civil rights movement as established by its early leaders, like Dr. King and the Southern Christian Leadership Conference. The history as lived in real time was defined by debates and conflict inside the black community.

Professor and author Michael Eric Dyson has commented that "there was always a 'self-help' strain that spurned some of the methodology of the civil rights movement, beginning in a conservative way with Booker T. Washington's pull-yourself-up-by-your-bootstraps approach, but there were 'bootstrappers' who were not accommodationists in the same way that Booker T. Washington was. It was the [Godfather of Soul] James Brown approach: 'I don't want nobody to give me nothing—open the door and I can get it myself.'

"This was part of a critique of the methodology of non-violence in the face of white violence. Malcolm and Black Nationalist organizations said, 'We want to operate in our own world, with our own pace, with our own goals without asking anybody for anything.' No hat in hand, but the demand for respect."

According to Dr. Dyson, it is crucial to understand that

people like Brown, Ali, and Malcolm X were still a part of a broader overarching struggle even if their agenda was not aligned with King's civil rights movement. The movement consisted of all types of approaches and philosophies, but the civil rights movement was the most widely elevated by the dominant society "because it ceded the humanity of white people and their consciences as the linchpin [for] the doors of justice to open. Jim Brown was certainly part of the black freedom struggle, but it was an assertion of manhood, an assertion of blacks' humanity . . . an assertion of the economic power of black people."

Before the Black Panthers, the most prominent organized black critics of Dr. King and the civil rights movement could be found in the separatist organization of Malcolm X and Elijah Muhammad, the Nation of Islam, referred to first in the white press and therefore popularly known as "the Black Muslims." Their ideas were far more in line with the thinking of Jim Brown than the philosophies of Dr. King. In *Off My Chest*, Brown stunned the sports world when, just after Muhammad Ali joined their ranks, he defended the Nation. Brown spoke out because he was unabashedly in regular debate, discussion, and conversation with their members. He wrote:

"I am not a Black Muslim, but rather a member of the more rational NAACP, and yet I'm all for the Black Muslims. We need every possible element going for us, whether it be a radical sect, a CORE picket line, or a team of NAACP lawyers arguing in court. The more commotion the better. . . . It is indicative of the white man's ignorance of our attitudes that when you ask whites—intelligent whites—what sort of organization they

think the Muslims are, they almost invariably answer something like this: 'The Muslims are extremists. They're the counter-
part of the Ku Klux Klan.' The fact is, they are not. They don't
stalk into the night and burn crosses and terrorize people and
flog them."

The Nation of Islam's ideology dovetailed with Brown's
conservative ideas about gender relations and economic policy,
but it also connected with his frustration over integrationist politics and anger toward the bloody history of white
supremacy.

Brown's public defense of and dialogue with the Nation of
Islam also help explain what took place in Miami on February
25, 1964, when a young boxer, Cassius Marcellus Clay, Jr., in
his own words, "shook up the world" after winning the heavyweight championship over the supposedly unstoppable Charles
"Sonny" Liston. But that alone is not what makes February 25,
1964, such a seminal moment. It was what happened after the
fight. Clay did not celebrate or—as his trainer predicted—spend
the night in the hospital. Instead he sat in his hotel room eating
ice cream with some interesting company: Jim Brown, music
legend Sam Cooke, and Malcolm X.

They had not gathered just for ice cream and conversation.
Clay was considering a decision already hotly rumored in the
papers: that he would join the Nation of Islam and speak out in
sharp opposition to the civil rights movement of Dr. King. The
following day, Clay announced to the world that he would in
fact join the NOI, saying, "I ain't no Christian. I can't be when
I see all the colored people fighting for forced integration get
blown up. They get hit by the stones and chewed by dogs and

then [racists] blow up a Negro church. . . . People are always telling me what a good example I would be if I just wasn't Muslim. I've heard over and over why couldn't I just be more like Joe Louis and Sugar Ray. Well, they are gone and the black man's condition is just the same, ain't it? We're still catching hell."

These four people represented a stunning panorama of cultural capital: black men who for decades to come would symbolize the idea of using manhood, personal pride, and cultural excellence as tools to resist racism. Yet within a year of this meeting, only Brown and Ali would still be alive.

Ali died in 2016, after decades of being rendered largely voiceless because of Parkinson's disease, so only Brown is capable of communicating what actually was discussed on that fateful night in Miami. Brown's first memory was that it almost didn't happen. As he remembers, "I told Ali we had planned a huge postfight party at the Fontainebleau Hotel. I told him that all the sharp chicks and happening little girls would be there and he should show up. Ali said he would only come through if he beat Sonny Liston. After the fight I ran to find Ali. I was so happy. I wanted to get our asses to that party."

But Muhammad Ali did not have partying on his mind. Instead he looked at Brown and said, "No, Jim. There's this little black hotel. Let's go over there. I want to talk to you."

That "little black hotel" was called Hampton House, a refuge for black entertainers and athletes in a time when Miami had more in common with Dixie than the multiracial, international city it would soon become.

The four men differed in their personalities and politics but were bound, as Brown put it, "because of race." Sam Cooke, in particular, was someone who embodied a bootstrap ethos mixed with a strong sense of black nationalism and pride. Cooke started as a gospel singer with the Soul Stirrers. He went on to have thirty hits land in the Top 40, including "You Send Me," "Chain Gang," and "Everybody Loves to Cha Cha Cha." But Cooke's most memorable song was the civil rights anthem "A Change Is Gonna Come," which he wrote after feeling frustrated that Bob Dylan had a higher platform as a civil rights troubadour than any black artist.

Yet Cooke was more than a songwriter and performer. He owned his record label and the publishing rights to his songs. He wanted to blaze a trail so other black artists would not continue to be robbed blind by the record industry. Brown remembers, "Sam Cooke was one of our favorite singers, and I liked him. But during that time, it was always about change. The stars were not just stars on the laundry list, singing or acting or whatever. People were conscientious about being good black citizens. People were deciding how they wanted to resist. And Malcolm was one extreme. Most people were afraid to be around Malcolm. We were not scared."

Many people have always assumed that the conversations Cooke, Brown, and Malcolm had with Ali at Hampton House were about giving the young champion the moral support to "come out" the next day and announce that he would join the Nation of Islam. After all, Brown and Cooke both stood strongly with the economic black nationalism that the NOI preached. Malcolm's presence makes a great deal of sense since he had developed a close friendship with the young fighter, traveling with him to his Miami training camp in the lead-up to the Liston fight. He was also the Nation's most prominent member, the number-two person in the organization under Elijah Muhammad.

As Ali himself remembered decades later to his biographer Thomas Hauser, "Malcolm was very intelligent, with a good sense of humor, a wise man. When he talked, he held me spellbound for hours."

Yet there were always holes in this assumed history, most pointedly that Malcolm was already clearly on the outs with the Nation of Islam. The minister had been suspended for comments he made soon after the November 1963 assassination of John F. Kennedy, saying that it was a case of "chickens coming home to roost." Malcolm had also been increasingly public about his dissatisfaction with the NOI's abstention from the activist part of the black freedom struggle. There was also his private anger, revealed in his posthumous autobiography published two years later, focusing on Elijah Muhammad's hypocrisy in having fathered children out of wedlock with young women in the Nation. Brown remembers, "We used to go down to the beach in Miami and talk. And I admired his courage because at this moment, he was going against Elijah Muhammad and his life wasn't worth a dime. He was lonely."

By February, Malcolm was already planning what his political and religious life would be when he was out from under the leadership of Elijah Muhammad. Would he really have been encouraging one of the most famous athletes in the world, and a dear friend, to join an organization he was leaving, an organization that he believed was threatening his life?

Brown revealed what actually went down in that hotel room, painting a picture of Malcolm X trying to figure out if the young, impossibly charismatic champion would in fact join him in his imminent exodus. He wasn't making a "hard sell" to Ali to disavow the Nation, but he was probing the possibilities. When asked if he tried to steer Ali more toward Malcolm X and away from the NOI, Brown said:

"Actually, I did just the opposite because I was living in the real world. If you are Muhammad Ali, you are going to have to live your life. You had to take a plane to get to Miami. You had to get a hotel room, and you had to deal with the federal agents that the government had and you would want the protection and support of the Nation of Islam. Something could break out at any time. So, I was interested in Ali himself, his safety and state of mind, and I was absorbing what he was telling me. Malcolm was who got Ali truly interested in the Nation of Islam and Ali was close to Malcolm, but he was a free thinker. He was making moves and making other people adjust. He knew that he wasn't a second-class citizen and he knew that no Viet Cong ever called him 'nigger.'"

Brown remembers that he was asked by Ali to provide some balance against Malcolm's pressuring the new champ to leave.

He said, "Muhammad Ali was a freethinker. Don't let anyone ever tell you that he was somebody's monkey. I say that because many assume—and books have been written talking this junk—that he was some kind of a puppet for the Nation. No, he wasn't any kind of puppet. He had a mind of his own. He liked the manhood that the Nation displayed—it appealed to him. His intelligence and his logic were such that he knew he wasn't a second-class citizen and the Nation allowed him to respect that. He had such respect for Elijah Muhammad that he would never have gone with Malcolm. But Malcolm, all he truly wanted, if Ali would not go with him, was to keep up the friendship. It was a very intense time. We knew that we were a part of making history but we were also living in the reality of that moment. It wasn't like we all said, 'Let's go to the motel and talk about revolution.' Shit was going on. Malcolm was on the outs with the Nation of Islam, and Ali let it be known that he was not going to go with him. Ali said he was 'going to be a true follower of Elijah.' Malcolm wanted to keep their friendship. Life goes on. It was history, but every day was like history. Every day was history and you felt it."

The strength of Elijah Muhammad's organization as well as his stature as a father figure and mentor to Ali proved to be stronger than Malcolm's friendship.

Brown acknowledged that Elijah Muhammad's power also came from the millions of dollars his followers donated to the Nation of Islam. "His representation and appeal to Ali was, 'You know, you're a great fighter, but that's minuscule to what I got: power, people, wealth, and I don't have to dance for anybody.'"

Brown becomes something close to animated when discussing Ali, jutting back and forth in his chair, as if shadowboxing from the sitting position. "Do you remember when Ali was in Miami and he came in with that denim jacket on with the lights on the jackets flashing, and it read, 'Bear-hunting'? [Ali famously taunted Sonny Liston by calling him "the big ugly bear."] Ali was a funny guy. But Ali was also a shot-caller. He put his ass on the line. To become a Black Muslim and talking what he was talking? He had a lot of heart."

Then Brown stops shifting in his seat and his face falls half an inch, which, on his impassive visage, is the equivalent of an avalanche, as he mentions Ali's late-in-life infirmities: "They broke him, too."

That night in 1964, four of the most dynamic men in the United States decided that together and separately they would chart a path toward asserting their manhood and cultural strength as a bulwark against racism. They would not be integrationists; they would be symbols of independent strength. Within one year, two were dead by gunshot.

Malcolm was killed at the Audubon Ballroom in Harlem by assassins, and Sam Cooke was felled at the Hacienda Motel by the building manager, Bertha Franklin. The circumstances surrounding both deaths have raised eyebrows for decades. Malcolm's assassination, it was widely believed, was the result of his feud with the Nation of Islam. Yet two of three men convicted in his killing long maintained their innocence. Newly classified government documents, CNN reported in 2015, show how deeply the federal government had infiltrated, surveilled, and attempted to disrupt the Nation of Islam as well as the forces in Malcolm's inner circle. These documents also demonstrate just how slipshod the investigation was into Malcolm X's killing. As Zaheer Ali wrote for CNN, "These questions [surrounding the assassination] deserve answers. They call upon us to revisit not just the political significance of Malcolm X's life, but the implications of his murder. Our government especially deserves scrutiny for its covert information gathering, disinformation campaigns, and even violence waged against its own citizens. Fifty years later, we still have more to learn from Malcolm X's life, and his death, and our government's actions toward him."

Sam Cooke's family has long questioned the official version of his death, which was ruled a justifiable homicide. Bertha Franklin's claim was that Cooke had arrived at the motel with a woman named Elisa Boyer. He was acting violently and tackled Franklin, so she pulled her gun and shot him four times. But it was later revealed that Boyer was a sex worker and Franklin a onetime madam, facts that were not revealed at trial. The theory is that Cooke was drugged by Boyer and killed by Franklin. This theory, advanced by Cooke's family, is that his enemies in the mobbed-up music business did not want a black man with this much power and set him up to die.

Whatever the truth in the deaths of Malcolm and Cooke, their removal from this foursome in Miami undoubtedly left a terrible scar on Brown and Ali.

The meeting of these four men did not make the papers the next day. But the excitement and possibility that Jim Brown saw in Muhammad Ali was crackling inside him. On March 1, in his otherwise milquetoast Cleveland *Plain Dealer* column, Brown wrote about going to the fight in Miami. Normally this was a space where Brown urged kids to exercise, eat healthy foods, and take their vitamins. But on this day, he told his audience about how exciting the Liston and Clay contest was to witness. He then wrote, "A few hours after the fight I was sitting with Cassius and some friends of his in an out of the way motel room." ("Some friends of his" might be the most understated way imaginable to identify Malcolm X and Sam Cooke.)

After spending most of the column talking about their friendship, Brown wrote: "Cassius loves people but has been disillusioned and hurt by some of the falseness in our society. This could be the reason for his association with the Black Muslims. Regardless of what religion or political views Cassius has it doesn't change the facts. He's a clean living young man and he did exactly what he said he would . . . beat Sonny Liston and become the heavyweight champion of the world."

He included this cryptic phrase at the end: "One more thing before I get away from the typewriter: I enjoy reading letters from all those folks who have opinions about Cassius Clay. The new heavyweight boxing champion is an unusual fellow. I may have more to say about him soon."

He would, at that. On May 21, after it was known across the country that Clay had joined the Nation of Islam, and he was being trashed in all the newspapers—black press and white press alike—around the country, Brown took to the *Plain Dealer*, in what must have been a stunner for readers:

> Columns all over the country downgraded Clay. They pointed out that he was detrimental to boxing. Although I never could see eye-to-eye with Cassius on his way of worship, I would never criticize his chosen path. And I feel very bad seeing so many slanted articles about Clay and the Muslims.
>
> There are many subversive organizations. To me the Black Muslims do not represent the greatest threat. They were born only because there was so much hate for the Negro generally. It would seem that if this hate was not so

evident, the Muslims would fade away. There are many southern gentlemen who pledged to keep the Civil Rights Bill from becoming a reality. None of them is a Muslim.

We can see that there are more important haters than Cassius Clay could ever be. It is a fact that there are many more white hate groups than black. It also is true that these white groups can spread their hate more easily if only because they have the freedom to travel undisturbed wherever they please. This is impossible for a Malcolm X or the heavyweight champion of the world, or a non-member of the Muslims like Jimmy Brown or even a Nobel Peace Prize winner like Ralph Bunche.

Jim Brown never joined the Nation of Islam, and was never close to considering membership, but the FBI assumed otherwise. He says, "Well, that's a funny thing. I got a lawyer to use the Freedom of Information Act to see my FBI file. What the federal government kept saying over and over was, 'We think he is going to join the Nation. We think he is going to join the Nation. We think he is going to join the Nation.'

"So they kept waiting, expecting me to the join the Nation, because in their minds that was my inclination. But I never would have joined the Nation, because it was too limited from my way of looking at things. I liked what they were doing: cleaning up the neighborhoods, cleaning up the men, being respectful, working in the prisons, standing up and so forth. But I would be bored to death to be standing in a rigid position for five hours, going with the minister here, going with the minister there. It really just seemed to me to be too boring. So I never really thought about being a part of the Nation, but I was a friend. I even had a title. I was 'First Friend of the Nation.' They actually listed that. But I think Elijah Muhammad knew that I wasn't going to join because I was too independent and had my own thoughts."

Brown was independent and certainly had his own thoughts, but he also could never have abided the ascetic, monogamous lifestyle demanded of NOI members. While he appreciated the political theory that white racism can be mitigated only if you're able to build your own institutions, Brown was too committed to the idea of his own autonomy to bend to any organization that he would not lead. But he did learn from the Nation of Islam and it led him to discovering his place in the movement. It wouldn't be building protests, but institutions to aid black economic development.

By 1966, retired from football and thirty years old, Jim Brown could have done nothing and remained a powerful symbol of the times. He could have booked speaking gigs where he would lecture abstractly about the importance of economic self-reliance. He could have been content to forge a path in Hollywood as a "New Black Man" in the cinema. He could have joined the Nation of Islam or been welcomed into a civil rights movement that sought his star power. He chose to do none of those things. Instead he formed the Negro Industrial and Economic Union, later known as the Black Economic Union. (He changed the name because, he says, "I had to spend too much time explaining why I sanction the word 'Negro.' Personally it doesn't matter to me one way or another. 'Black, Negro, spook, blood, spade, boo-boo,' whatever the fuck, you know?")

The Black Economic Union is credited with the launch of at least four hundred black-owned businesses between 1965 and 1972. On March 8, 1968, the BEU received a $520,000 grant from the Ford Foundation that allowed it to open national offices in Cleveland and New York City. They also had locales in Los Angeles, Kansas City, Philadelphia, and Washington, D.C. The BEU gospel, according to Brown, was "to make more black Americans rich and powerful. We wanted them spending their hours building their economics and to stop marching, singing, kneeling, and praying." The BEUs were for-profit institutions and pooled together donations from athletes, corporations, and nonprofit foundations. Their slogan was "Produce, Achieve, and Prosper."

Brown said at the time, and repeated often, "What I'm interested in is green power—money. You can't begin to talk about equality or integration until you've given black people the opportunity to make good bread and to run things, to learn about what they can and can't do. What we need is to own businesses, to do the hiring and firing, not just be applying. We have to get black people participating in the American economy, and the major step in this direction is establishing them as producers as well as consumers. They have to create a market of products for consumers, both black and white, to compete with—and thereby actually help—the white market."

In a few short years, Brown was leading what was the largest independently organized black economic development organization in the country. It had a meteoric rise and, as it frayed for a host of reasons, an equally rapid fall. But by 1971, he was feeling nothing but hopeful about its future prospects. "We have black graduate students at Harvard, the University of Chicago and UCLA who will move into the organization and provide business expertise," he said at the time. "We have the kind of group that can exist with everybody because everybody needs what we're talking about: food, clothing, shelter, and jobs. You tell me somebody that doesn't need that: militant, Uncle Tom, black, white or bigot."

Brown's goal was to produce a network of MBAs who were sent through graduate school with BEU scholarships and then connected with a network of athletes to "build and utilize the struggle." He enlisted other NFL players—John Wooten, John Mackey, Irv Cross, among them—to be point people for the BEU, attempting to create a synthesis between the economic and cultural power of black athletes and impoverished parts of the black community. Many of them worked for free to expand the BEU until that 1968 grant finally allowed them to hire an actual paid staff.

The athletic component was a critical ingredient of the BEU–Jim Brown formula. Almost all the local organizations were connected to a professional athlete, creating a cultural cachet around each office. Bobby Mitchell, Brown's Hall of Fame backfield partner in Cleveland, was one of those athletes. He said, "We walked the streets and told people you don't have to be afraid anymore. Just do it."

"It may sound immodest, but it's a fact that we tend to be heroes among black people, especially black youth," Brown told Alex Haley in 1968. "Something that's haunted me for years is that look I have seen so many times in some of those black teenagers' eyes looking at me up close: For just an instant, that animal hipness and suspicion leaves the face and you see a look in the eyes that seems to say, 'For God's sake, for just a minute, will *somebody* care?' It gets to me, because *I* was that kid once. . . .

"So it's one of those 'There but for the grace of God' things with me—and it's the same for all the other athletes I know. . . . On the field, cats were trying to run over each other, break each other in half; then the evening after the game, we're all huddled together excitedly discussing this new project. Guys like John Wooten and Walter Beach of the Browns, Bernie Casey of the Atlanta Falcons, Brady Keys of the Pittsburgh Steelers, Bobby Mitchell of the Redskins, Leroy Kelly, Bill Russell, Curtis McClinton, Timmy Brown, lots of others.

"We mapped out an organization that would sell memberships to anybody and everybody for from $2 to $100, to raise money to finance good ideas for small black businesses, because so many good black ideas can't obtain financing. And we decided to make use of black professional people—these 'middle-class Negroes' we hear so much talk about—to draw them in with us, to lend their talents to young Negroes in all the various ways they could. And we decided to use the image value of black athletes in personal-contact programs with black youth, especially in the ghettos. We all put in some of our own money to get it started. I personally donated more than $50,000. Then we hired a secretary and rented an office in the ghetto area of Cleveland, where people wouldn't feel uncomfortable coming to see us."

Brown minces no words today when talking about the legacy of the BEU: "I'll say this: the greatest concept that came out of the movement of black people was the Black Economic Union. There was nothing else close to it. And it was put together basically on intelligence of how to function within this society and how to make a better life for your people.

"We live in a country that has only a certain amount of freedom," Brown says. "The most important freedom we do have is to try and practice its economic principles. And if you practice those economic principles successfully, it allows you to be an almost independent nation within a nation because all power flows from the power of economics. I've always studied the Jewish community and they had it down pat. So, my thing was, I could take a lesson from Jewish people and concentrate on economic development and we can start black businesses, clean up black communities, and circulate the money. We don't have to ask for a lot of favors or be dependent on a government that could take those favors away."

This sounds in many respects like conservative rhetoric—no handouts!—but Brown also did not conceive of executing this plan in conservative terms. Instead he was challenging the United States to live up to its promises of economic freedom or expose itself for letting racism prevail. He said, "The thing about me is that my philosophy can't really be attacked. They can't fight the philosophy, but they can cut off areas where funds must be obtained to develop black people economically. They don't want my independence to be used as an example for others to follow."

For Brown, black ownership was a tool of resistance that many activists overlooked. "It was always about what was being done to us, and that would motivate us to action, and that action would be protest," he says. "But after the protest you still ain't got shit because you ain't got no capital to work with, you ain't got no banks, you ain't got shit other than you done protested to get somebody else to go to the government to give you funds. You're making yourself work for no reason."

Part of this attraction to economic development as a weapon against racism was because he thought the "integrationist" civil rights movement offered no solutions for the reality of the problems black Americans faced.

"Everything was channeled to 'integration,'" Brown says, making a familiar point he has echoed for decades. "I don't want no fucking integration, I don't need to live with nobody that don't want to live with me. Fuck your neighborhood; I don't need to live by you. I want to build my own shit. Other groups come over here and build their own communities and use those principles to gain footholds and, at some point, really profit—as damn near a whole community."

He then pauses and erupts in a deep laugh, the kind of laugh that sounds friendly, but his broad craggy face does not complement the laugh with a smile. "'We Shall Overcome,'" he says. "I hated that song. It was about marching and singing—I didn't like marching; I didn't march. I didn't like singing to get my freedom. And I damn sure didn't like singing 'We Shall Overcome.' To me, that was weak."

In the ultimate slight, Brown compared Dr. King's methods to his former coach Paul "Little Caesar" Brown's brand of football. He also did so after King was assassinated and critiques of him were rare. Brown told Haley, "Like King, [Coach] Brown was a genius in his time, but he refused to change and finally he became outdated. I think the sit-ins, walk-ins, wade-ins, pray-ins and all those other -ins advanced the movement tremendously by awakening the nation's conscience—making millions of white people aware of and sympathetic to the wrongs suffered by black people.

"When the white population was at that point, I think the movement's direction should have been altered toward economic programming for Negro self-help, with white assistance. Think what could have been accomplished if the nation's black leaders, at that time, had actively mobilized the goodwill of all the millions of white people who were willing, even anxious, to help the Negro help himself. We could have had millions, white and black, working toward that goal, with tremendous results.

"That was what I felt and what I tried to do, in forming my National Negro Industrial and Economic Union. But no one listened—not in the movement and not in Washington. What happened, instead, was that the marching went on and on, getting more and more militant, until a lot of white people began to resent it—and to feel threatened. Whenever any human being feels threatened—it doesn't matter if he's right or wrong—he starts reacting defensively, negatively. We lost the white sympathy and support we'd fought so hard to win: Badly needed new civil rights legislation began to die on the vine; existing laws were loopholed, modified or ignored; poverty funds dried up. On the threshold of real progress, the door simply closed in our faces. The inevitable consequences of that frustration set fire to Watts, Detroit, Newark, and two dozen other cities."

Part of why Brown launched the BEU was also his personal

and political rejection of the Pan-Africanism that was common currency in the movement. Brown told journalist James Toback in 1971, "Look. An American black cat, no matter what he may want to think or what you think, is more American than African. His roots are in Cleveland or LA or New York not Mali or Timbuktu. He digs cars and records and sports and movies and air conditioners. I'm working within the system."

Today he says that the twenty-first-century rhetoric of calling for "diversity" as a goal is just the same "snake-oil integration" in a new bottle. "Diversity has nothing to do with our rights. Our rights are bigger than diversity. And so, we have allowed the issue to be misrepresented. In other words, it has looked like we were fighting to be with white people, as if we wanted to be a part of the white community: 'We want to buy from your store, man! You going to let us in there so we can spend this money!?'"

It was a hell of a vision but also, by 1975, for all intents and purposes a failed experiment. Ironically, the BEU ended just as the advent of free agency and unionization was about to launch salaries into a stratosphere unimaginable to the players of Jim Brown's day. Linking the modern salary to this concept would have exponentially increased its power.

It must be noted that the Black Economic Union of Kansas City still exists. It was founded in 1968 by Jim Brown and former Kansas City Chiefs halfback Curtis McClinton. The Kansas City BEU is the oldest community development corporation in the city and helps put on the Kansas City Jazz and Heritage Festival. According to its literature, "BEU was responsible for leading Kansas City's urban core redevelopment efforts in the areas of housing and commercial developments including: 635 affordable multi-family units; 320 elderly units; 85 single-family homes; 720,902 square feet of office, commercial and business development." But this is the lone exception.

Dr. Robert Bennett, the only person to have written a doctoral dissertation on the Black Economic Unions, has his own theories about why the BEU did not take root across the country. "It's not complicated. Guys took on different interests. Jim, as he said, never wanted to be behind a desk all his life. But if you look at Jim Brown, the centrality of black development with a social component never ceased."

BEU's social mission was particularly strong in Cleveland and served many of the city's black adolescents through four components: a program called "World of Work," a "Future Businessmen Club," a mentoring initiative known as "Project Men," and a scholarship program.

"When you read about these things, you also wonder, who are the people that were impacted?" Dr. Bennett says. "It's impossible to get a full accounting of that. The brother of a classmate of mine was an actual recipient of this scholarship, and he attended Ohio State. Their whole thing was providing scholarships for high school graduates who seek a higher education degree or even trade school."

Brown has his own thoughts about why the BEU did not have staying power. "It's funny . . . one of the things I think about is that there's no answer to solve the major problems in this country. The poor ain't going to catch up with the rich. Not in the next ten million years. It's not structured to happen. It's structured so certain individuals can emerge and enjoy life on the highest levels of society, and they think they are empowering the less powerful by being an example of what you can do if you're a strong individual.

"But if you work about it in that manner, it'll take you another hundred thousand years to break into the good ol' boys' club. So I was thinking, how do we know when we are successful in bringing about change? I decided to do my part with like-minded people and tried to be intelligent about it. The best way would be to plant the seeds of how to succeed in this country that will be carried on forever and would happen through the Black Economic Unions.

"It was designed not to become a major institution unto itself. It was meant to create a certain kind of education and a certain kind of economic availability as well as access to money. It would be able to lay out the principle of how to succeed and people would then on an individual level, be able to move forward successfully."

This sounds like Brown is saying that it did not fail. It just faded away, having served its purpose of laying the groundwork for future generations of black entrepreneurs.

But Brown also blames the collapse of the BEU on the inability of the succeeding generations of black athletes—those who arrived after Bill Russell and Bobby Mitchell—to pick up the baton. People from big-name sports columnists to Kobe Bryant have wondered why Brown is always so quick to chastise the black jocks who have come after him. It is rooted in the BEU and his belief that so much could happen—especially as salaries have ballooned—if they worked together.

Brown said in the 1980s, "Those who have the ability as

African men to bring a change in a community that so desperately needs it are concentrating only on their own careers, some charities and how much money they can make. The ones that are most popular and most powerful. Michael Jordan would be one. Charles [Barkley] is talking about issues, but I don't think Charles is in touch with the community. They're all nice guys, now—don't misunderstand me. But they have the ears of the general public, they have the money, and they could call together a hundred black athletes and solve so many problems in these inner cities, it would be unbelievable."

This abrasive approach may have made Brown catnip for reporters and increased his reputation as a tough-as-nails truth-teller, but it did not serve to actually bring people in to do the work. He wouldn't plead with the next generation of athletes or try to organize them. He expected them to "get it" and then would lash out when they lacked his consciousness. There was no bend on either side. Star athletes are not exactly inclined to meet others halfway.

Longtime *New York Times* scribe Robert Lipsyte speaks wistfully about what the BEU—and by extension Brown—could have been. "Jim should have been taken even more seriously than he was. Ali was incredibly important symbolically, and everybody could attach their own symbols to him, and he made people feel brave.

"But I think Jim Brown was kind of sui generis. He was this really tough guy who was willing to take whitey's money and be a gladiator. But as soon as he didn't have to anymore, he creates his own economic organization. I really thought that he was going to take that somewhere. I was disappointed that he didn't. I think that he could have been a very important figure just for that. When you think about the symbolism of this black gladiator, Jim Brown, who'd rather run over you than run around you while also having this kind of smarts and collective will to put these things together, it could have been very powerful. I think that he somehow let this slip through his fingers."

Brown's entire commitment to the BEU also represents a central contradiction within the Black Power movement. "I am a man" could be used by Memphis sanitation workers fighting for union rights or black men trying to start their own businesses. It explains how Brown can be pro Black Power and yet hostile to the NFL Players Association.

According to NFLPA executive director DeMaurice Smith, "Jim Brown had some choice words for the union before I took the job. I can remember calling him one day after I was elected and we were on the phone for about an hour. I talked to him about where I was coming from and what my thoughts were and how I thought the union should be focused 100 percent on players, and he didn't mince words. He wanted no part of it."

Smith believes that Brown has long disparaged the union because of the history of racism in the labor movement. "Let's not kid ourselves," Smith says. "Dr. King forged a lot of alliances with the AFL-CIO and the Teamsters at the time, but the reality was that many of those unions also closed their doors to African-Americans."

Nonetheless, Brown had a deep friendship and business relationship with Hall of Fame tight end John Mackey, who died in 2011. There is no player more responsible for the existence of the NFL Players Association than Mackey, who tirelessly organized his fellow players, earning him the enmity of NFL owners. Mackey and Brown were so tight that in 1982 Brown threatened to remove his plaque and jersey from the Pro Football Hall of Fame when it became painfully obvious that Mackey was being blackballed from induction because of his union history.

Smith understands how this seeming paradox of the anti-union Brown being a brother in arms to the union-diehard Mackey could exist. "Both of them were, when it came to their principles, utterly solid. And there's a cost to that. That forged a mutual respect between two grown-ass men. The connection was made because they were both extremely tough guys in extremely tough times who looked out for one another."

Dave Meggyesy—who was also very close to Mackey—was a politically radical athlete who contributed to the New Left–leaning *Ramparts* magazine in the Bay Area and saw himself as part of the Woodstock generation. In addition to writing his groundbreaking memoir, *Out of Their League*, Meggyesy gave talks around the country on why he left the NFL and how sports could be leveraged to build a movement for social justice. He described Brown's politics this way: "Jim was really into making moves for 'access.' Access to this society, access to opportunity, access to being full-fledged citizens. And at the time, I was critical of that. I was on the side of, 'We don't need access to this system. We've got to overturn it.' In retrospect what the BEU was doing was a very positive kind of thing. But in those days we thought wanting to start businesses meant, 'These guys are just selling out.'"

Meggyesy was a strong union guy who quit the league as an act of protest against the war in Vietnam. This put him in an alternative 1960s universe with respect to Jim Brown.

"I was in D.C. hooking up with [gonzo journalist] Hunter S. Thompson, and we got a little blazed one night," Meggyesy said. "The next day, I hook up with John Mackey and John picks me up in a Bentley, wearing a fur coat. I'm in my blue jeans and an army fatigue jacket. He invited me over to his house for dinner, which was great because I knew his wife, Sylvia, and his kids. After dinner, we went downstairs and John just basically talked for two hours about the whole struggle that he was going through with the NFL owners because he was head of the Players Association. And then in the next breath he was talking about the food markets and business ventures that he had been setting up with Jim Brown. It seemed like a hell of a contrast. But then I think of my own contrast: here I am hanging with Hunter the night before—and I see Mackey pulling up with his Bentley and his mink coat and it was like 'What!?'"

The line between those trying to get their share of the system and those trying to overthrow it was never a clear one in those days of social tumult. This was especially seen in what became known as the "Ali Summit" in 1967.

Coaches and team executives tend to be conservative creatures who believe that any engagement in the outside world by "their players" qualifies as a distraction from what happens inside the lines and will lead to the short-circuiting of their well-tuned machines. This trope is used to whip players into line and coerce them to just "shut up and play." But there is one moment, one press conference, one photo that reveals this directive to be the mendacious and self-serving tripe that it is. The photo was taken on June 4, 1967. Jim Brown, the greatest runner in NFL history and member of the 1964 champion Cleveland Browns, sits alongside the greatest winner in team sports history, Bill Russell of the Boston Celtics. Next to them is the linchpin of the most dominant team in college basketball history, the twenty-year-old Lew Alcindor (later to be known as Kareem Abdul-Jabbar) of the UCLA Bruins. They are surrounded by a collection of black pro athletes including NFL players Bobby Mitchell, Walter Beach, John Wooten, and Curtis McClinton. Also at the table is future Cleveland mayor Carl Stokes.

At the center of them all is Muhammad Ali, by this time the champ-in-exile, his heavyweight title stripped for his opposition to the war in Vietnam and refusal to submit his name for the military draft. He was facing five years in a federal prison for his stance, and few athletes in professional sports were ready to openly support him. Until the Ali Summit.

"The principal for this meeting of course was Ali," McClinton told journalist Branson Wright of the Cleveland *Plain Dealer*. "The principal of leadership for us was Jim Brown. Jim's championship leadership filtered to all of us."

This collection of men had gathered at the Cleveland offices of the Black Economic Union, and all of them—with the exception of young Alcindor—had either contributed money to or were members of the BEU. Hundreds gathered outside to get a sense of what could be happening and why these stars were congregating. "It represents the philosophy that we were establishing in the BEU and beyond," Brown says of this epic collection of heroes. "It represents so many things because, man, I'm proud of it. I'm proud of the people that came. When we reached out to everybody, nobody talked about getting any money, and I guess everybody paid their way to fly there and nobody refused. Let me put it to you this way: to me, there was no one at that table but soldiers."

Every athlete in that photo was at risk of jeopardizing his career by appearing alongside Ali. As Brown remembers, "The fact that they were at that table meant that whatever they felt, whatever nerves they had, they controlled it. They said, 'Fuck the nerves.' Kareem was the youngest, and he was up there standing tall. All the individuals were there because they wanted to be. That's the kind of thing that will get you blackballed forever."

By holding that press conference, Brown was also resisting pressure from his friends and allies in the Nation of Islam. We now know from declassified FBI transcripts that the Nation did not want Ali opposing the war in Vietnam for a variety of reasons. They wanted him in the ring where he could earn millions, much of which he gave to the organization. They also did not want the pressure of increased federal government surveillance, which had stepped up dramatically against black revolutionaries who opposed the war. And there were certainly people in the Nation who cared deeply for Ali and feared he would be a target for assassination if he took such a public stance. Elijah Muhammad's son Herbert was Ali's manager. Herbert did not believe he could sway Ali, so he asked Brown to do it for him.

"Herbert wanting Ali to go into the service was a shocker," Brown revealed. "I thought the Nation of Islam would never look at it that way. But Herbert figured the Army would give Ali special consideration so he would be able to continue his career. But he couldn't talk to Ali about that, so he reached out to me and I had the dilemma of finding a way to give Ali the opportunity to express his views without any influence. I never told Ali about my conversation with Herbert. I never told anyone, really."

Instead of using his gravitas to undermine Ali, Brown built him a stronghold of solidarity.

"Herbert wanted me to talk with Ali, but I felt with Ali taking the position he was taking, and with him losing the crown, and with the government coming at him with everything they had, that we as a body of prominent athletes could . . . stand behind Ali and give him the necessary support."

It wasn't only pressure from the Nation of Islam that Brown resisted. He was a financial partner at the time in boxing impresario Bob Arum's Main Bout, Inc., the promotions company that staged Ali's fights. Arum wanted to negotiate a scenario with the army in which Ali could fight exhibitions, do his service in the ring, and continue to make money. Brown, for all his talk of "green power" and the need to leverage capitalism as the most pressing of tasks, did not see that as more important than Ali's principled opposition to the war. Within months, Arum would call Ali "a dead piece of merchandise."

Everyone present that day at the Ali Summit may have been a soldier, but before standing with Ali, they wanted to hear directly from the champ-in-exile. Before that press conference, they gathered for two and half hours because they wanted Ali to explain why he was choosing this path of most resistance. He told them that his religion made fighting for the United States in a war on "the darker nations of the world" something he simply would not do.

Bill Russell remembered Ali's words: "He said, 'I know I'm right. And if you want to talk me out of it, that's not going to happen.'"

Shortly after the summit, Russell told *Sports Illustrated*, for its June 19, 1967, issue: "I envy Muhammad Ali. . . . He has something I have never been able to attain and something very few people I know possess. He has an absolute and sincere faith. . . . I'm not worried about Muhammad Ali. He is better equipped than anyone I know to withstand the trials in store for him. What I'm worried about is the rest of us."

Brown sat at the center of their press conference and proclaimed to the media, "After two and a half hours of discussion, we decided that the champ is sincere in his religious beliefs."

Brown has spoken with admiration of Ali's ability to never waver in this difficult period. In Thomas Hauser's *Muhammad Ali: His Life and Times*, Brown said, "Ali, before he came back, was a true warrior. It was unbelievable, the courage he had. He wasn't just a championship athlete. He was a champion who fought for his people. He was above sports; he was part of history. The man used his athletic ability as a platform to project himself right up there with world leaders, taking chances that absolutely no one else took. . . . From the standpoint of his ability to perform and his ability to be involved with the world, Ali was the most important sports figure in history."

Reflecting on the offer to sit at this prestigious table, Abdul-Jabbar said, "I was just happy to be invited. I was told they wanted me to be there because the youth of America, black youth, needed someone who more or less represented their point of view. And Jim Brown at that point was already thinking about economic issues and the black community; business being a crucial aspect of black liberation. . . . I didn't feel any butterflies but I probably should have."

Brown said, "In the '60s, when I called the athletes to come and talk to Ali, they didn't bring their agents, managers and lawyers. They came because they thought it was worthwhile. . . . We athletes were just like normal citizens in those days, fighting for our rights. We didn't put our sport before our manhood."

Inspired by this event, Dr. Harry Edwards, who was organizing the Olympic Project for Human Rights, asked Brown to join the OPHR effort to get black American athletes to boycott the 1968 Mexico City Olympics unless demands were met regarding hiring black coaches and disinviting the apartheid countries of South Africa and Rhodesia from the games. In synergy with the Ali Summit press conference, the activist-athletes of the OPHR added another demand: to restore Muhammad Ali's title; they were calling him "the warrior saint of the black athletes' revolt."

Dr. Edwards said, "When I was looking for support for the Olympic Project for Human Rights, there were two black superstars in the country that young people identified with. I mean true superstars, where when they walked into the room, everybody had this sense of it being appropriate to bow from the ankles. One was Bill Russell, and the second was Jim Brown.

Jim epitomized what it meant to be a black man. Bill was the greatest winner in team sports history. He was political, he was outspoken. But Jim was out there, every week, taking those hits, and still speaking out, speaking up, while he was playing. Jim was the quintessential gladiator. And so in 1968, the first person to support us was Bill Russell. The second was Jim Brown. At that point I really came into a personal appreciation of who he was as a man and as a warrior."

Brown was not only organizing Ali Summits and supporting Dr. Edwards at this time; he was also endorsing Republican Richard Nixon in his successful run for the U.S. presidency. This shows starkly how the politics of Black Power could be used and refashioned to mean different things in different situations.

In a newspaper interview that year, Brown was asked what he feared above all else. He said, "Nothing . . ." and after a pause, followed up with: "Being an Uncle Tom." He certainly risked being seen as such by supporting Nixon. Brown did this partially because the Nixon of 1968 was not the Nixon who would dominate the 1972 elections by adopting the "Southern Strategy," which aimed to connect with the racism and resentments in the South toward the civil rights movement. Instead, at least part of Nixon's strategy against liberal Democrat Hubert Humphrey was an effort to co-opt the rhetoric of Black Power and appeal to its entrepreneurial, nonrevolutionary wing. Nixon said in a 1968 speech that "what most of the militants are asking is not separation, but to be included in—not as suppliants, but as owners, as entrepreneurs—to have a share of the wealth and a piece of the action." Federal government programs, Nixon said, should "be oriented toward more black ownership, for from this can flow the rest—black pride, black jobs, black opportunity and, yes, black power."

This meshed with Brown's perspective that you needed to work the system, not try to dismantle it. "Even if it meant dealing with the devil or getting his hands dirty, access to resources, not purity, was the greater good in a capitalist country," one friend said of Brown's approach.

Brown was not the only prominent black cultural figure to support Tricky Dick. Both "Godfather of Soul" James Brown and Sammy Davis, Jr., sided with Nixon as well. There are numerous accounts of the two singers' feeling a significant backlash for their Nixon endorsements. They were shunned by the liberal establishment, criticized by the black press, and skewered mercilessly by black radicals. Jim Brown, however, emerged unscathed, attracting no public criticism. He was Teflon. The assumption—one can only assume—was that whatever Jim Brown was doing, people believed it was for the greater good.

It is also almost certainly because even though Brown's actual politics could be quite conservative, he remained shielded from criticism by memories of what he represented on that football field and in Hollywood movies: black pride, black manhood, and a quiet intelligence spliced with reservoirs of rage.

Robert Lipsyte tells the following story: "In 1966, we're in Toronto for the Muhammad Ali–George Chuvalo fight. We go out to a Chinese restaurant with Dick Gregory, Jim Brown, and Carl Stokes. Three very important black guys and me. With those guys, I just listened, and Jim tended to dominate the conversation.

"When the dinner was over, the waiter brought me the bill—the only white guy at the table. Gregory made a joke. Stokes, the politician, made some sort of remark about, 'Wow, that's where we are in 1966.' But Jim Brown becomes enraged. He jumps up. We think he's going to hit the guy. He just rages at him. The whole idea about, 'Here is another example of the white power structure, the brainwashing of people's minds, and how even waiters go right to the white guy because he thinks that's where the money and power is.' And he kind of goes on for a while. Finally, Gregory keeps making jokes and brings him down, and we go off for the night. And I'm thinking, holy shit. This is where this guy's energy comes from. Everybody's strength is their weakness and in Jim Brown's case it is that rage. But at the same time he was right, of course. What would be a greater example, of the normalcy of racism: three of the most important black guys in America, and the bill goes to some white boxing writer sitting there at the table. And yet, he was the only one who had that energy to react."

Stories like this about Brown are legion. You would not mock him for supporting Nixon when he lived his life like a shaken can of soda, ready to explode with what has been called "the gift of fury."

Even with Brown's Nixon endorsement, Dr. Harry Edwards still sought—and Jim Brown gave—his support for the 1968 Olympic boycott. But while Brown backed the proposed boycott, there were limits to his support for this new "revolt of the black athlete" and the most politically incendiary of the

Olympic protesters. The 200-meter gold medalist Tommie Smith, who raised his fist from the stand in Mexico City alongside bronze medalist John Carlos, wrote in his 2007 autobiography *Silent Gesture* about his treatment by Brown afterward, and his remembrance is stunning, but consistent with Brown's politics on the economically conservative edge of black nationalism.

Smith, who had been drafted by the Los Angeles Rams in 1967, was looking forward to an NFL career after the Olympics. At the time, Brown had started a sports agency called the United Athletic Association: the first NFL player to use an agent would have an agency of his own so that young athletes would not be run over by teams in negotiations. Smith signed with UAA, and Brown gave him a $2,000 loan against future earnings, typical for an agency. By now Brown's reputation as a leading strong black man was unimpeachable, and Smith was thrilled with the association. Then Smith went to Mexico City and made the silent gesture heard around the world. When Rams training camp opened in June 1969, Smith tried to contact the UAA office in Los Angeles, but he didn't hear anything. He finally got Brown on the phone, and in Smith's words, "He was very vague. He did say that what I had done in Mexico City had made everything null and void. He also asked for his $2,000 back. Here I was, 24 years old, without a job, without a degree yet, with a wife and an eight-month-old son, trying to finish school and get some sort of career started, and he asked for his money back. The great Jim Brown. I was very hurt, and I let him know how hurt I was and how disenchanted I was, and that what he had done and what he said was uncalled for, and I hung

up on him. . . . I paid it all back. But we needed that money."
Years later, Smith recalled, he saw Brown at a fund-raiser and
was snubbed. Smith wrote: "People now talk about Jim Brown
this and Jim Brown that, on camera taking a stand and helping
brothers out. That's not the Jim Brown I know, because that Jim
Brown's mind wasn't on helping this young brother out. What
he is to me is the guy who asked for his two grand back, money
he had given me that I needed to stay solvent, because I had
stood up on the victory stand." It seems likely that Tommie
Smith's NFL dreams went up in smoke after his Mexico City
protest, and given that he would not be a profitable client,
Brown unceremoniously let him go. No profit potential to
build the agency, no time for Smith—no matter his need for
political, not to mention financial, solidarity.

But the man who did not see the importance of standing
with Tommie Smith sought the company of Huey Newton, the
leader of the Black Panthers, and this was reciprocated. Newton
desired Brown's friendship and was a fixture at his house. He
loved Jim, though in a 1969 *Ebony* interview Newton stated:
"Black capitalism is a hoax. Black capitalism is represented as a
great step toward black liberation. It isn't. It is a giant stride
away from liberation. No black capitalist can function unless he
plays the white man's game. Worse still, while the black capitalist wants to think he functions on his own terms, he doesn't. He
is always subject to the whims of the white capitalist."

Brown says of Newton, "Huey and I spent days talking. Not
just us. Richard Pryor and Huey and myself. Yeah, I dealt with
all the organizations. I dealt with the Panthers. But I would
push economic development on a different level. The Panthers

were like a ground-level organization that dealt with the people. The Panthers were attractive, but they weren't smart. But I didn't argue with Huey. He was my favorite Panther. He was intelligent and bold: a young dude that was dedicated. Had a style of his own, women were attracted to him, and he was like a soldier. A great young soldier."

Brown says he never argued politics with Huey. "I never had to argue with anybody because we were doing what we were doing, and they were doing what they were doing. We were in a partnership, and everybody doesn't have to do the same things. It also wasn't just about the struggle. Huey, Richard, and me were relating as men."

Even in the world of the civil rights movement of which Brown was so critical, his presence was sought. After Martin Luther King, Jr., was assassinated, on April 4, 1968, Brown was asked to attend the funeral and sit inside the church. He of course accepted that invitation. He said, "Listen to the tape they played of Martin speaking and you'll know how I felt."

These are the words that were played at the funeral: "If any of you are around when I have to meet my day, I don't want a long funeral. . . . Tell them not to mention that I have a Nobel Peace Prize, that isn't important. . . . I'd like somebody to mention . . . that Martin Luther King, Jr., tried to love somebody . . . that I did try to feed the hungry . . . that I did try, in my life, to clothe those who were naked . . . that I tried to love and serve humanity."

Brown was on the inside absorbing these words, yet people including U.S. senators Charles Percy, Edmund Muskie, and Ralph Yarborough had to stand outside. Neither Brown nor the

Black Economic Unions were bystanders after King was killed and urban uprisings erupted in cities across the country. They attempted to organize athletes to go into the streets and try to use their cultural capital to assuage the anger. Jim Brown was seen as having the power—as was once said famously about Malcolm X—to start or stop a riot.

Similarly, when Dr. King's young protégé the Reverend Jesse Jackson started Operation PUSH after his break from the Southern Christian Leadership Conference in 1971 and gathered more than a thousand people at the Metropolitan Theater on Chicago's South Side, he asked Jim Brown to attend, and Brown was there. Despite Brown's critique of this method of struggle, it was a priority for Jackson to have Brown in attendance. Jackson says, "It was validation. And he identified with our negotiations and boycotts in the cities. I worked with youth, and of course, he worked with youth, so we worked together, trying to get the gang members to change their ways and use better options in their lives. Jim Brown remains true to his basic commitment, to raise up a new generation of young people with vision."

Brown may have had his head in the business side of Black Power and his heart in its reformist wing, but each side had its own pitfalls regarding gender equality. A strain in the Black Power political ethos was about the assertion of black masculinity at the expense of black women.

As onetime Black Panther Party leader Elaine Brown wrote in her memoir, *A Taste of Power*, "A woman in the Black Power movement was considered, at best, irrelevant. A woman asserting herself was a pariah. A woman attempting the role of leadership was, to my proud black Brothers, making an alliance with the 'counter-revolutionary, man-hating, lesbian, feminist white bitches.' It was a violation of some Black Power principle that was left undefined. If a black woman assumed a role of leadership, she was said to be eroding black manhood, to be hindering the progress of the black race. She was an enemy of black people."

Professor and author Dr. Jared Ball contests this, as well as sociologist bell hooks's statement that Black Power somehow undermined what under the leadership of Dr. King could have flowered into "a movement of gender uplift." He said, "I don't want Black Power to get some special blame or attention for patriarchy or misogyny, as if those things didn't exist in the pre-1965 civil rights movement. Dr. King did not exactly represent the vanguard of a black, radical, feminist movement. Ella Baker had to force them to look at young people, force them to look at women. What I always like to remind people is that the Black Power movement did not become the target of the most powerful state in the history of humanity because it was patriarchal and misogynistic. The Black Power era also inspired black radical feminists and the activity of African women and shouldn't be singled out as ushering in some new era of patriarchy or misogyny."

The author of *From #BlackLivesMatter to Black Liberation*, Dr. Keeanga-Yamahtta Taylor, gives another perspective to Elaine Brown, saying, "I don't know if the sexism of the New Left and the Black Panther Party were any more virulent than sexism that was pervasive throughout American society. By 1970, the Black Panther Party had five thousand members and forty-five chapters; and it was two-thirds women! There was incredible sexism within the party, but there was also a formal commitment to anti-sexism. In the 1970s, they passed a resolution for women's liberation, they conducted classes on women's liberation. There was a gap, clearly, between the formal positions of the party and what actually happened. But we fall into a trap by treating these women as passive objects of the movement who weren't thinking, fighting, and trying to exert their own influence over the direction of things. Dismissing them as victims of sexism and the Black Panther Party as a masculinist, sexist entity that was hostile to black women just does not fit with the facts."

As the 1960s became the 1970s, women's issues and women's leadership intervened even more sharply into Black Power circles. The leadership of people like Nikki Giovanni, Elaine Brown, and Kathleen Cleaver forced people inside the movement to adapt. In the sports world, the stance of tennis legend Billie Jean King and the push for equality found in the groundbreaking 1972 Title IX legislation put these concerns on the front burner. Men had to adapt or risk falling behind.

In the Olympic Project for Human Rights, many calls to action had statements about "reclaiming manhood," as if African-American women weren't victimized by racism or couldn't be part of a strong voice against it.

Despite this exclusion, many women athletes eventually became critical voices of solidarity. "I'd like to say that we dedicate our relay win to John Carlos and Tommie Smith," said Wyomia Tyus, anchor of the women's gold-medal-winning 4x100-meter relay team. John Carlos later commented, "That was an education right there. Honestly, it was uplifting and downright humbling that they had the courage to give their support. It was uplifting because everyone else had run away from us. It was humbling because they were very much shut out of the process of building the Olympic Project for Human Rights. . . . Years later, Tyus took OPHR to the woodshed, saying, 'It appalled me that the men simply took us for granted. They assumed we had no minds of our own and that we'd do whatever we were told.' She was right to do it."

AS THE PAST SEVERAL DECADES HAVE SHOWN, THE TOXIC masculinity that pervades resistance movements eventually becomes a fetter on expanding and advancing the struggle. At some point the men involved are faced with the question of whether they will help push forward or see it all evaporate. Robert Lipsyte said of Jim Brown:

"His manhood is really throwback macho. We're willing to understand it in Lawrence Taylor or any number of other guys. But Jim Brown had so much more to offer. He was smart, he had a touch of the visionary. He had this incredible passion. He was not the only one. You have Bill Russell, there's Kareem . . . but none of them have that game face, none of them are as intimidating, none of them have that combination of powerful politics and righteous thinking, and it's undermined by that kind of stupid, outworn, subverting macho. He really seems like a man fighting himself. Malcolm X was growing out of that. I interviewed him in his final days and I'm convinced that

Malcolm would have been amazing in the years to come. He came out of a deeper pit materially than Jim Brown ever came out of. He would have evolved as someone who would also be against sexism. He would have seen all of this as part of the way of muting and dividing the entire black community. I don't think Jim figured that part of it out."

Brown says now that the struggle for women—black or white—was simply not his fight. His vision of black liberation involved only half of the black community. He said, "No matter what, I knew I would always be in the struggle: the race struggle for self-determination and manhood."

The question, however, of what that struggle encompassed would change. As the movements of the 1960s faded and Jim Brown made his home in the Hollywood Hills, his struggle turned for a time into one against the movie industry, against his friends, and eventually against the people closest to him.

# FIVE

# ALMOST A LEADING MAN: THE HOLLYWOOD HUSTLE

—

*You are in a hip singles club. It's the type of place where a young actor goes to see and be seen. You work out. You have a thin gold chain with a cross that rests right between your health-club pecs. You are drinking some rum concoction with a fancy name. You took some dynamite pills and topped them off in the bathroom with a bump of coke. Everyone says you're going to be an action star someday on the big screen. You've got a mouth full of teeth, as square and white as Chiclets, and a dimple poised to break hearts. You are talking up this chick with hoop earrings and long fingernails creeping up your thigh. Life is too sweet.*

*Then you hear a bit of a commotion, a buzz reserved for those who are already known instead of almost famous. You move to the back of the club right by the not-so-secret entrance—and there is Jim Brown. Holy shit. The football God. The man from* The Dirty Dozen *himself. The black John Wayne. You walk up to him. Maybe he knows you. Maybe he saw that western where you had a line and spat some fake tobacco. "Hey! Jim Brown!" you call out. "The baad mother-fucker!" You go in for a high five and are ignored. You are left hanging in the breeze, and it might be your imagination but you swear you hear a titter of giggles around you. You double down. "Oh, too big for us? Too big for me?" A friend of Brown's rises out of his seat with a "Be cool, muscleman. We're just here for some fun." You say, "Fuck you, flunky." A crowd is gathering. That chick with the hoop earrings is fading back.*

*It's time to be bold—to be the star you want to be. You put your foot up on his table and lean in like you're stretching before a workout. "You're not so big and bad, Jim Brown. You're looking a little old to me."*

*Now he sees you. He looks briefly into your eyes and stands. It has a sobering effect, like a pot of coffee . . . being thrown into your face. He didn't seem so big sitting down, but once he's standing, you see that he seems cut from a different cloth. You're gym-strong. He looks like he's been drawn by a comic book artist. He gets up and takes two steps for-ward. You smell his cologne, and your breath gets caught in your mouth. Then he walks right past you toward the front door. Your ego recharges. "Yeah! You better leave," you chirp. Everyone is laughing. That chick you were talking to slides back by your side. The tension leaks out as Brown reaches for the door. Then he does something curious. He doesn't leave. Instead he locks it. Then he turns around and for first time makes eye contact. "I'm not leaving," he says. "You're staying."*

*The story of what happens next becomes Hollywood lore, the "great Jim Brown ass-kicking." Twenty years later, you are long done with that Hollywood game. One night, flipping channels, you come across the movie* A Bronx Tale *with Robert De Niro. A version of what you went through appears on screen. The locked door. The beating. You smile. You finally made it.*

THE HOLLYWOOD WHERE JIM BROWN INITIALLY BUILT HIS film career in the late 1960s and the 1970s was a unique time in the history of the movie business. It was when a young generation of filmmakers were turning on to sex, drugs, and social struggles and creating a new commerce that fit the tastes of the baby boomer/flower power era.

Before this time, Hollywood was a top-down, vertically operated system controlled by wealthy overlords: studio chiefs who ran star-system assembly lines that were populated almost entirely by white actors and actresses. But in the late 1960s and the 1970s, just as on campuses and in communities throughout the country, things ceased to be the way they had always been. Movies like *The Graduate, Easy Rider,* and *Bonnie and Clyde* signaled an utter reorganization of the studio system. A new generation of young directors—auteurs—like Spielberg, Coppola, Lucas, and Scorsese were given an unprecedented amount of power to realize their visions.

This new paradigm could not have taken shape without the movements of the 1960s, and these struggles also created space for a rugged black presence like Jim Brown to emerge as a new kind of screen star. But there were still limitations. While this was the era when auteurs could challenge studio chiefs for creative supremacy, these auteurs were almost invariably white men, albeit with shaggier hair, and weed on their breath instead of whiskey. Not even someone with the fame and drive of Jim Brown was able to chart his own path in a Hollywood dream factory just awakening from a monochromatic reverie.

Brown, with his NFL stardom, good looks, and powerful frame, was approached about acting while still an active player. He was in Los Angeles for the 1964 Pro Bowl, and "a guy from 20th Century Fox" walked up to him and said he should come down to the studio lot for a screen test. As Brown remembered, "I broke into Hollywood the old-fashioned way. I knew somebody." Even though Brown had no acting experience, he quickly "caught the bug." Brown first arrived in Hollywood during the NFL off-season. His debut film was a 1964 western, *Rio Conchos*; he played a U.S. Cavalry officer, a Buffalo soldier, sent to investigate how Apaches in Mexico were getting their hands on powerful U.S. Army rifles. The film is a liberal morality play. Star Richard Boone is a highly trained ex–Confederate soldier who hates the Apaches because they killed his family. Early in the film, his character is arrested and forced to lead a ragtag, multicultural scout team made up of a Union officer, an Apache woman, a "knife-wielding Mexican" played by Tony Franciosa, and Jim Brown. They discover that the person who is supplying the Apaches with weapons is actually another ex–Confederate soldier, played by Edmond O'Brien. The film ends with Boone's character overcoming his racism and dying to save the Apache woman and the Union officer. Brown's character is killed as well, which may have been the official start of an ignominious Hollywood tradition that has since become cliché: the black guy in an action ensemble always getting killed by the final reel.

*Rio Conchos* was a modest success. It wasn't high art, but it didn't have to be. The very existence of a black cowboy on the silver screen turned more than a few heads.

Brown saw his role in *Rio Conchos* and those first years of his movie career as a cultural expression of the new assertion of black manhood. He said in one 1968 interview, "Have you ever been to any Negro theater with a movie going, with a Negro in it? Well, you can just feel the tension of that audience, pulling for this guy to do something good, something that will give them a little pride. That's why I feel so good that Negroes are finally starting to play roles that other Negroes watching will feel proud of and respond to, and identify with, and feel real about, instead of being crushed by some Uncle Tom on the screen making a fool of himself. You're not going to find any of us playing Uncle Toms anymore."

In a gushing November 11, 1968, article about Brown for *New York* magazine titled "The Black John Wayne," Gloria Steinem wrote, "He's [become] a black John Wayne; or maybe John Wayne with just a hint of Malcolm X thrown in."

What is remarkable, in retrospect, is the excited expectation that this archetype of the mainstream black action star—part John Wayne, part Malcolm—would fly in the Hollywood of 1970. It was at best overly optimistic, if not naive. Seventeen years later, in Robert Townsend's *Hollywood Shuffle*, a movie about the experience of being a black actor in Tinseltown, a character says, "We never play Rambo until we stop playing Sambo."

Jim Brown was not a great actor, although he is a surprisingly effective on-screen presence. He certainly deserved better than the backhanded compliment delivered by his *Dirty Dozen* costar Lee Marvin, who said, "Well, Brown's a better actor than Sir Laurence Olivier would be as a member of the Cleveland Browns."

In other words, he was an action star: a charismatic, brutal, and physically powerful presence. He became at least as effective an actor as a certain bodybuilder who made the 1987 film *The Running Man*, costarring Brown, and later became governor of California. The space for black action stars was extremely narrow, but Brown held out the hope that he could blaze a trail for a new archetype. He was not alone.

Author Michael Eric Dyson says, "My first awareness of Jim Brown was as an action hero: a very strong, chiseled black man who was unapologetic. He was not a shucker and jiver. He was not shuffling along. So, for me, at my age, his iconography was first as a strong black man on film. Then, curious about his exploits on screen, I began to discover what he had done on the gridiron. And that presented, again, a fearless, no-nonsense, take-no-prisoners approach that he was exemplifying on screen. When Sidney Poitier, as Mr. Tibbs, slapped back that white man who slapped him [in the 1969 film *In the Heat of the Night*], that was the Slap Heard 'Round the World: that first inkling of the awakening of black masculinity on screen. But with Jim Brown, it exploded. He was still in that playing shape. That was a dangerous image in the late sixties and the seventies."

Brown wanted to stay on that John Wayne trajectory. He aspired to be the strong, silent action hero: the cowboy. It's fitting that this was his ambition. In the history of this country's popular culture, that archetype is uniquely American. As sociologist Orlando Patterson wrote, "The quintessential American myth is that of the cowboy. . . . Central to that myth are the role of violence and the reverence for the gun. . . . Thus violence is . . . embraced and romanticized."

But with rare exceptions—Will Smith in the box-office clunker *Wild Wild West* and the little-seen Mario Van Peebles movie *Posse*—the cowboy has been a white cultural archetype. Brown was threatening to rewrite that script. At the start of his film career, Brown told the *Atlanta Daily World*, "I don't want to play 'Negro parts.' Just cool tough modern men who are also Negroes. And not good guys all the time. If a kid comes out of the movie feeling strong saying, 'Hey, that's a man,' then he'll feel like a man too."

He also wanted to be something that had never been seen on screen before, not even from the great Sidney Poitier or the impossibly handsome Harry Belafonte: a black man who was not just sexy but overtly sexual. Film historian Donald Bogle said that the now painfully dated film *Guess Who's Coming to Dinner*, where the liberalism of a white couple, played by Spencer Tracy and Katharine Hepburn, is challenged by the presence of their daughter's new fiancé, played by Sidney Poitier, "might as well be called 'Fear of a Black Penis.'" Reacting to Jim Brown's emergence, Bogle said, "The audience is going to know that not only does he have a penis but it's erect and he's going to know how to use it."

It was a new kind of black masculinity and it fit the moment. In Brown's breakout role as Robert Jefferson in *The Dirty Dozen*, his first line brought viewers' attention immediately to his politicized member. Lee Marvin's Major John Reisman interviews

Jefferson, a condemned man on a military death row, and asks if he wants to volunteer for a new special squad of soldiers. Brown as Jefferson says, "Don't sweet-talk me, whitey. You know why I'm here. Or maybe you think I should've let those cracker bastards go right ahead and castrate me? . . . That's your war, man, not mine. You don't like the Krauts, Major, you fight them. Me, I'll pick my own enemies."

Brown thought this sort of role was his future. He told Alex Haley, "I [played] Robert Jefferson, a college-trained soldier condemned to death for murdering a white racist who had brutally assaulted me. I strongly identified with Jefferson. I could feel and understand why he did what he did. I just made myself Robert Jefferson in my mind."

Jefferson meets his end on film when, amid the Dozen's suicide mission into the enemy Nazi hideout, he runs at full Jim Brown speed across a clearing, looking more authentic than any mere actor. He is then mercilessly chopped down by machine-gun fire, limping through the bullets like they are would-be tacklers before he falls to his knees.

Dr. Jared Ball, who watched this film as a child, later recalled the feeling of witnessing Jefferson's death. "That was one of the most traumatic media experiences I've ever had. I was a kid who was not ready for that. I didn't know that Hollywood killed off major characters. I was broken. I said, 'No way! That's Jim Brown!' He's not just this character in a movie. He doesn't get killed. He doesn't get hurt. He's got to get up. He's going to be okay. This can't be happening. It was the most unexpected, most unnatural thing. And again, looking back, I'm sure now it was because he had become for me this important figure as a man, and seeing him gunned down, even though I understood it was a movie, was impacting me beyond the screen."

Brown also stood out by making it clear to the Hollywood establishment that he would not play roles that demeaned black men. Before the release of the 1968 film *Ice Station Zebra*, he expressed excitement about playing a Marine captain, Leslie Anders. He said, "Anders is my kind of officer—a man, self-sufficient as hell, bad, uptight, ready to do a hell of a job. He doesn't care who likes him or who doesn't, so he doesn't try to be liked."

Early supporting roles in *Rio Conchos*, *The Dirty Dozen*, and *Ice Station Zebra* were somewhat close to the political persona he wanted to build for himself in Hollywood, because that was a role he played off camera as well: an unquestioned man, highly principled, violent if necessary, at times solitary, and also very sexual. Ultimately these kinds of roles for black men were rarely on offer in major Hollywood productions.

"I began to wonder," he remembered to *Sports Illustrated* in 1994, "'Do I have to be called nigger in *every* script?'" That meant he wouldn't play a stereotype. Instead, he was, as Bogle analyzed, "leading the way toward meeting the demands of a younger audience for more assertive and powerful black characters."

Brown said of his black contemporaries in Hollywood, "They come in shuffling and rolling their eyes and 'yes sirring' everybody and I get so embarrassed I'd slide way down in my seat. That's one good thing about being thought of as 'a bad cat' and 'arrogant.' Nobody's going to bring a shuffling part to me."

Despite his resistance to stereotypical parts, there was one that Brown played to the hilt in his personal life: the sexually liberated lothario, or more bluntly, the stud. In 1969, he spoke to *The New York Times* about his recent on-screen heat with Raquel Welch in the western *100 Rifles*: "The filming of our love scene was just like any other scene. I just had to follow directions and remember to hit certain marks. . . . When I'm really making love I don't have to follow directions."

In 1973, Brown posed completely naked for *Playgirl*. The photos present Brown as oddly vulnerable, unsmiling, and facing away from the camera. His only comments on this choice to display his body for consumption was, "If women like to look at a thirty-eight-year-old man and think he looks sexy, what am I to say?"

Professor and author Dr. Mark Anthony Neal describes Brown's film persona as "the smart brute, the sexual brute. The desire by an audience to see a black man in that kind of role is driven by a . . . thinking that if you're that kind of cool black man, you're an outlaw. And the mythology of the outlaw is that you're exempt from responsibilities that a white, browbeaten, middle-class guy would have to deal with."

Brown could represent the fantasy of escape for a heterosexual male audience and a different fantasy to those in the audience attracted to his chiseled frame.

At no time were Brown's screen persona and sexuality under a more political microscope than when he made *100 Rifles*. The film borders on unwatchable, but the on-screen heat and interracial sex with Raquel Welch was groundbreaking for its time, shocking critics and audiences. As Brown said, "We were trying to send a message to America."

These scenes were also central to how the film attempted to turn a profit. Even though *100 Rifles* stars other famous actors, including Burt Reynolds, the poster for the film shows a shirtless Brown and the petite Welch curling her body around him from behind. This gives an idea of what the filmmakers and studio marketers thought about Brown's potent sexuality: he is in a film with Raquel Welch and it is *his chest* that gets front billing.

Dr. Ball recalled that poster and other promotional material. "They had almost as much impact as the films themselves. Just seeing him in magazine ads, depicted with white film stars, was something. This black man, cinematically at least, in love with or in physical relationships with white women made me believe that this is exactly what I would've thought a strong black man was supposed to do. Obviously I see all kinds of problems with that as an adult, but at the time, that was, consciously, what I was feeling."

It also enraged members of the FBI. According to an interview sportswriter Mike Freeman did with an FBI whistleblower for his biography of Brown, *100 Rifles* was "infuriating to members of the bureau" and on its own spurred members to step up surveillance on Brown for his off-screen activities.

As for the filming itself, the big love scene between Brown and Welch was scheduled for the first day of production, when the two actors had barely met. Brown was supposed to act, in his own words, "sex starved" while Welch squirmed beneath him before—bosom heaving—she succumbed to his power and their shared passion. It's a scene with roots in Hollywood cinema dating back at least to *Gone with the Wind*: a woman resists a man's violent seizing of her body, but his kiss and rough embrace break down her defenses. She says no, but her eyes—as judged by the man—say yes. The idea that this could be construed as rape goes entirely unexamined.

Amusingly, the competing narratives from Welch and Brown about the filming of the scene tell their own story about the different ways men and women could view a steamy love scene. In *Out of Bounds*, Brown recalled, "I kissed Raquel's ear, and her body jumped. Hmmmmm. I stuck my tongue in softly. Raquel started heating up, so did the scene."

When Spike Lee interviewed her in his documentary *Jim Brown: All American*, Raquel Welch did not describe herself as "heating up." Instead, she said, "I'm getting a squeegee on the side of my face. No one does this who's a real actor. It's a guy thing. . . . He was acting out all these male fantasies of physical prowess. He was gladiator and now he had to win in this arena too."

Welch had another observation about Brown, whom she would later date and with whom she would maintain a friendship. She said, with a touch of pity, that Brown as an actor was "not ideal because an actress has to be a little bit more than a woman and an actor has to be little bit less than a man. You need that femininity there. Jim does not have an ounce of femininity in him."

The main feature, however, whether it was *100 Rifles* or the 1972 film *Slaughter*, where Brown had a torrid scene with the alabaster blonde Stella Stevens, was the aggressiveness, even brutality, that Brown was directed to show his love interests on screen. The white male writers and white male directors of these films wanted that to be step one toward seduction. Being the "first black actor with an erect penis," even in liberal Hollywood, meant playing out the domination fantasies of those behind the camera. One of Brown's film producers, Robert Chartoff, praised him this way: "Women are afraid of him but they're attracted to him at the same time. He satisfies women's masochistic need."

As with the early pornography of the 1970s, which gained an art-house following of middle-class audiences who saw attending porn in large groups as a sign of sophistication, there was a fine line between sexual liberation on film and exploitation, whether in the form of the exploitation of women or of a black man's sexuality for a titillated white audience. That fine line was explored famously in Melvin Van Peebles's 1971 classic film *Sweet Sweetback's Baadasssss Song*. The movie is about a black man whose job is to have sex in a brothel for a wealthy white audience of voyeurs. When he is framed for murder, Sweetback—so nicknamed for his massive penis—goes on the run while handcuffed to a member of the Black Panther Party. Huey Newton wanted the film to be required viewing for new inductees into the Party. It was an examination of the black masculine id unbound.

The line between film and reality was also blurry. Van Peebles performed his own sex scenes—some not merely simulated—and contracted gonorrhea. He used his gonorrhea diagnosis to sue successfully, amid filming, for workers' compensation, and then used this windfall to purchase more film so he could complete the project. *Sweet Sweetback* is a critique of white fascination with black male sexuality, but it also, uncritically, presents black male sexuality as a tool for revolution, something that could be used to hypnotize the ladies or lead a revolt against the police.

*Sweet Sweetback* was extremely profitable and is recognized as the film that spawned the blaxploitation genre that flourished in the 1970s. But *Sweetback*, strongly influenced by French New Wave filmmaker Jean-Luc Godard, is far more artistic, measured, and political than slapdash films like *Blacula* and *Disco Godfather*. Its most distinguishing feature was the presence of Van Peebles himself, behind the camera. It was a black man's vision, not a white director's caricature. But its success did not spawn a flowering of opportunities for black filmmakers influenced by French cinema. Instead, Hollywood saw an opportunity to commodify black rebellion and a fiercely heterosexual black masculinity: a masculinity strong enough to control women, beat up racist pigs, and assert domination over any setting.

In many ways, the character of Sweetback was modeled after Jim Brown or, at the very least, the fantasy of Jim Brown conjured by Melvin Van Peebles. As Van Peebles said, "Jim was our hero." One result of *Sweet Sweetback* and the spawn of blaxploitation is that it gave Hollywood a place, a ghettoized genre, to slot Brown without worrying about him challenging black archetypes and being the "black John Wayne" in mainstream, well-funded blockbusters. Throughout the 1970s, Brown would be shut out of mainstream films, cast instead in this subgenre. But he still continued to fight, even in the context of the blaxploitation world, to never play a drug dealer, a pimp, or anyone he thought would bring shame to young black kids sitting in that theater.

He told the *Los Angeles Press* in 1973, "You've got to think of entertainment for the whole market but I feel I'll be doing something just by being aware of the state of mind of the black man and try to represent something on the screen that will be inspirational in him; something that he can identify with and something that will make him feel he's got a chance too. We're trying to become citizens of an industry we've breathed life into."

Yes, they breathed life into the film world, but moving beyond the blaxploitation era's limitations proved impossible for a generation of actors, and Jim Brown was no exception. Even with everything the industry knew about his political beliefs and standing in the black community, he was offered the title role in *Mandingo*, an infamous 1975 film about a big black stud on an antebellum southern plantation. Brown turned it down and the producers gave the role to another star athlete, former boxing champion Ken Norton. It is stunning—and it says a great deal—that Hollywood would even have the gall to approach Brown with such an offer. Asking him to play a slave who in the end gets boiled alive and turned into soup is like asking Steven Spielberg to direct a remake of *Triumph of the Will*. Film critic Roger Ebert called *Mandingo* a "piece of manure . . . racist trash, obscene in its manipulation of human beings and feelings, and excruciating to sit through." When it was greenlit for a sequel, its producers again asked Jim Brown if he had any interest in a starring role: this time playing Mandingo's father, out for revenge. Brown's response: "Give me one billion dollars and I'll do it. . . . Hollywood wants to project a view that white liberals freed blacks. They're comfortable with that. When a black man stands up there's an entirely different reaction. Racism in Hollywood? Absolutely."

It is worth noting that there was a range of quality in blaxploitation cinema, and several of the most important films of the era strove to carry a political message that had nuance and brought a sense of empowerment, not caricature. Brown, as well, with a set of very limited choices, turned down the pimp roles and never stopped trying to find projects that stretched boundaries. One example was the film *Slaughter*, where he played a part described as "the black 007." But even if these characters had dignity, the films in which they appeared also possessed the elements common in the genre: shoddy direction and scripts and dreadful portrayals of women (Pam Grier and Tamara Dobson excepted). When Brown entered the genre, most famously in *Three the Hard Way* with Fred Williamson and Jim Kelly, he elevated the surroundings probably more than they deserved. Brown was able with every part, no matter how poor the film, to emanate charisma, maintain his dignity, and still be the person whose performances could "give black people a lift."

But being a black actor in the Hollywood of the 1970s also meant being without power, and this absence of self-determination was frustrating for Brown. Hollywood had damaged his ample ego. He interpreted his own inability to elevate his position in the movie business not only on the grounds of the industry's racism but because, in his estimation, they couldn't handle "real men."

In *Out of Bounds* he expressed his frustration about how the Hollywood community did not measure up to his macho code.

"I have not found entertainers to be half as secure as athletes," he wrote. "And I think I understand it, at least regarding guys who played football. A man who has experienced fear and physical hardship . . . doesn't have to advertise his toughness. He's just tough, you know? Men like [football tough guys] Bubba Smith and Ray Nitschke now live gentle lives. Give them sufficient reason they could still whip ten men. That kind of man doesn't have to stuff his pants."

By 1978, Brown was largely done trying to become the black John Wayne. He was forty-two years old, tired of the Hollywood hustle. He instead attempted an audacious power move from actor to movie mogul, applying everything he learned and preached from his days with the Black Economic Unions. He wanted to be a boss. Yet meetings to get other people to fund his projects were largely unsuccessful. One producer, among the few women in Hollywood with the money to bankroll projects and speaking on the condition of anonymity, met with Brown and described him as serious, prepared, and motivated. She also said that she couldn't concentrate on what he was saying because "I couldn't stop looking at his thighs. They were just bursting through the seams of his pants." He was a body, not a brain, and was experiencing what women in Hollywood had confronted for decades.

Faced with these obstacles, Brown, just as he had done so successfully as an NFL "locker room lawyer" and the first modern pro athlete in sports history, tried to change the game. He saw the opportunity to leverage his friendship with a black film star who shone even brighter than he did, and set up a new sort of film studio. It would promote intelligent parts for black actors and develop black talent in front of and behind the camera. The studio would provide a space to tell black stories under black creative control. This dream almost came to pass, but ultimately it didn't, because making it happen meant having to handle the wickedly talented and deeply damaged genius of Richard Pryor.

Brown's friendship with the comic legend might seem on paper like an odd coupling: the taciturn football player who eschewed drugs and the frenetic comedian who wrestled with substance abuse throughout his adult life. But the bond was deep, and Brown felt it before they were friends. He wrote in *Out of Bounds*, "Even before we met I identified with Richard. He was always getting in scrapes, so was I. One of the first times I saw him, Richard was sitting behind bars. I went to the jail to visit, didn't say much. Told him I liked him, appreciated his comedy. Next time I saw Richard he was in a hospital, for drug abuse. I stuck around. We had a bond."

But for both, the friendship clearly touched on many tender psychological pressure points. Brown has described Pryor as "the only man I ever truly loved." For a person who was raised by generations of women and without men in his immediate family, Pryor was the little brother to protect that Brown never had. For Pryor, the relationship was even more fraught. Scott Saul, author of the biography *Becoming Richard Pryor*, said, "Richard hungered to have a strong father figure who could supply the forcefulness that his father had, but also the gentleness that his father lacked. That's what he might have been looking for in Jim Brown. He had a father who beat him for no reason. His father was just a brutal person: a pimp. He's always kind of searching for a brother figure who can lead him out of the trauma of his past."

Brown saw himself as that brother figure: the person who tried to get Pryor onto a healthier path and off hard drugs, particularly freebase cocaine. In the classic comedy concert film *Richard Pryor: Live on the Sunset Strip*, Pryor has a whole segment on Jim Brown. It captures just how low the pipe brought Pryor and the way he turned to Brown as the powerful presence who could get him off "base":

> Ain't been out of my room in eight weeks. Funk is my shadow. Funk be just hanging all over me, talkin' about . . . "Hey, don't wash." Then finally, my old lady called Jim Brown up. She said, "Jim gonna come over."
> "Fuck Jim Brown! I'll show Jim Brown. I don't give a fuck. Nobody afraid of Jim Brown here." [*The audience laughs.*]
> Jim was coming in the driveway. I got all nervous. [*Shaking*] "Oh, shit! This motherfucker ain't gonna scare me. Let me get my pipe."

The friendship between Brown and Pryor did not transition into a business relationship over dinner or in a boardroom surrounded by lawyers and agents. It happened after Pryor set himself on fire and almost burned to death. There is a myth that Pryor became engulfed in flames accidentally while freebasing cocaine. It is true that Pryor was freebasing, but his self-immolation was actually an attempted suicide. Pryor struck a match after dousing himself in 151-proof rum. He jumped out a window and ran down the street as his clothes melted into his skin, and he suffered horrendous burns over most of his body. "One thing I learned," said Pryor, "was that you can run *really fast* when you're on fire." As Pryor fought for his life in a hospital room, Jim Brown was there, refusing to leave his friend's side. According to some of Pryor's relatives on the scene, he would not leave even when asked by family and hospital staff. It was over-the-top, but in Brown's mind, he was determined to protect Pryor, to nurse him to health and get him clean.

Pryor touched on this again in *Live on the Sunset Strip*: "Jim was in the hospital every day when I was getting well. He'd be there every day. Fire don't mean shit to Jim. Fire jumped on Jim once, he said, 'Hey!' [*Brushes jacket*] Jim would be there giving me strength. I say, 'Jim ain't never been hurt, so I can't show no pain. I gotta show my strength, try to get well.'"

There is a more terrifying version of that story from the perspective of Richard's widow, Jennifer Pryor—who had an extremely stormy on-and-off relationship with him from 1978 until his death in 2005, and was separated from him when he attempted suicide. She is also no fan of Jim Brown.

Jennifer, who had suffered from drug addiction, stopped using after her own near-death experiences. She tried to get Richard help before the night he set himself on fire, and turned to Brown, with whom she spoke on a regular basis at the time.

"Jim said, 'Oh, don't worry, Jennifer. Everything's going to be okay, we're going to get him help. I just saw him and he'll be okay,' and a bunch of bullshit," she remembered.

Brown said that Richard had promised to check himself into

a hospital, but she was unconvinced. On the day Richard set himself on fire she had pleaded with him once again to get help. He refused. "He said, 'Jennifer, you better get the fuck out of here. I've made up my mind there's no way out of here. If you don't leave, you're going to get hurt too.'"

Richard, she knew, wasn't one to make idle threats. She ran to the kitchen and appealed to Richard's entourage, but they only laughed her off. She then drove back to her apartment. With no one else to call, she tried Brown.

The housekeeper answered the phone and told Jennifer that Brown was roller-skating.

When she finally caught up with him, she says, he told her to "just calm down" and she wondered, "Why is he talking to me like I'm the person who's lost it? Why doesn't anyone fucking listen to me?"

"Nothing's going to happen, Jennifer," Brown continued. "I'll call him later and talk."

Jennifer slammed the phone down and called Pryor's house. By that point, the ambulances already had been called.

As Brown describes it, while Pryor lay burned in a hospital bed, waiting for extensive skin grafts, Brown cared for him like a baby. Brown has said that his absence in the lives of his children is his greatest regret. If Brown did not care for his own babies, he poured that love into Richard, keeping a bedside vigil, wiping his behind, and putting cream on his wounds. Jennifer Pryor recalled, "He wouldn't leave. The nurse had to be called to tell Jim Brown that he would have to go. Jim Brown said, 'Make me.'"

Brown confirms this story but says that he wouldn't leave

because he was concerned that Pryor was not getting adequate care. He wasn't being intrusive. He was being paternal.

Jennifer does not agree. She believes that others would say equally cruel things about Brown, but they are frightened of him, even at his advanced age. She described a scene at the hospital where Jim took control of the surroundings. She believes that Brown had other motives and points to the fact that it was during Pryor's recovery period when he signed papers to name Brown the president of Pryor's burgeoning production company, Indigo Pictures.

She said, "He was preying on a vulnerable creature. Richard was burned up, and that's where Jim got his talons in."

Brown disputes this entirely. But it is true that after Pryor was able to leave the hospital, he and Brown launched Indigo Pictures as a company that would make black films above and beyond the parameters imposed by blaxploitation. They owned the rights to *The Color Purple* and were approached about producing a film starring a young singer named Prince; the film was called *Purple Rain*. They passed on both. Today, watching footage of the press conference announcing their new venture in May 1983, you can see the potential in their plans and the cracks in the partnership. Brown said to the assembled cameras that Indigo would be a place for black artists to grow. Pryor, out of the hospital and appearing very frail, looked unnerved by Brown's confidence and said, "No one [white people] will be excluded" from working with Indigo.

That proved not to be the case. Someone was excluded. It was Jim Brown. Pryor fired Brown by December of that same year. Pryor decided that he had no desire to oversee the production of other people's films and just wanted to work on his own projects. He said, "I thought I could do this. I made a mistake."

Why their partnership failed depends on who is doing the telling. In his 1997 memoir *Pryor Convictions, and Other Life Sentences*, the comedic giant—by then stricken with multiple sclerosis—wrote, "Indigo was a fiasco, something much bigger than I could handle. I didn't know how to run a company, and, come to think of it, I didn't even want a company. . . . Jim Brown did, though. I made my friend, Jim, president. At the end of 1983, I fired him and all hell came down on top of me. Jim, a complex man, liked running the company more than I liked having it. He hired lots of people. He made lots of noise. He commissioned numerous scripts. Started up all sorts of projects. . . . I wasn't happy about where the company was going. The only thing I cared about was the work, and when I sat down to read the scripts that had been developed, I couldn't find one that stood out as special. Not one screamed to be made. . . . I had to ask myself a serious question, something I tried my damnedest to avoid. 'Rich, do you want the company?' 'No.' And that's basically what I decided to tell Jim when I fired him. I caught shit, though. The black film community was outraged. The NAACP turned on me. Everybody . . . acted like it was my obligation to employ people just because of their skin color. They didn't understand. I didn't want to employ anybody— black, white, or purple. I didn't give a shit anymore."

Journalist Greg Tate's interview with Richard and Jennifer Pryor about this chapter of Richard's life appeared in the August 1995 issue of *Vibe*. Pryor started by speaking about Brown as if he was a bully who needed to be confronted and vanquished. "I hired Jim Brown to run [Indigo] and realized I made a mistake. And I said to myself, If I don't knock this motherfucker out, or at least make the attempt, then I ain't never gonna hit nobody, ever again. And that's the truth. I said, You know, I'm so bad. I bulldoze people all over, but I ain't bulldozed this motherfucker, so there ain't shit to my stuff."

Then Pryor pivoted and said the breaking point was when Brown passed on the chance to work with Prince and produce the smash summer movie *Purple Rain*. The film established Prince as a pop culture sensation and provided one of the biggest-selling soundtracks of all time. Adjusted for inflation, it would today be a $200 million blockbuster in domestic ticket sales. "He fucked around and turned down Prince's *Purple Rain*," Pryor said, not exactly beating around the bush. "That movie would've been great for us. But Jim thought it didn't have enough black people among the production assistants or whatever. I said, 'So?' 'No, see. You got to have black people. This is a black thing.' I said, 'What we going to do, Jim?' I felt like I was mad. I was insane. I told Jim Brown over lunch that I didn't want this company and Jim cried. Jim Brown, you dig? I was either going to die right there or live with a broken face. I didn't care because I was tired of his shit."

Brown told a very different version of the *Purple Rain* story: "The movie *Purple Rain* was really the first venture I wanted, and I said, 'Richard! This is it, man! Prince is about to break out!' But Richard didn't know who Prince was and we passed on it."

For his book *Let's Go Crazy: Prince and the Making of* Purple

Rain, Alan Light interviewed the film's producer Roberto Cavallo, who remembers the disagreement in a way that favors
Pryor's account. "I pretty much had a deal and [Brown is] saying, 'Look, I'll be executive producer and you run everything
by me,' and I said, 'Well, I've hired a cameraman—one of my
best friends is a five-time Academy Award nominee.' I tell Jim
Brown that and he says, 'How many times have I told you that
you have to run it by me?' So I go over to him and say, 'Listen,
Jim . . .' I put my hand on his back, and I knew that was a
mistake—someone had to jump in between us and block him
from killing me. So that was that—fuck him, I was gone."

Cavallo's director of choice, Albert Magnoli, had a bit of a
different spin on it but still put the weight of the decision on
Brown. "Jim Brown took one look at us and said, 'What is this,
the Italian Mafia in front of me? I wouldn't make this movie
with you clowns. I wouldn't make a movie with a black artist
and no black people [behind the camera].'"

As with many stories involving Brown, several versions of
the truth battle for space around what actually happened. But
several facts are certain. Clearly Brown had a vision for Indigo
that involved the promotion and development of not only black
talent but black filmmakers and employees. Clearly the producers of *Purple Rain* did not see a problem with developing a film
around a young black superstar without hiring a black crew.
Clearly Richard Pryor did not want to be a film mogul and had
deep problems with sharing any alpha-male status with Jim
Brown, who was—in Pryor's mind—some sort of representation of his bullying father. A final *Purple Rain* note: The character of Prince's abusive dad, who was portrayed by Clarence

Williams III, was done up to strongly resemble Jim Brown, down to the mustache and hair.

Brown, when speaking about the dissolution of the partnership over the past thirty-five years, has always been open about feeling not merely hurt but heartbroken by the entire ordeal. "Richard fooled me," he said in a 1986 interview. "I'd known him as a person who would come into [my] life, usually when he was in trouble. I was foolish enough to think he really cared about me."

Brown said he took over Pryor's affairs out of altruistic concerns, noting, "People wanted the combination to his safe, I kept that from happening. With his feeble hand I got him to write a check so his family could have money for the house. I worked closely with the doctors. I kept one of his daughters at my house. I dealt with all of his ex-wives. I mean, everything you could think of."

According to Brown, Pryor went off to somewhere on the African continent. "When he came back, he said he wanted his company back. He said, 'If you're here, I won't be here.' So I just got my little stuff and left. He wrote me a strange letter. Said something about 'differences of opinion, but if you ever need me . . .' I feel sadness. There's no animosity. See, I never depend on anybody anyway. I thought Richard cared about me. But he didn't care about anybody else. I knew he didn't care about his kids, I knew he didn't care about his wife. I knew he didn't care about anybody. But, shit, he suckered me."

Jennifer Pryor says, "The day that Richard fired him, it was at the Sony lot. They're outside in the lot and he's telling Jim that it's over and Jim left. Richard said to me, 'Jim must've thought I had a gun.' I said, 'Well, did you?' and Richard said, 'Of course I did.' So Richard was afraid of Jim, too. Jim's heartbreak just stems from a crushed ego and crushed chances in Hollywood."

She also says, "Indigo was Jim's shot to legitimize himself, to prove himself. To elevate himself. To validate himself. And I think that all fell apart. That was his one big moment—his pie in the sky just disintegrated."

This is a story of damaged, talented people that in retrospect seems like an idea that was ahead of its time but with a combustible combination of personalities that appeared destined to fail. What Brown saw as "tough love," Pryor saw as bullying: two alpha males with deep wounds who were unable to connect. But to understand how Pryor could flip against Brown, it is worth looking at one scene in a movie from earlier in Pryor's career, *The Mack*.

Released in 1973, *The Mack* is considered a blaxploitation classic. It is about a pimp named Goldy who fights cops and the mob while psychologically manipulating the sex workers in his "stable." With its extensive discussions about how to "run game" on women and its footage from an actual Players Ball with pimps wearing their finest and walking the runway, the film has influenced everyone from Dave Chappelle to Quentin Tarantino to Snoop Dogg. There has probably never been a film more sampled in the history of hip-hop.

Pryor plays Goldy's best friend, Slim, and was allowed to ad-lib at will. He is also clearly under the influence. In one scene that is unbearable to watch, Goldy (Max Julien) and Slim are brought out to a dark alley behind a bar by two corrupt white cops who tell them to "go on home. Walk away," so they can shoot them in the back. Taking over the scene in a frenzied fit of improvisation that seems confuse the B-list actors sharing his screen, Pryor starts shrieking that they should just shoot them now and that they "ain't shit." His volume brings other people from the bar outside and the police slink away. Pryor is left on screen, his body shaking, saying, "We are going to get those motherfuckers!" On the DVD commentary, Julien marvels at Pryor's improv and says that he looks like "a woman standing up to an abusive husband."

Pryor wanted strong people around him, but he also had a hair-trigger hatred of people who he felt were projecting that power in a paternalistic manner that intruded on his space. Scott Saul said, "Richard was looking for somebody who could be some kind of father-figure of strength. But that could also tip into a situation where he felt like he was being taken advantage of, if not bullied."

Sure enough, in an interview with *Essence* magazine the spring after their partnership dissolved, Pryor said of Brown, "He was a bully. And there was a point when I had to say, 'All you can do is kill me, but you can't be the president of my company, because I'm not going to take any more of this shit.'"

When Pryor fired Brown, it also provoked the anger of the local NAACP. Willis Edwards, leader of the Beverly Hills/Hollywood NAACP, said, "It's a slap in the face because we were working very hard with Jim Brown. . . . Richard Pryor couldn't just fire Jim Brown by himself. . . . I think they're using Pryor as a scapegoat, making everybody think he did this

when in fact it was Coke and Columbia making the move."
This was vociferously denied by all parties involved.

Ross Greenburg, former head of HBO Sports, said, "Hollywood was not ready for black ownership. Even though they
were giving Pryor a check, they were doing it really for Pryor
to make his own films. I think [Brown] struggled with that for
many years."

There may be truth in what Greenburg says, but Indigo
never had the chance to find out. The actual truth might be this
was simply a case of two personalities, one Jim Brown who
needed to be in control and one Richard Pryor who could not
stand to feel controlled. As a result, what could have been an
era-shifting pivot for black filmmaking was lost.

One of the few times you see Brown's face visibly fall and
appear melancholy is when he speaks about Pryor. He says, "I
tried to keep him alive. And the funny thing to tell you is that
I think the only person in my life that I ever looked upon as
having the ability to disappoint me—because I don't have certain expectations, about people—was Richard. I was like, 'I'm
not fucking with you because you're Richard Pryor. I care
about you, man. And here I am. And shit, I'm wiping your ass
when you go to the bathroom—I don't do that shit! There's
some things I don't do, but I do it for you because of the friendship and the struggle that you have. I'm not fucking with you
like no flunky. You know, you're my friend, man. And you
have some problems that I was able to come and help you with.'

"And he accepted that and accepted me, and I allowed him
to see places that you don't want people to go. And he and I
were cool, regardless of what the fuck was going on, and now

he's going to sell out on me? It's like he fucked me up on a whole other level! And that shit sounds crazy. Shit, I'm cold, I'm a soldier, I'm going to continue my work and I'm going to go on. I don't have that sensitivity, but then there's that break-through with a certain issue, and it touches you that way. . . . Richard was sick. I can blame his family or his hangers-on, but Richard was sick. He had the drug problem when he was dealing with Indigo."

Brown has other suspicions about why Richard fired him, saying, "I had invited their company [Indigo's financial backers] to meet most of our company when we were in town. And I invited them to come and meet up. And this one girl—I think she was Jewish—I think she went back and told them that I was a Farrakhan-lover, and so on. And the company, I think, must have gotten the hint, pulled Richard to the side, and told him that, 'We got to get rid of this guy over here.' They gave him an ultimatum behind my back. So, one day, I reached out to them, and I'm sitting in my office, and he comes in and he says, 'Hey, man, I want my company back.' I said, 'You want your com-pany back? That ain't no problem.' And he got up, and that was that. He just didn't want to do it. He wanted the company back."

Brown then slows down. Usually, everything he says is mea-sured, every word considered, the profanity that peppers his speech acting like commas so he can pause and collect his thoughts before continuing. But on the subject of Pryor, he is talking too fast, and he slows it down.

"Yeah, yeah, yeah . . . It hurt, you know? Because the deal was him and me against the world. And we were winning. And when he said that he wanted his company back, I just got up, man. It was like, 'Fuck. Can't go through this shit.' And I don't want nothing from nobody. There are no false pretenses. He was scared to death and that's what happened."

Brown could not be fake with Pryor and his inability to be fake also hurt him in Hollywood. Brown may not have been a Farrakhan disciple—in actuality, he is an admirer of Jewish life and culture—but he wanted to know if someone was going to judge him for having Farrakhan as a friend. Brown may not have been able to "get real" with Richard Pryor, but he also had no ability to "get fake" with anyone else.

One of Brown's closest compatriots was a high-ranking longtime LAPD officer who had a short run in the NFL, George Hughley. A physically imposing individual, who died in a motorcycle crash in 1999, Hughley was always a reliable defender of Brown in front of the cameras and behind the scenes. Hughley observed of his friend, "There's a lot of posing and ass-kissing that goes down in that business. If he'd done some of that, he might be working more. Of course, if he'd done some of that he wouldn't be who he is."

Brown couldn't live with being that kind of person. He said, "If you kiss somebody's ass for a hundred thousand dollars, the hundred thousand can go pretty fast, but ten years down the road you still kissed the ass. It all comes around."

The fall of Indigo meant that Brown, other than the infrequent acting gigs, started to look for other challenges. And these challenges needed to have an element of being, as Don McPherson puts it, "that bad motherfucker." He had walked so many of the machismo stations of the cross: football, Hollywood action star, sex symbol. But he found himself stymied in attempting to synthesize Black Power and economics, and then after playing the sex symbol/Hollywood game, he found himself being treated on each of these canvases as "something less than a man." He told Gloria Steinem for her 1968 *New York* magazine article, "Well, I couldn't stay in this Hollywood business if I weren't doing other things. The ghettos, that's really where it's at. If those black kids look at you with respect, then you know you're a *man*."

# SIX

# MAN UP: GANGSTERS, SHOT-CALLERS, AND FIGHTING TO MAKE PEACE

—

*You are Rockhead Johnson, legendary Compton Crip. You were raised not so much by a family as by the prison system. You were kicked out of juvenile hall at age eleven, kicked out of the youth authority prisons by fourteen, and ended up going to a grown-up correctional facility by age fifteen. You were paroled six months into a six-year sentence, and then in short order were sent back for eleven years. You get out, finally, in 1992 and hear that this old football player named Jim Brown was having all the Crips and Bloods over to his mansion in the West Hollywood Hills. That sounds like a party, so you pick up about sixty Compton Crips and roll on up. What you didn't realize was that he was having both Crips and Bloods over at the same time. You feel disrespected. An Original Blood puts his hand out and says, "Glad to have you here, brother."*

*"Don't touch me!" you shout. You get your crew together and you*

*leave. As you shut the door, you hear Jim Brown say in a booming voice, "That's Rockhead. Don't worry. That was just a misunderstanding. He isn't staying today, but maybe tomorrow."*

*It sticks in your head: he's as respectful as you were disrespectful. Then you get a call the next day and it's Jim Brown. You hang up. He calls back and you hang up again. Finally you take a deep breath and say, "Why are you calling me, man?" He says, "Are you a fucking bitch or are you a fucking man?" For a second you are stunned, but you quickly correct yourself and make clear you're a motherfucking man and you're ready to prove it. You jump in your car, put your "trey-fifty-seven" in your waistband, and drive to his house. He answers the door and repeats, "Like I said, brother, are you a fucking bitch or are you a motherfucking man?"*

*You show your gun and say, "I'm a motherfucking man!" He says, "Put it away and let's talk like men, then." And before you know it, you're talking.*

**IF THE 1970S SAW THE UNITED STATES DRIFT FROM THE** movements that animated the previous decade, the 1980s were the era of the "backlash." In Los Angeles, a spike in unemployment, cuts in social programs, and the explosion of the crack cocaine trade turned poor neighborhoods into open-air drug markets and street gangs into eager employers. Violence, turf wars, and automatic-weapon fire that occasionally strayed into white middle-class suburbs created a hysteria unto itself. The death tolls were met with a malignant public indifference as long as the murders and drug trade continued to be contained in black and brown communities. Once the artillery entered affluent neighborhoods, the LAPD set about attempting to put out these fires with gasoline.

The police were given license to go into South Central and East Los Angeles and bust heads. They all too often acted little differently from how the gangs they were meant to police acted. This was revealed most jarringly in the Rampart scandal that played out from 1997 to 2001, with tales of widespread corruption of then police chief Daryl Gates's once storied Community Resources Against Street Hoodlums (CRASH) anti-gang unit of the LAPD's Rampart Division. More than seventy officers were implicated in crimes ranging from evidence-tampering to narcotics-dealing to backing up this behavior with organized and systematic violence.

Yet in the 1980s, years before Rodney King, before the L.A. riots, before the O. J. Simpson verdict, and before the Ramparts scandal revealed just how deeply the divisions ran in Los Angeles, few outside the black community raised a peep about the actions taking place in plain sight. Chief Gates would signal a new raid by saying things like, "This is war. . . . We want to get the message out to the cowards out there, and that's what they are, rotten little cowards—we want the message to go out that we're going to come and get them." The head of the District Attorney's Hardcore Drug Unit followed that up with the statement "This is Vietnam here."

It wasn't Vietnam. It was an economically lucrative turf war that exploded with the widespread use of crack cocaine in 1984, creating an illegal economy that easily took root in the absence of jobs and infrastructure. The green power of the

Black Economic Unions never flourished. Black Power was of the past. Instead there was the crack trade and the even more lucrative war on drugs, or as author Mike Davis called it, "the drug 'war' the LAPD secretly loves losing." The hysteria around this war built the careers of future political power brokers throughout the state of California. It also laid the groundwork for a heightened level of police brutality that publicly revealed itself to white America in the video that captured the savage police beating of Rodney King.

It is also worth noting that while gunfire, police brutality, and broken families defined entire sections of Los Angeles County, the Hollywood glitterati existed in a state of oblivion. As many in the fame bubble lived the lifestyles of the rich and famous, easily ignoring the reality of the Los Angeles streets, fifty-year-old ex–NFL player and actor Jim Brown made the decision to stand against the current and work with thousands of young people that the system was more than ready to write off.

In the early 1980s, Brown was somewhat lost. After the collapse of Indigo Pictures, he found that there was not a lot of work for middle-aged black action heroes in Hollywood. Profiles of him in that period find him working out obsessively, roller-skating, and dating teenagers. With his still muscular frame, receding hairline, and swinger lifestyle, he had become, in a phrase coined by Chris Rock, "the old guy at the club." Brown, always so proud, seemed to be doing things for the sake of getting attention, like posing on the cover of *Sports Illustrated* in a Raiders uniform, threatening to make a return to the NFL to prevent future Hall of Fame running back Franco Harris from taking his rushing record. Brown was quoted: "Who's to say a 47-year-old can't do it? I'm not talking about being Jim Brown of 1965. I'm talking about being Jim Brown of 1984. If Franco Harris is gonna creep to my record, I might as well come back and creep, too."

Brown also called out Harris's football manhood, saying, "Franco is having a lovely performance in his twilight years. . . . If [he] hangs around long enough and keeps running out of bounds, he'll get my record."

Much of Brown's 1989 book *Out of Bounds* is midlife crisis as text, entertaining but animated by an anger over his legacy's being underappreciated and the fact that his activism was not being taken up by that era's generation of players. "When I look at the black stars today," he wrote, "I wonder if they ever study history. How do they think they got in the position they're in? Blacks who came before them paved the way, blacks who had to do more than just play good football, who had to endure some bitter cruelties. A lot of them did more than endure. They spoke out, provoked some thought, took some damn chances, instead of saying, 'Hey, I've got mine. Everything is cool.' If we had done that, the guys today would be starting from scratch. And that is my crucial point: it's thirty years later, but everything is *not* cool. If blacks start taking their gains for granted, future generations will have serious trouble. I don't want the guys today to give *me* their damn time and money. I want them to wake up."

Brown was simply too restless to just sit in the West Hollywood Hills and do nothing. Instead, he looked to use his fame, his connections, and even his home to help stop gang violence. This was far from the first time Brown had wrestled with these issues. In the Cleveland of the 1960s, he would walk the meanest streets and speak to young men about alternatives to gang life. After retirement, he tried to get the Black Economic Unions off the ground and spoke about using them as a means to move young people from gangs into business. He did not think that God or family would save young people from gangs, but what could save them was a job that gave them pride and dignity.

One can see the seeds of his gang-intervention methodologies in an interview he gave after the 1967 urban uprisings. "It was unrealistic, it seems to me, to expect that the people sealed up in these ghettos would remain quiet in them forever," he told Alex Haley. "I know what I'm talking about; I've seen what can happen with these people. You've got to persuade the black men who are respected in their area to go in and crack the door, crack the ice.

"I've been able to do this myself a few times in a few places. The ghetto people know I'm straight, that I speak up and stand up and I wouldn't betray them. I've gone into ghettos and talked with the toughest cats. I've told them, 'Now, look I think you know I'm my own man. Now, here's what seems to me a hell of a program, but it needs your help to get wide community support behind it.'

"In most cases, these guys will give 100-percent support. Give the toughest cats a certain respect, because *they* have respect from the people you're trying to reach with help, and they'll work with you. Sure, they're hostile and suspicious, but they'll talk sincerely with you if they figure you're *with* them. You find their greatest disappointment and bitterness come from promises, promises that proved later to be some political sham or that just weren't followed up. Whatever program there is has to be followed up, day to day. And the best people to monitor that is these tough guys: Give them jobs doing it. All they want is decent salaries; they have to eat, to live, just like anyone else. But I find that city administrations don't like this idea. They're still after political points. They want to dictate the terms, and the ghetto people resent anybody bringing them any program with white strings, so naturally it gets nowhere."

He would create a program where the only string was that you had to listen to Jim Brown.

The gang world can be like a pure, uncut dose of toxic machismo, a place where, in the words of bell hooks, one can find "the simplest way to assert patriarchal manhood" in a culture that condones "violence as a means of social control" and "identifies patriarchal masculinity by the will to do violence." This would be Jim Brown's turf: a terrain, unlike the backbiting world of Hollywood, that he believed he understood and where he felt he could assert a measure of control.

Dr. Mark Anthony Neal says, "Jim Brown's hypermasculine persona made him uniquely able to enter the world of the gangster. There are a lot of folks who pretend to be OGs [original gangsters, older gang leaders who command respect]. Jim Brown was a real OG. And out in L.A., a lot of those gang members respect what he's historically represented. He never bent. Jim Brown was always Jim Brown. Sometimes, you'll see the more intellectual types who are committed to that type of work, but can't thrive in those spaces. The fact that he was an ex-jock, and this perfectly distilled version of hyper black masculinity, gave him a credibility in these spaces that others wouldn't have. Barry Bonds, Marcus Allen, Walter Payton . . . no. I don't think even Kareem or Bill Russell have that kind of level . . . Ali, maybe, if he was healthy. Jim Brown is a rare breed in that regard."

Brown approached this work in a way that sharply contrasted with the "war" aims of the Los Angeles Police Department. His relationship with the LAPD at this time was, as always, on a knife's edge. He had buddies on the force—his best friend, longtime LAPD Officer George Hughley, was a prominent presence—but he had certainly made his share of enemies in the department as well. Brown taunted them in *Out of Bounds*, like someone waving raw meat in front of a half-starved pit bull: "There are cops in Los Angeles who would love to be the guy who sent me to San Quentin for 49,000 years. If they can't accomplish that, they'll settle for taking me in, leaking it to the press, getting a headline, their name in print, for the type of incident they would not even respond to if my name was John Doe. . . . I'm not saying the only reasons I've gotten in trouble with the police [are that] I'm black and outspoken, though if you study American history those are two damn good reasons."

Brown set about making his mark by launching a for-profit gang-intervention foundation, Amer-I-Can, in 1986. The name was coined by Dionne Warwick, and embedded within the pun is the central aim: to take individual responsibility and to rise up in the narrow space allowed for social mobility. Its initial aims were to teach basic life skills to gang members and soon-to-be-released convicts. The skills curriculum had a specific, unconventional focus, which Connie Rice, a civil rights activist and longtime Amer-I-Can supporter, described as "a kind of Gangsters Anonymous that aimed to break addictions to impulsive destruction and expose them to the ABCs of rational thought, self-control and a vision of advancement that replaced the cult of death."

Amer-I-Can truly took off after a joint event featuring Louis Farrakhan and Brown in 1989, organized in response to the skyrocketing number of gang-related deaths. It was called "Stop the Killing" and it brought thousands to the L.A. Coliseum. "The next night we met up with some gang members—shotcallers—at my house, hoping that, maybe, it would have an effect on them," Brown remembered. "We invited some gang members up and Minister Farrakhan talked and they talked and we talked, and most of these guys were just human beings that respected the minister, because he was defiant, and they liked somebody that was defiant like that. So we had a lot of kids all standing in the room, and certain subjects were very sensitive because a lot of guys that had made it that night were looking across the room at someone that had killed somebody in their gang and they had to refrain from going off. It was tense.

"So when the minister left town, I continued to have these meetings. And sometimes, seven days a week in my house, looking out at these very hills. But what changed everything was the life skills curriculum. It was like the Bible for what we [were] trying to do. With a life skills curriculum, Amer-I-Can could be a business, because if we got a contract for teaching in the schools, we could teach our gang leaders how to teach it, so they could make a living as professors of life skills in

Amer-I-Can. We were able to get quite a few contracts and hire individuals that worked in the prisons, and schools."

Brown opened up his West Hollywood Hills home to leaders from rival gangs so they could work out their differences in advance of entering his program. The next step was arduously training and then employing these shot-callers as paid Amer-I-Can facilitators. This is the crux of the Amer-I-Can program: in Brown's words, "training gangsters to be professors." If they made it through the demanding self-help curriculum, shot-callers were then tapped to teach the curriculum. For that teaching, they were paid a true living wage, a salary that would bring status and be a disincentive to go back into "the life."

According to Dr. Harry Edwards, "Dick Gregory liked to say that Jim Brown had people in his house 'whose own folks was afraid of 'em.' And he never locked his door. He never had any guards around or anybody. They came in, and because of the level of respect that he commanded, of dignity that he commanded, he would have guys in there, sitting in his living room, who if they had met each other on the streets, it would have been a shootout. But they would come up to his house, sit down and have a conversation with him sitting there, and he was the anchor, he was the cover, he was the one that made it all possible through the weight of his stature."

Brown says, "I share what I have. Everybody comes to my house because it's open and everyone feels accepted. They feel trusted. The sharing of a home is very important to me to bring about the kind of change we need."

He says that the young men from the roughest neighborhoods in Los Angeles have come to his home "looking for peace and . . . dignity, and some kind of dignified economics. Because the main thing I give would be 'respect.' That word is used a lot by us because the cry is, 'You gotta respect me. If you disrespect me, we have a problem.' This word 'respect' is not used properly all the time, but it's very important. And what we say here is always private. You don't tell on anybody. Snitching is not an acceptable alternative."

Brown's home was the site of numerous gang peace treaties. The night before the 1992 verdict in the Rodney King case—a verdict that acquitted four LAPD officers who were caught on tape beating the black motorist—Brown helped orchestrate a massive treaty that took place with "guys from gangs. Guys no longer from gangs. Guys who never belonged to gangs. Guys from 'the jungle' in the Crenshaw district. Guys from Imperial Courts [a public housing project in Watts], where the peace talks would go down. Guys who wanted to talk about keeping the city cool."

These people "already were worried that there could be a tremendous eruption," Brown explains. "They didn't want things to decay. They wanted to see if there was a way to keep things from erupting."

As riots spread and flames engulfed Los Angeles, Brown's largely ignored work from the last decade suddenly had cachet and received a great deal of media attention. The "Chief Daryl Gates Way" had produced a social explosion that resembled a postmodern Armageddon, where National Guard troops protected Frederick's of Hollywood as huge swaths of the city burned. Now Jim Brown's credo, of dealing with young people who had been marginalized and insisting for years that they not be rendered voiceless or expendable, was seen by politicians—at least publicly—as vital to achieving a measure of civic peace.

While the riots were still roaring, his work with gang members was profiled heavily in the *Los Angeles Times*, which highlighted his hands-on approach to helping gang members change their lives:

> He was doing something last Wednesday, before the startling King-case verdicts came down. He was inside a penitentiary at Wasco, northwest of Bakersfield, accompanied by actor Blair Underwood of the ironically named television series "L.A. Law," presiding over a graduation ceremony for men involved in his Amer-ICAN Program— emphasis on the "I can"—dedicated to prepare inmates for a life beyond bars.
>
> This is not some charity. The organization is a profit-making corporation that actively solicits contracts with civic and private enterprises in pursuit of business opportunities for people in need. Not only has the Amer-ICAN Program educated its hundreds of constituents in both personal and professional "life-management skills," it has at times persuaded judges to release offenders to its recognizance rather than task an already overcrowded prison system.

To put it mildly, Brown was hands-on. *Sports Illustrated* covered Brown and Amer-I-Can in 1994, and recounted a meeting where a young man openly resisted Brown's attempts to establish a dialogue. After repeatedly refusing Brown's requests to excuse himself, the young man instead challenged the fifty-eight-year-old to a fight. "Brown and the gang-banger wound up rolling out the back door in a comic-book ball of dust," wrote Steve Rushin. "Shortly thereafter they reappeared and shook hands, and the meeting resumed. One of Brown's charges—'one of my gangsters,' as Brown calls them—recently got out of his gang, got a job and got married. The wedding was held at Brown's house."

The programs were also having a serious impact inside prison walls. In the Pitchess Detention Center, as Connie Rice recalled, "less than 12 percent of the Amer-I-Can graduates violated probation, and those who did took three times as long to do so. This was in contrast to over 60 percent of the other prisoners."

Amer-I-Can by this time was running programs in fourteen penal institutions and wanted to expand to even more. Brown said, "We save the state of California $30 million [annually]. It costs anywhere from $19,000 to $45,000 per inmate, per year, to be incarcerated. If we find them work out here, they won't be in *there*."

Brown heard about the Rodney King verdict while traveling back from California's Wasco State Prison, and he immediately grasped the serious repercussions of the officers' exoneration—for the young men he worked with and the entire L.A. community.

"I got a sick feeling in my stomach," he says. "I knew we could be in for major problems. Even if some of them were let off, I thought there had to be at least some guilty verdicts. I mean, for something so blatant. But you know, thinking back, it was like they prepared us. There was [Police Chief] Daryl Gates, preparing his officers for trouble in case of a not-guilty verdict. There were ministers, cautioning everybody not to overreact. Everybody seemed to be prepping us for these guys being found innocent. And that kind of warning actually might have inflamed it, put the idea across that they were going to get off."

Brown had a new platform, and not surprisingly, he used this moment to not only preach the virtues of Amer-I-Can but also to harangue the athletes of the 1990s for their apathy, just as he had in previous decades. This is something Brown always goes back to: that in his mind, athletes have fumbled the baton passed to them and surrendered an awesome opportunity to affect seismic social change. "If I had the participation of the top twenty athletes in this country, we could probably create a nationwide gang truce," Brown has said. "These athletes represent such a great amount of resources and influence. These kids would be flattered to have their lives changed by them. Prisons are overcrowded, recidivism is at an all-time high, the education system is going downhill, there's this new culture of drugs and gangsters and killing without any thought. Kids are shooting each other at thirteen and fourteen, and all of a sudden it's not gonna stay in the inner city."

Brown's oft-repeated disgust over the last forty years with modern athletes and their political commitment (calling them "worthless," "pathetic," and far worse) was, in his mind, well earned. In the 1980s and 1990s, he made an effort to connect the work in Amer-I-Can with the modern generation of athletes, but found little success. During the 1991 NBA Finals, which pitted the Chicago Bulls against the Los Angeles Lakers, Bulls guard Craig Hodges, one of the most politically conscious athletes of his generation and a Chicago volunteer at Amer-I-Can, was asked by Brown to bring the team to his West Hollywood home.

As Hodges wrote in his memoir *Long Shot*, "I couldn't wait to go to Jim's house. . . . Trying to negotiate a truce between the rival LA gangs the Crips and the Bloods, [Jim] wanted the support and input of the Bulls. I explained this to the team but quickly saw that I was the only one interested in the meeting. 'I want to stay focused on the series, but ask Jim how he made all his money,' said [Michael] Jordan."

Even without the money and presence of other sports stars, Brown led a 1990s expansion of Amer-I-Can in cities around the country. By this time, he had roughly fifty "facilitators" who had been through the Amer-I-Can program, representing and leading the work. But the nucleus of the work still centered on the presence of Jim Brown.

Brown, almost thirty years after the founding of Amer-I-Can, easily explains his reasons for choosing to work with gangs. "Well, the starting point of everything is trying to analyze how to best affect positive change, and if everything has to end in violence and death, we might as well all go home.

"First off, I drew a conclusion that I had to get to know that culture. The gang culture is entrenched because of the way the education, economic, and criminal justice systems are set up. Even if they do the right thing, they often get cut down. So what I had to do was try to devise a way to reach that culture, influence that culture, and reintroduce these guys back into society. And then there is the in-prison work. I had to break through prison doors and make professors out of these so-called gang leaders and shot-callers."

Explaining the "life management skills" that his "gangster professors" teach, he says, "These skills are the ones that are missing when a father leaves, or a mother is not doing the right thing, or when people are not getting educated. It's not advanced arithmetic; it's common sense that you can live with: the problem-solving techniques you use, the decision-making techniques that you use, how you make important decisions in your life. Those fundamentals will allow you to eventually be successful. Without them, you just end up drowning in a goddamned lake, hoping to be rescued."

The successes of Amer-I-Can created a network of true believers. Gina Belafonte, longtime social justice activist and daughter of civil rights legend Harry Belafonte, says of Amer-I-Can, "What is great about it is that it transcends a person's socioeconomic situation and backgrounds; it transcends gender, transcends age; it transcends all isms and stigmas. So it is really a transformational self-help program that anyone can use, whether it's for our incarcerated brothers and sisters or whether it's in the community or in a corporate firm. I think that it's a very useful tool. It gives many incarcerated individuals a doorway into their own humanity and the opportunity to take a deeper look at their early childhood development and what pushed them into the space they find themselves in today. So it helps them create and develop tools of reconciliation and forgiveness within themselves and in their community." Further, Belafonte says, "it gives them tools to communicate with a language and request forgiveness from their loved ones. It's a life management skills course that enables individuals to develop their own language around healing and community participation and communication."

Gina Belafonte believes that his experience with Amer-I-Can was transformative for Brown as well, and that it continues to be a part of his "personal journey."

This transformation, however, did not include a willingness to cede control of Amer-I-Can. The program has improved the lives of countless numbers of people, but the bumps in the road often come back to that matter of control, whether it was a city bureaucracy wanting control over Brown or whether it was some of the young people trained through Amer-I-Can who wanted control over the organization itself and more of a voice in its direction. This was the string attached to Amer-I-Can. As one Amer-I-Can volunteer said, "It was Jim's way or don't let the door hit you."

There is so little give in Jim Brown that even—or especially— in this world of competing male egos and unfettered ids, he needed to be the one answered to. That rigidity has helped him stay the course through the various frustrations and pitfalls of doing this type of work, but it has also moved him to push away people he mentored, people who loved him and simply wanted to be appreciated as equals; to be recognized as the men they had become.

For Brown, this demeanor was conscious. He thought of himself as a very exacting father figure whom shot-callers would actually listen to. He says, "You have to care about them. When I would go into prisons, I used to always get up and say, 'I'm going to say something to you guys, and I challenge you to disagree with it, and I know that nobody's going to disagree with it.' The prisoners would say. 'Oh, you're an idiot.' I'd say, 'Is there anybody in this room that doesn't want to be loved or cared for by somebody? I want you to stand up.' Nobody has ever stood up."

Brown has put himself forward as this kind of father figure. But even fathers have to give a little if they don't want to push their sons and daughters away.

Aqeela Sherrills, who today is the principal of the Reverence Project, helped found Amer-I-Can as well as write and develop the Amer-I-Can curriculum. Three decades younger than Brown, he recalls their first contact. "I met Jim through the 'Stop the Killing' movement that Minister Farrakhan was doing across the country in November of '89. Jim hosted a meeting with Minster Farrakhan and a small group of folks. We went up to Jim's house, and we all sat around the table and talked about pulling together key members of the city to talk about trying to organize a peace treaty."

This meeting was a turning point for peace activists trying to find a solution to not only gang violence but also the drug trade.

That first meeting with Sherrills brought together "brothers from across the city." It was the first of several gatherings, all at Brown's house. Each meeting was bigger in size. Eventually it grew to hundreds of gang members and activists. "No violent incidents happened out of respect to the Nation and out of respect to Jim. What came out of that conversation was a smaller, tighter group of individuals that Jim decided to work with to end the killing in the streets." This is how that first class of "gangster-professors" came into being.

For these younger people, Brown's status came less from his football exploits or acting chops than the role he played on the streets in trying to bring people together and the simple fact that he was willing to let people into his home.

"It was hilarious," recalls Sherrills. "I told him, 'On behalf of the brothers from the Jordan Downs, we wanted to just let you know that we appreciate you opening up your house.' And he said, 'Hey, man, if you ever want to get out of the hood, and bring your ladies up, call me.' So he gave me his number, and we were just doing all sorts of crazy stuff up in his house."

Brown was involved at every level, Sherrills says. "I put together a proposal and told Jim, 'Hey, we've got a little storefront across the street from the projects. We're selling T-shirts and buttons and all different types of things with messages about the need to stop the killing.' Jim loved what we were doing and started paying the rent on our storefront, about four hundred dollars a month."

Sherrills tells one illustrative story of the time they didn't go to Jim Brown's hood but Jim Brown came to theirs: "Jim used to have this 1969 brown Mercedes convertible. He had it for years. So Jim pulls up in the parking lot in the gym, behind the projects, and he has this black tank top, that red, black, and green kufi he wore, some sweatpants, and his flip-flops. He comes walking across the field. And we're sitting there, and some cats are like, 'Man, that's Jim Brown!' They know everything Jim ever did. So dudes are like, 'Oh my god, we got Jim Brown in the hood, what!?'

"Jim walks up, and everybody is shaking hands, going home to go get cameras. And one of my boys, Chop, was there. Chop had just got out [of prison] and he had, like, twenty-four-inch biceps, and he walked up to Jim, and said, 'Jim, hey, Jim! Give me some money, Jim! And Jim looked at him—you know Jim has this crooked look, he can't just turn his whole body around. So Jim turns his head at an angle and says, 'You ain't got no panties on, man. Shit. I only give money to women,' and everybody just started laughing. Chop looked struck for a moment, and then he just started laughing and he was like, 'Jim, you cool as a motherfucker, man.' And that was just the relationship, and it developed from there. Somebody else that was in that circle probably would've gotten defensive or something, but this is Big Jim. Big Jim done seen it and done it. He just says, 'I ain't worried about you, this is what it is, this is what I do.'"

Brown was putting money into Aqeela's storefront and other Amer-I-Can projects, but he was getting something back: his own street-level education of both youth and gang life. He says, "If I don't know this culture, then I couldn't change this culture." He sponged up every bit of knowledge this new generation of gangsters could give him. This is a characteristic of his personality, and it is an O. Henryesque curse: he is a man most comfortable hearing other people talk and soaking up the wisdom of what they have to say, yet he is constantly the one to whom people are asking questions. But in this world he found people eager to share their experiences with a famous person who was willing to listen. Brown went to communities and neighborhoods that few in Los Angeles traveled to unless they lived there or were part of Daryl Gates's Operation Hammer, and he listened. He wanted to understand, and in the words of one Amer-I-Can graduate named Julius, "He wanted to feel the gang culture down to its last compound. He wanted to get to know the root causes of gang violence, beyond the media bullshit—that it wasn't just war because we hate each other, that it was deeper than that. That it was rooted in opportunity and economics as much as anything else."

Brown invested more than $400,000 of his savings to get Amer-I-Can off the ground. He said, "If you brothers give me ten years, I'll show you how to access your tax dollars, work the system, invest in your own community, save money for your families and never have to worry about taking care of yourself for the rest of your life."

Sherrills connected with that message and committed with a broader group to do the work. "I tell you," says Sherrills, "what he said came to pass. We organized. We founded Amer-I-Can. We got a contract with the Department of Corrections and Rehab with nineteen correctional facilities in the state and we ran the program inside the prisons. Then my brother got the idea that instead of trying to focus the peace treaty on the whole city, we would try and focus it just on the neighborhood, on Watts. If we brought together the four major housing developments, we would create a domino effect for peace throughout the city because Watts is the trendsetting community. It took us four years, developing the contracts inside the jail facility, then getting the contract with L.A. County probation to provide services in the summer camps, and then working with key brothers throughout the neighborhood, hosting meetings and conversations and dialogues. We used to have these meetings up at Jim's house every Wednesday night."

The cornerstone of all this work was the Amer-I-Can

curriculum. "We would have classes in the community," Sherrills says. "We could have these Wednesday nights up at Jim's house where we would invite new people to learn about what we were doing to bring about an end to the killing. Everybody would come up there. Celebrities from Chuck D and Flava Flav, to Queen Latifah to Dionne Warwick, to shot-callers like Rockhead Johnson from Compton to Big U from the Rollin' 60s. They all got enrolled and introduced to the movement that we were engaged in and it formed the basis of keeping the peace treaty in place."

Sherrills also incisively points out that while the reputation of "black Superman Jim Brown" may have gotten him through the door, it's not what made people want him to stay. "Who Big Jim is gives him access. But people respected that he was really interested in people, and understanding how he can be of service to help folks have a better quality of life. I think he's always wanted to give that gift. Some of it is the machismo, but some of it is just that he gave a shit. I think that the machismo stuff was probably the worst quality, if anything. People don't respond to that machismo shit. It wasn't the macho stuff. It was the gentle Jim, that's why all of these gangster cats were so engaged in the organization. He had that soft side that he shows you, where he supports and helps you. Jim's a daddy."

The first two years of the treaty, gang-related homicides dropped by 44 percent—and Amer-I-Can expanded to even more cities. State by state, mayors were asking them to come in to organize gang truces. The first place they went was Las Vegas. The mayor, Jan Laverty Jones, warned them not to go into the projects, which were too dangerous to enter without proper introductions to gang leaders or accompaniment by a phalanx of police. But according to Sherrills, they went right in on their first night in town.

"One month later, we got two hundred and fifty Crips and Bloods shaking hands in the city hall of Las Vegas."

But Sherrills, whose love for Jim Brown seems to beat visibly through his chest even today, had to leave Amer-I-Can because there wasn't space for a fully grown Aqeela Sherrills at Brown's table. Sherrills says, "The analogy is that the mother bird pushes the baby bird out of the nest, and it's not always on agreeable terms. I connect with that. I had been in service to Amer-I-Can and to Jim for ten years, and we just weren't seeing eye to eye how to move things forward. I would say that Jim's vision was to see it expand into different states across the country. But we needed people to be there in those places to put in the time to train staff and make it work. . . . My vision was that we should really be building roots in L.A., digging down a little deeper, and expanding the services that we're providing. That we're not this virtual organization that's just a curriculum that just kind of drops in and does its thing and then comes out."

Yet it wasn't just a disagreement about tactics. It was also about communication and the process, or lack of process, that existed for making these kinds of decisions.

"Jim has a certain style of leadership," Sherrills observes. "He has to be the one in control and make all the decisions. After two years at his side, that's still great. After four years, after six years, it starts to become old. Because at this point we're colleagues in the business now, because we run a company called Amer-I-Can, so some of the control has to be relinquished so we can manage the organization better."

The deep relationship between the two men frayed the more Sherrills drifted from Brown's control, and it continued to unravel when he created his own organization, the Community Self-Determination Institute. "Jim never came down to the building, to the organization. . . . And then over the years, all of the cats that were working for him ended up coming to work for me and they told me all types of crazy stories and stuff about what Jim said to them about me, about how I wasn't going to be nothing but a pimp politician. It broke my heart. I liken it to a breakup. Then sometimes I think, maybe he's just trying to teach me a lesson. Always about teaching a lesson. Jim is a know-it-all, and he's smart as a motherfucker, and he makes sure you know it. I love him still."

In 2016, Sherrills joined with Brown again, for an initiative in New Jersey, and was deeply moved by how Brown had changed with age. "In his eighties he's a new cat. He's talking about things I had never heard him speak to before, speaking about spiritual things and God. He's evolved and I'm so grateful for it. It was deep. It was transformative."

But the greatest moment was when they had a conflict that needed to be resolved. As Sherrills tells it, Brown realized that he was in the wrong, looked at his former protégé, and said, "Aqeela. I'm sorry." Sherrills takes a breath when telling this story. "I really couldn't believe it. Usually he wouldn't apologize for shit. He was apologizing. It was a small issue, but that he was willing to give me that, it meant so much."

Jim Brown today may have more "give." But twenty years

ago, his rigid "I'm gonna throw your ass in the fire" approach could go only so far. This is seen in his work with onetime Crips leader Rudolph "Rockhead" Johnson.

Rockhead Johnson was raised in Compton, California, and is one of the most respected and reputedly fearless members of the Original Compton Crips. "Jim Brown spoke to me like a man," remembers Rockhead. "And I realized his childhood was little different than mine. He ran away at a young age at one point. He felt like his mother chose her boyfriends over him. If it wasn't for his girlfriend's parents taking him in, there's no telling where he would be. His past in most ways was a lot different from mine. It wasn't as violent, but I related to his story. And then he starts telling me about his trials and tribulations.

"He told me about how he wanted to quit Syracuse, and used that lesson of sticking it out to say, 'Don't quit at anything.' And he started really addressing issues with me. He explained to me how he stood beside Muhammad Ali, and I'm listening to this guy, and he's telling me about the Amer-I-Can program and I'm listening. And as I'm hearing it, I'm thinking, 'This dude really might care about people like me!'"

Brown invited Rockhead to be a part of the Amer-I-Can program. Rockhead was interested, but his attitude toward the instructors, former shot-callers all of them, was, "Y'all can't teach me shit. Man, I'm good."

They reported to Brown that Rockhead didn't want to listen.

Rockhead recounted Brown's frustration with his most difficult protégé:

"Jim called me to his house and said, 'What's up, man? I thought you wanted to learn.'

"I said, 'Man, I'm trying, I'm learning! These motherfuckers don't know what the fuck they're talking about, Mr. Brown!'

"He was like, 'You got to listen to somebody.'

"I said, 'I ain't never had no respect for no adults, man. Never in my life, since I was twelve years old. If it wasn't for you dealing with me as a man, I wouldn't respect your ass. But I'll sit back and go through your program if you personally do it with me.' And he did. We did the program together at his house. I started listening and it made me deal with myself. It made me look deep inside my belly and deal with my childhood conditioning. Once I understood my childhood conditioning, it started helping me change my life for the better. Then I started believing in what he was telling and preaching all this time."

The bonds between Brown and Rockhead Johnson were fully forged at the moment Brown chose to be there for him in a manner above and beyond what anyone could have expected. Rockhead tells this story: "I got in my car to take some youngsters to this swimming pool party. And as we were going, I'm noticing this car following me. The next thing I know, I'm hearing gunshots. My car was being shot up on the freeway. The youngsters, in retaliation—they had guns on them—started shooting back from out of the window. And I'm like, 'Shit, I have two strikes on me. I'm fitting to go to jail forever.' And I jumped off the freeway, told the youngsters to get out and run. Three minutes later, about thirty police cars pull me over and [the policemen] say that I was just involved in a drive-by shooting on the freeway. And I told them, 'It wasn't me! I was shot at in my car.'

"And they said, 'Man, step out of the car and put your hands up.' I had over fifty shots penetrate my car, so they searched my trunk and found a banana clip in the trunk tied in a black bandanna. So I'm sitting in jail, I'm wondering what I'm gonna do.

"I called my house and somebody yelled, 'Jim wants to talk to you.'

"I said, 'Man, I don't want to hear that shit Jim got to talk about right now. I gotta figure out the way I'm going to get out of this bullshit.'

"And they said, 'No, man. He heard what happened and he wants to help you!'

"So I called Jim. I told him that if I had to stay in jail, I'll never get out. I will become the person I was and I'll kill or be killed. I said, 'If you can help me get out of this thing, Mr. Brown, I can give you Compton.'

"He said, 'What do I care? I don't want Compton, Rockhead. I want your mind.'"

Jim Brown went to the parole board hearing and stated that Rockhead was in the process of changing his life. He went through the legal case to show that there was little evidence against Rockhead. It was a case of an ex-convict victimized by a drive-by shooting and that was all there was to it. Brown explained that the board would be doing the community a disservice if they sent Rockhead back inside; he vouched for him, saying that Rockhead Johnson could make a difference through the Amer-I-Can program. The parole board sentenced Johnson to three months' time served and released him. But there were two stipulations: he had to go through the Amer-I-Can program, and he had to deal with Jim Brown directly.

Brown tested Rockhead Johnson immediately. He sent him out of his comfort zone, to San Francisco, to the Geneva Towers and Sunnydale Projects, two places with reputations for being impenetrable. Rockhead's mission was to create a peace training program with the existing gang leaders. There were people in those projects whom he knew from the inside, people he could reach.

As Rockhead remembers, "That was my first experience doing the work of Amer-I-Can, and I went crazy over it. I fell in love with it. And I felt happy about doing something that could help change things. Then [Jim] asked me to go to Oregon with him. We met with the director of corrections, the right-hand man of the governor, the head of schools, and they're all in this room with him and me. Me! And Jim is talking to them, and they're all debating and arguing with each other about where Amer-I-Can is going to start first—the jails, the streets, or the schools. I watched him bring them all together, and that's when I truly believed in Jim, that he could bring these people together to sit with and listen to me. He left me in Oregon for over a year and a half, and I ran the programs—in the jails, the community, and the schools—and graduated a lot of young people. He just kept believing in me and kept putting me out there, and I eventually mastered the life skills program and ran his program to a point where by 1994 I knew how to approach young people and get them out of the game."

The drama with Rockhead Johnson did not end, however.

He remained connected to a community steeped in violence and the drug trade. That is what made him effective as an organizer—and also what made him vulnerable. Post-riots L.A. was still a place where the economics of dealing drugs was seen as a fast track to status, wealth, and manhood. While Rockhead was holed up in Oregon, a local South Central "wannabe shot-caller" tried to recruit into his narcotics distribution network the young people Rockhead was trying to mentor out of gangs. They resisted, saying it was not for them. Then they were shot in the kneecaps. Rockhead heard and was on the next plane back home.

"I went back out to Compton, and I challenged this so-called leader in front of two or three other guys. And I told him, 'They want to change their lives—they don't want to sell your dope no more, man. They good.' He got smart with me in front of this group and I slapped him and he didn't do nothing. So I said to all of the folks watching, 'This is who y'all think your leader is? He's not a man. He can shoot these youngsters, but he can't stand up to a man and deal with me.'"

Yet stories like this rarely end with a shot-caller getting publicly slapped in the face and everyone learning a lesson as if they were living out an afterschool special. Rockhead returned to Oregon, but on his next trip back to Compton, he was approached by a group connected to the person whose manhood he had so publicly challenged. They shot him eleven times.

Rockhead survived. When he woke up in the hospital, Jim Brown was at his bedside and he wasn't alone. As Rockhead tells it, there were Crips and Bloods in the room—both sets now bound to him because of the gang truce—and they begged

Rockhead to give them the names and descriptions of whoever had shot him so they could mete out some street justice.

Jim Brown stood over Rockhead's bed and didn't lecture about peace. He didn't beg people to seek nonviolence. He simply said, "Rock, what do you want to do?"

Rockhead's answer was, "I don't know, but I better figure out how to walk first."

Brown insisted that Rockhead stay at his house while he recuperated. During that arduous process, Rockhead saw "a different side of Jim Brown," someone who took care not only of Rockhead but of his daughters as well, playing "ghost" with them and making them laugh. While at Jim's, Rockhead had more space to think and "reject the revenge path" so he could continue doing his work.

That wasn't the last time the violence that marked his past came back to haunt him. And the next time, it almost ended his relationship with Jim Brown and all the effort he had invested into building his new life. It was January 13, 1998. Rockhead was celebrating his birthday with a party at his house, and he started receiving emergency-signal pager texts. He thought this was just friends trying to find the party. Then someone came to the house and told him that his sixteen-year-old daughter, Mercedes Mendenhall Johnson, had just been killed.

Rockhead responded with every old instinct. He assembled a crew of young men with TEC-9s to go out and find out what had happened and who would have to pay the price. Then, as if entering one of his old films right on cue, Jim Brown showed up at Rockhead's door. His people tried to keep Brown from coming in, saying, "Rock, we ain't hearing that shit he's talking, man. Let's go kill who did this. Ain't no peace."

Rockhead told them, "Man, I owe him a conversation. He saved my life. I been out of jail now for seven or eight years because of him, because he gave me the opportunity. I can at least listen to him."

Rockhead's friends persisted, with a lot of calls of "Fuck that," but they allowed the sixty-one-year-old Brown to pass through.

Rockhead recalls: "He came in the house, man, and we went into my room, closed the door and had some privacy. He didn't talk. He just took me in those big arms, and for the first time in my life, a grown man saw me cry. And I just cried, and he held me in his arms."

After Rockhead cried himself dry, Brown said, "Rock, I know how bad you want to get revenge. But if we cross this line, there's no turning back."

"What do you mean 'we,' Jim?" said Rockhead. "This is my thing."

"No, man. 'We.' Because I invested in you, Rock. I want you to think about all them kids' lives you saved and got out of gangs. I mean, what are they going to say if you do this?"

"They're going to understand me, because that's my daughter, man, and I got to kill this dude."

"Look, Rock. Again. If that's what you want to do, if *we* cross this line, there's no turning back."

Rockhead then looked at him and started crying again, because, he remembers, "I understood that he was just as serious as I was. He was deadly serious." Rockhead told him, "No, I can't let you do this, man."

"All right, then, if it's not good for me, then it's not good for you," Brown replied. "Let's just think about it. Let's sit back."

At this time, Rockhead's friends, armed to the teeth, started trying to break down the door. "Are we going to do this or what?" they said. "Fuck this old nigga!"

This set Rockhead off. "I said, 'Now look, you're going to respect this man and we're going to respect his opinions. And if you don't like it, get the fuck out of my house.'

"After that, I lost guys who I thought were friends. They really weren't, because they wanted me to go out there and go back to jail. And Jim again saved my life, because when I turned my cheek at that moment, I understood what the bigger picture was. I got on the phone with my other daughter, who told me that her sister would want me to continue the work I'm doing, and not go backwards. They made me understand that. I turned a cheek and left it alone. You know, my file from when I was inside the California state prison system is probably one of the thickest on record. I have stabbing after stabbing. Even when I was in the hole, I was making spears and dart guns, trying to stab people walking by my cell. And all I understood was violence. And this man made me take that negative attitude I've had all my life, and helped me."

Rockhead still loves Jim Brown, but love alone was not enough to keep them working together. Once again Brown had difficulty, no matter how deep the bond, reimagining the relationship as one of equals.

The ensuing narrative is very similar to the one with Aqeela Sherrills. After six years, Rockhead wanted to start a basketball program for at-risk young people, to be called the Jim Brown Amer-I-Can All-Stars.

"He said, 'Well, do what you got to do. How much is it

going to cost?' I knew nothing about costs, nothing about uniforms, nothing about nothing! So I had some people help me put a budget together and came up with a figure of about fifteen grand. I went to Jim with the budget and he gave me the fifteen grand—first time I had fifteen thousand dollars in my hand legally! I went to the bank and they showed me how to cash this check—I knew nothing about any of that—and I learned. I took him and we'd go to every game, and the joy in the kids' eyes, the fun of just being out of Compton, being out of L.A., being out of Watts. Except Jim told me one day, 'Rock, you're doing too much basketball. I need you to deal with this gang stuff.'

"I said, 'Jim, I'm dealing with this gang stuff through basketball. Teaching kids life skills through sports.' And he didn't understand that, and made me make a choice." Rockhead chose his basketball program. He took Jim Brown's name off it, so it was just the I-Can All-Stars, and the formal relationship between these two men was severed.

Rockhead says, "When I ran with the Amer-I-Can program, I became his top facilitator. I opened programs up in ten different states. I was the person who didn't go backwards, who didn't try to sell dope while I was changing lives, who wasn't still playing gangster behind closed doors. I was the true example of change for him, and still am.

"He did what a father would have done for me. When we had no money for Amer-I-Can facilitators, Jim made sure we were paid every month. I never had a father. As controversial as people say he is, his passion is what it is. He taught me years ago that if you only deal with facts, you won't lose debates. Jim taught me how to take advantage of my strengths in the right way. He taught me to eliminate the negative path and choose my best options. He taught me what a man really is. He taught me how to have respect for myself first in order to have respect for others. I also know that without Jim Brown I'd be dead. He don't owe me nothing. I owe him."

Rockhead has thought about why Amer-I-Can did not expand to a greater extent. He believes that the forces holding it back are a combination of racism against programs that try to help young black men demonized by their association with gangs as well as Brown's own personal reputation.

"People look at who he is, and not what the program has done for us. He has saved thousands of lives across the board. Our program was in the county jail for thirteen years, and we stopped riots. People don't understand that this program that Jim created transcends race, religious, or socioeconomic status. And the program is still broke."

Through this gang and prison work, Jim Brown met a man on death row who is often credited with founding the nation's most infamous street gang, shot-caller Stan "Tookie" Williams. This relationship put Brown in a position where he had to publicly defend someone his old *Running Man* costar Governor Arnold Schwarzenegger wanted to put to death.

Brown fought to prevent Tookie's execution, in the face of overwhelming sentiment in California to see him die. Williams cofounded the Crips in 1971. Ten years later, amid the dawning of the antigang hysteria that would swallow Los Angeles County, he was convicted of the murders of Albert Owens, Tsai-Shai Yang, Yen-I Yang, and Yee-Chen Lin, in two separate 1979 robberies. Williams always maintained his innocence but was convicted in a trial where prosecutor Robert Martin likened him to "a Bengal tiger in captivity in a zoo" and his South Central home to "a jungle." Martin removed three black jurors from the jury pool—a practice he had been warned against by judges on two prior occasions. Subsequently, an all-white jury found Williams guilty and he was sentenced to death.

But the unexpected happened on the way to the gallows. From the confines of his six-by-ten-foot cell, Tookie Williams decided to make a difference. "I no longer participate in the so-called gangster lifestyle, and I deeply regret that I ever did," he wrote. "I vow to spend the rest of my life working toward solutions."

He spent the twenty years of his life on death row intervening in gang disputes and cowrote a children's book series, Tookie Speaks Out Against Gang Violence.

"Don't join a gang," he preached. "You won't find what you're looking for. All you will find is trouble, pain and sadness. I know. I did."

More than seventy thousand people sent e-mails to the SaveTookie.org website to thank him for providing them with the inspiration and motivation to leave gang life behind. He was nominated five times for the Nobel Peace Prize, and his books were honored with awards. He even received a President's Call to Service Award from none other than George W. Bush—an award that the Bush administration then tried to revoke after a law-and-order outcry. Both the *Los Angeles Times* and the *San Francisco Chronicle* printed editorials calling on Governor Schwarzenegger to grant clemency, writing that Williams was more valuable alive than strapped to a gurney.

Brown intimately knew the value of Williams's work. The year before Williams was due to be executed, Brown spoke out on his behalf, saying, "To get to real change, you have to have systems in place. Then, you put a powerful voice with that system and you get the result. [Amer-I-Can] has worked for years to put a system in place and has now joined forces with the powerful voice of Stanley Williams. Tookie is brilliant and has a fantastic spirit."

Brown took this fight on and became Tookie's most prominent advocate as the clock toward execution ticked down. Brown went on talk radio, in very hostile environments, saying, "When someone like Tookie says, 'This is not the way to do it. I made a mistake in my life,' yes, literally, lives are saved."

Brown wanted to save Tookie but it wasn't just about one individual. He took this opportunity to come out publicly against the eye-for-an-eye politics of state-sanctioned executions. "I oppose the death penalty with all my heart," he said. "Death is absolute. Innocent people have been put to death. You can say, 'It's only three percent found to be innocent.' Oh shit. Who's in that three percent? Your sister? Your brother? You can make a mistake that can't be rectified. People with life sentences have been found innocent but death is absolute. Also death is not a deterrent from anything. The studies over time have proven that."

Despite Brown's efforts—and the work of thousands of death penalty abolitionists around the country—Stan Tookie Williams was executed at midnight on December 13, 2005. Governor Schwarzenegger waited until the day of the execution to announce that there would be no clemency, raising hopes and then dashing them, to the devastation of those who had been touched by Tookie's efforts at redemption.

Four separate demonstrations took place across Los Angeles on the night of Tookie's execution. The crowd outside San Quentin swelled to as many as five thousand people.

The night Tookie was executed, five hundred gang members came to Jim Brown's house. Brown believes that if Tookie had decided to go down shooting, he would have had an army at his disposal and the city would have erupted. But Tookie did not call for violence, and Brown, as well as the people working alongside him, helped keep Los Angeles calmer than it would have been, even though protests sprouted across the city.

Today Amer-I-Can is still doing the work. It partnered with Mayor Ras Baraka in Newark, New Jersey, on an interventionist task force, and has produced a film titled *Jim Brown's Amer-I-Can Dream*. It used Brown's eightieth birthday in 2016 to bring together athletes such as Marcus Allen, Rod Woodson, and Ray Lewis to raise $150,000 to continue its outreach programs. But it is a constant effort to keep Amer-I-Can going. Brown says, "We do all this good work. We have all kinds of data. But the struggle to keep everybody eating . . . it really puts the squeeze on you. We had a contract for years in the prisons here. And then this year we had to wait about three months to get it renewed. But these guys [the facilitators] got to eat every month. So I struggle my ass off every day, trying to raise money to keep payroll. This is a hell of a job. In one area of the city, for fifteen years, we had virtually no homicides because we had peace treaties, but that's just not a priority for a lot of folks in politics."

Brown says that he often keeps his Amer-I-Can work separate from his friendships in the entertainment and sports worlds because "not everyone is suited for this kind of work." Then he names the one person who, surprisingly, had stepped up to help. "Bill Belichick is a great Amer-I-Can supporter. He spoke to our guys; he donated money to the organization's foundations. He went to the prisons, one of the schools in Arizona when they had the Super Bowl, he came and spent about two or three hours with the students. A great contributor."

He smiled as he thought about the stone-faced New England Patriots coach and said, "You'd shock people to death, telling them about Bill. He's totally different than they think."

Their relationship was built when the revered Belichick was head coach in Cleveland more than twenty years before. Jim Brown, who had reconnected with the Browns franchise, engaged the coach on his work and was able to get Belichick to speak at a graduation ceremony for those who had completed the Amer-I-Can program. Describing the experience, Belichick said, "Brown was emotional, I was emotional, everyone was emotional. It was very moving. I would say right up there emotionally with winning a Super Bowl."

In another interview, Belichick said, "My concern with Jim is that as time goes by, people will forget just how important he was to sports and society. I just hope people don't forget that or remember him only for some of the controversies he was involved in. He is without question one of the top two or three human beings I have ever met. He makes me proud to know him and proud to be his friend. What is important about him is how he relates to people in the community. He can talk to anybody, whether it is the owner of an NFL team or a kid in the projects. I just hope his life, and how impressive it was, is never forgotten."

Brown can be morose when speaking about future prospects for the organization. "I think in the future we're going to say that we almost got over the hill, but in the end, the load was too heavy, because you have to get the funding. [The gangsters] we turned into professors . . . couldn't be professors in any other organization, because they were not qualified through their education. But they were definitely qualified through their intelligence and through their street knowledge and through their street power. And we are the only ones who will pay them to display this knowledge."

Amer-I-Can's influence and legacy are still being felt in corridors beyond antigang work. In 1992, Jodie Evans, a longtime activist, felt her own sense of urgency after the L.A. riots to do something in the community she called home. She reached out to Amer-I-Can after running Jerry Brown's Democratic Party campaign for president, which left her feeling "how stupid politics was."

Evans said, "First of all I was really impressed that [Jim] Brown was giving his all to these kids, courageously bringing them all up to his house and feeding them and nurturing them and nourishing their souls basically at a time when parts of the city were a really intense war zone. . . . He was layered, as are all people with power. He was not perfect. But what I appreciated was watching him empower these young kids."

The work in Amer-I-Can also inspired Evans to co-launch

Code Pink, an antiwar organization that aimed to challenge the endless U.S. wars overseas in the post-9/11 era. This epiphany came during one of the life skills classes where "every single gang member's dad had been in Vietnam and had come home damaged. They described them being strung out on drugs or pushing a shopping cart and at the end of that I was just like, 'Oh my fucking god. The war did come home and we live in the war zone.'"

About gender politics in Amer-I-Can, Evans said, "Brown did not treat me any better or worse because I was a woman. I never experienced direct sexism in Amer-I-Can. He always treated me as well as he was treating anyone. He was still about being in the center of the room, so he wasn't necessarily all about reaching out to include and empower, but that wasn't necessary. I wasn't in the room except to support the same people he was supporting. It was his program that we were using in South Central."

Rockhead Johnson also talked about a "Criplette" (female Crip member) out of Watts named Sister whom Brown helped launch a nonprofit organization to help women transition out of gang life. Rockhead said, "If wasn't for Jim, there'd be no telling where she would be. When her son got killed, she came to Jim. When her nieces got killed, he was right there with her. Jim went to the projects with her to show the community that she was working with Jim, hands-on. And I actually put her on payroll." Rockhead remembered other women-focused programs that Brown created, taking young women out of the projects to go through the life skills program. According to Rockhead, "At Amer-I-Can, we didn't care about whether you were a woman or gay or a police officer or a gang member. We just wanted to work with people."

Brown did not treat anybody differently in this work. It was tough love all around. He saw part of it—for better and worse—as breaking people down and rebuilding them. There are numerous tales of gangsters broken down to tears. Jim Brown never cried, but they did.

Michael O'Keeffe, an award-winning sports journalist for the New York *Daily News*, interacted with Brown when he was working as a cub crime reporter at the Denver *Rocky Mountain News* in the mid-1990s.

"I was doing a lot of street stories then," O'Keeffe says. "I knew a lot of gang members: Crips and Bloods, a lot of the Latino gang kids. I knew the skinheads in town. I was just on that sort of beat. I was sitting around the newsroom one day. The city editor said, 'Why don't you go find out what happened to Michael Asberry?'"

Asberry was a founder of the Denver Crips. Built like "a brick shithouse," he was a sophisticated, high-IQ enforcer who was able to practice a lucrative form of violence while staying ahead of the law. Then his luck ran out. According to Asberry, frustrated Denver police beat him until he finally resisted and then arrested him for assaulting a police officer. Judge Lynn Hufnagel, at significant political cost, gave Asberry the choice of jail or enrolling in the Amer-I-Can program out in Los Angeles under the watchful eye of Jim Brown.

O'Keeffe's boss told him to go out to report on Asberry's experience. "I flew out to L.A. with a photographer," says O'Keeffe. "Michael went to the Amer-I-Can program, and he flunked out. He had a hard time being a link in a chain. He always had to be the big man . . . the top dog. In Denver he was the toughest gang member in the city, but in L.A. he was just another tough guy. So he flunked out. He was homeless for a while. He got arrested with a gun, which was a violation of his probation. . . .

"One day we're going to Jim Brown's house and Michael's very excited. We get to the house, and I don't remember who answered the door, but Michael comes running in and goes straight to the pool and that magnificent view. Michael's talking a mile a minute: 'Can you see this? Can you see that?' He was like a little kid, excited to show us from Denver the kind of place where he was spending his time. Then Jim Brown comes in, and he's wearing a T-shirt and shorts. I remember thinking, 'This guy looks like he can take on an NFL team now.' And he doesn't yell. He just says, 'Michael, whose home is this? Who do you think you are, coming into my home acting all familiar? Who are you?' And it cast a pall over the whole proceeding. All of a sudden it went from this exciting, interesting time, like we were about to party with Jim Brown, to 'Oh shit, the shit's about to go down here.'

"Jim turned to me and said, 'I want everybody to sit down.' Everybody takes a seat, and Michael sits down on an ottoman in front of the chair where Jim is sitting. At some point, Jim pushes Michael off or he steps off, so Michael is literally sitting at Jim's feet during this conversation.

"They probably talked for an hour. He and Michael went back and forth, but it was mostly Jim. Basically, Jim was saying to Michael, 'You could've made something out of the program.

Instead, you're confrontational with other people, and then you drop out. We don't hear from you anymore. And now that the press is interested in this story, you're comin' up. . . .' And they go back and forth. And Michael was brought to the edge of tears. He was very moved and very shaken. He was very humbled by the whole experience. At one point I realize that this is all being done by Jim for my benefit and for the benefit of the photographer I was with. Jim was trying to send a message to Michael, but also to the rest of the world that 'I'm serious about what I'm doing. There's a method. There's a reason why we have this program. It works. In this program, you have to address your own shortcomings.' And that's what it was really about.

"Michael was very excited about the fact that a newspaper reporter had come to Los Angeles to write about him, and he was looking at himself like he'd gone Hollywood. Jim beat that out of him, not by yelling, and not by screaming, but by holding him accountable, by using his own words. 'You told me you were gonna do this. You told me you were going to do that. Did you do this? Did you get a job? Did you write a letter apologizing for this action? Have you made amends with this person?' And the answer was always 'No. No. No.' Michael was really brought down many, many notches over the course of that hour or so.

"And then, when it ended, Jim lightened up, and he became very warm toward me and the photographer, as if, 'I put you guys through shit, but I just want you to know I'm not as big of an asshole as I've been acting.' Then, after tearing Michael down for an hour, he built him back up, saying, 'Michael, I know you're smart. I know you're tough. I just need you to try.' He sent him away with a sense of optimism. With a sense of 'You fucked up. You did this wrong. You're arrogant. You're not following the program. You think you're smarter than you are. But we're here to help you, and we're gonna help you.' It didn't work out for Michael in the end [Asberry was shot and killed in Aurora, Colorado, in May 2008], but I think that's part of this work. There are a lot of people who don't make it. I think that's part of the burden that Jim Brown carries."

Brown doesn't yell at the Michael Asberrys or Rockhead Johnsons. But he challenges them. Paradoxically, he leverages his masculinity to make gangsters more sensitive, more in touch with who they are. Of all the things he could do with his sharply honed sense of manhood, Brown has in part at least tried to wield it as a force of reclamation. He has reached out to people without world-class athletic skills who have felt that toxic brand of masculinity become an anchor around their necks.

Connie Rice shared her personal insights on the role of masculinity in this nature of work. Rice is a Harvard-educated lawyer, a civil rights advocate, and one of the most powerful political players in the city of Los Angeles. Recognizing the problem of gangs in Los Angeles, she was determined to enter this fray. "I think there has to be room for the hypermasculinity for at least a little bit of it, for the guys who have been emasculated," she says. "You have to give them room to bounce back, which means they're going to go for the hypermasculinity of the gangster. That's what they're all about. And I think if you suppress that, you're going to do even more damage than letting them act out."

She believes that the value of Brown's approach and the attraction to those he is trying to reach is "that he was offering a path to manhood that wasn't emasculating. He was letting them claim their inner lion and use it for good." She also says that Brown was "very adept at picking the most talented gangsters with the biggest brains. That's why we can work with them so well and why so many of the different intervention organizations have taken off."

Brown says, "I've had meetings seven days a week with the most powerful gangsters in the country and street gangsters. And the word that I always use is 'caring.' Not 'love,' but 'caring.' . . . We're a team, we're all in the same boat up here. The outside world doesn't realize that the gangster is highly sensitive. They're highly sensitive because they have low esteem. So you can't assault them, or make them feel smaller. And you find that if they are not dealing with mental illness, guys can do the right thing. A regular gangster out there, if he can get an opportunity, he would choose to do the right thing. But there are not so many choices for you because your father didn't lay out anything for you to follow in his footsteps. Usually, they don't have a father. So you start dealing with bravado, dealing with your woman a certain way, dealing with your children a certain way, and bullshitting yourself about life. And the system puts pressure on people to be their worst selves. I am combatting that by not talking about bullshit, I'm talking about jobs. Because I know what they need at the end of the tunnel: some kind of paycheck."

Brown is convinced that the ability to create jobs and have a salary that's attached to some self-esteem and community stature—"turning gangsters into professors"—is the only thing that can break masses of young people from gang life.

According to Brown, "If you get a million-dollar grant from the city, then that creates seventy jobs for those key gangsters that have stepped out with you. And you teach them how to train others. So they're making a legitimate living training people to do the right thing and following that righteousness themselves. Those guys are not going to want to go work at McDonald's. But they damn sure don't mind being a professor in the Amer-I-Can Program, where they can teach this new knowledge that they have."

Brown maintains that there are forces that don't want Amer-I-Can to be successful. The question hangs in the air: Who are these forces that would not want a program like this to succeed? Lobbyists who work for the prison industry? People in law enforcement? Other gangsters?

A few years ago, Brown said, "All of those. It comes down to the people and the position of power that they hold. For example, Antonio Villaraigosa, the [former] mayor of L.A. He was a negative force. He damn near destroyed all the activism in this city. I don't know why. I guess because he's a law enforcement guy who wants to just incarcerate everybody. The system does everything to destroy the work. . . . The business of prisons is a major business, so the only reason these people would have to be helpful is that they just have a good heart—it's not profitable for them. Instead, a lot of the bullshit is profitable."

Schwarzenegger, when he was governor of California, wanted to expand Amer-I-Can statewide, but was not going to do it for free. In return for that massive expansion of the program, "the

Governator" wanted a master list of all the people in the program. Even though it meant the organization had to refuse an unimaginable amount of money, Brown would not give up a list. "See, the big thing with the system is, they always want to turn you into an informant," he said. "That's their goal. Then you work for them, and forever you are an informant. But if you inform, you have created a self-inflicted wound that takes away your credibility."

He then took a deep breath, perhaps trying to choose his words even more carefully.

"What you learn in this country is that any time you can influence more than ten people to do anything, the government goes crazy. Therefore, if you are not controlled, it doesn't matter how much good you do. Only when they control you do you get assistance, and your greatest attribute to the government will be that you are a reliable source of information for the government to keep control of. So ultimately, the greatest thing that you can do as an advocate for our government is to be a snitch. That's patriotism to them. And that's also like a fucking grueling death, to be a snitch. It's the lowest form of life."

Brown then pointed out that there is a contradiction in the very nature of policing, because they can't have it known that a program like Amer-I-Can, run by former criminals, can bring results that mass incarceration or cracking heads cannot. "It's a conflict of interest," he said. "When the polls come out about lower crime rates, the headlines are always, 'Law enforcement has taken crime down.' It's always got to be them. But I have, on tape, gang-bangers training law enforcement officers. And law enforcement officers say it was the best training they ever had. We taught them how to interact with the community. You learn how to do your job better and be loved in your community because of the way that you conduct yourself and the way that you carry out the job. Policemen should not be disliked in the community. They should be loved. If they take the right approach, the citizens will help them. But when they abuse their power, it has the opposite effect. It's terrible."

Brown's comments were made during the 2014 protests after teenager Michael Brown was killed by Officer Darren Wilson in Ferguson, Missouri: demonstrations that helped launch the Black Lives Matter movement against police violence. A shocking amount of military hardware was being used to disperse protesters. "That's America, man," he said, "That reminds me of Kent State. You fight back, you get blown up."

Yet many of the problems that Amer-I-Can has faced have had less to do with conspiracy than with what all organizations face when they enter the public sector. Not even a gridiron opponent like Sam Huff was as intractable a force for Jim Brown as public bureaucracy. Walter Beach, the East Coast director of Amer-I-Can, said, "Everyone loves the product but there is a constant struggle to compete for resources. What happens more than anything is that there is a lack of commitment and honesty to solve the kind of problems that need to be solved. No one has the courage to just say, 'We don't want to see kids educated.' Instead we hear, 'We do want to see them educated, but can't put the resources into doing it.' Seeing Amer-I-Can through requires five to ten years of concentrated effort. After a year, [the bureaucrats are] looking for the quick fix."

To illustrate the funding obstacles Amer-I-Can faced, Brown

recalled an encounter with Marion Barry during the 1980s, when Barry was mayor of Washington, D.C. "Marion was a good friend of mine. . . . I'd taken my program to Marion and he refused it. He said, 'Man, why do you think I'm going to let you come to Washington, D.C., and bring something that's good for the people—that I didn't bring?' If somebody doesn't control me, they don't want it, not really."

Connie Rice described Brown as "a brilliant leader" and said that the program "has produced some of the most capable gang intervention experts in the country." She had been deeply affected by one of the Amer-I-Can protégés, a young man named Darren "Bo" Taylor, brilliant by all accounts, who died of cancer in 2008 at the age of forty-two. Taylor moved on from Amer-I-Can to become an activist, a radio host, and the founder of an organization called Unity One. He also was able to persuade then USC head football coach and current Seattle Seahawks head man Pete Carroll to start A Better LA, a non-profit aimed at giving money to "peace squads," who would mediate gang disputes throughout the city.

The stories that Rice tells in her memoir, *Power Concedes Nothing*, also illustrate the dramatic impact that Amer-I-Can has had on young people. "They had to claim responsibility for the damage they had inflicted on themselves and everyone else, and they gained Jim's slightly less harsh designation of 'former predator.' . . . I did not need to be a friend or even like Jim to respect what he had done for the men strolling around his garden, talking in his living room, and playing chess on his patio. He had extricated them from the streets and molded them into respectability, and they had gladly paid the price of self-transformation and loyalty to join his church of entrepreneurial self-reliance. . . . He did it every day, with real human beings."

Rice also approvingly remembers Jim's decision to bring white prisoners into Amer-I-Can's ranks. "The Amer-I-Can course was the only interracial oasis in a prison system structured around racial gang segregation. Their decision meant members of the white supremacist Aryan Nations would deconstruct their faults in the presence of the black, Latino, and Asian prisoners they were supposed to dominate."

At an Amer-I-Can graduation held at Pitchess Detention Center, a onetime Aryan Nations leader was the valedictorian. Covered in tattoos, some that marked the completion of violent crimes, he said, "I'm here to testify and you know nobody could've told me this would happen. NOBODY." He said that before Amer-I-Can, he was "a stone-cold hater . . . I was raised a hater. My daddy hated. My brothers hated. Hating is all I knew. It's what we did. But I know something different now."

He held up the curriculum in front of the crowd and said, "This here shit has totally blown open my mind to turn it totally around. Listen to me, I am telling you: I don't hate nobody. I don't need to hate anybody. When I get out of here my daddy ain't going to believe the change in me. You won't even know me. Because of this shit here I can say every last one of you is my brother. I love all you motherfuckers. Black, brown, yellow, white. I am a hater of nobody now. Nobody."

Rice thought the success of Amer-I-Can would lead to an embrace of the program throughout the prison system. That did not happen, "because no one's job depended on men not returning to prison. Because the prison industrial complex made more money the more men were locked up."

Despite years of working with each other, and a clear mutual respect, at a party they both attended in 2014, Rice and Brown spent the evening on opposite sides of the room, not making eye contact or interacting. Whatever bad feelings exist have nothing to do with the work itself.

Brown seemed bewildered by the chilliness between them, and looks wounded when discussing it. He wants the respect and comradeship of people like Connie Rice yet he also realizes that his time on this earth is limited, and many of the friendships in his life can't be rebuilt. He physically simply can't be rushing from meeting to meeting "seven days a week," the way he once could, to repair every relationship. Some bridges just have to stay burnt.

Brown has described what may be his heaviest regret with his Amer-I-Can work: "The one negative is that I can't supply what they need either economically or as the father figure they want me to be. There's one kid that just called, he's losing his sight. He said the left eye's gone, but the right eye might have a chance. I want to help him. . . . I can't help everyone."

There is a sense when Brown talks about this work that it's less of a calling and more a form of penance. When you speak to Aqeela Sherrills, Connie Rice, Rockhead Johnson, Gina Belafonte, or Jodie Evans, you hear the passion in their voice for the work. They are animated by it in a way that speaks to the life-sustaining aspects of social justice work. But Jim Brown sounds burdened. He is trying to rescue people from gang life by getting them in touch with a part of themselves that Brown himself has largely rejected.

Radio host and black feminist theorist Esther Armah said, "Jim Brown creates this phenomenal platform from which he does extraordinary work that should be remembered and re-vered. It has the capacity to make people more emotionally conscious. This is part of the movement that garners no ap-plause. It's the place where no one is going to give you a stand-ing ovation. But it's also the place where you very likely might save someone's life."

The question is whether Brown has used his implacable stat-ure to impose this level of emotional introspection on gang members because he cannot bear to impose it on himself. Rice describes one Amer-I-Can event, insisted upon by Brown, where male ex-cons and gangsters threw a surprise party for their mothers, wives, and girlfriends. When they entered the celebration, they were greeted by a banner that read: "To the women in our lives, thank you for loving us when we did not deserve to be loved." One by one, the men stood and asked for forgiveness "for any and all emotional or physical abuse." Jim Brown watched, but Jim Brown did not stand.

# SEVEN

# TOXIC: MANHOOD AND VIOLENCE AGAINST WOMEN

—

In the history of humanity, spouse-beating is a particularly odious tradition—one often employed by men looking to exert power over women. Just as lynching in America is not a phenomenon wholly confined to black people, spouse-beatings are not wholly confined to women. But in our actual history, women have largely been on the receiving end of spouse-beating. We have generally recognized this in our saner moments. There is a reason why we call it the "Violence Against Women Act" and not the "Brawling With Families Act." That is because we recognize that violence against women is an insidious, and sometimes lethal, tradition that deserves a special place in our customs and laws.

—Ta-Nehisi Coates

*You are Eva Bohn-Chin. You are an internationally successful model with dreams of the silver screen. Just twenty-two years old, you are from Germany, of German and Jamaican ancestry, giving you a degree of worldliness and exoticism that is catnip to the new fashion movement of the late 1960s. A movie star ten years older than you sidles up and asks you to be "Jim Brown's girl." That's how he says it: "Jim Brown's girl." He's not a smooth, beautiful man, like the models you meet backstage. But he's handsome and his body puts a catch in your throat. He was some kind of American football star, but you don't know much about that. Just that he has status, and people—Americans in particular—part when he enters a room. He's married, but he convinces you that his wife, a woman named Sue, accepts that he will never be faithful. "I believe in the European view of man-woman relations," he says. You know what that means. You begin a torrid affair, one with heat, fights, and makeup sex that shakes the chandeliers of fancy hotels throughout Europe and the United States.*

*One night, the fight is particularly bad and neighbors call the police. After the police struggle with Jim just to get through the door, investigators find blood on the walls as well as the floor and "a five-inch patch of hair on a large rug." You are found semiconscious below the balcony, after a twenty-foot fall onto concrete, the bones in your shoulder shattered. Your famous lover is charged with attempted murder and pins are put in your shoulder. When you revive in the hospital, you don't press charges, insisting that the entire ordeal was a misunderstanding. You tell* Jet *magazine, "I fell from the balcony by myself. Jim was nowhere near me at the time. He was just opening the door for the police when I went over the railing. I must have fainted before falling." Then you light a cigarette and comment cryptically, "That's not to say it wasn't a pretty bad fight we were having." You stay with your man after the "incident" and your asking price as a model soars, as you learn the value of being infamous. People make comments behind your back. You hear that the joke among sportswriters is, "Jim Brown's got to be the best lay in the world, because he'll throw you off a balcony and you won't even press charges." Let them joke. You're getting paid. But eventually you part ways, the offers dry up, and life sours as you go into hiding, reliving that night more than you will ever admit. Thirty years later, you speak to Spike Lee for a documentary on this lover from times long past. It's your first interview in years. The director tells you that Jim has said emphatically that he did nothing to you. You are asked to respond. Your voice shakes. Your confidence in your English has never been great, but you press on. You look at the camera and say, "He pushed me. He slammed me." You then point out scars on your body and say, "I was young, good-looking, a person who loved life. Why would I jump?"*

IN 1994, O. J. SIMPSON WAS ON THE RUN, HAVING FLED his home after the double homicide of his wife, Nicole Brown Simpson, and her acquaintance Ronald Goldman. The world was abuzz over the ex–football star whose friendly, smiling image was so at odds with someone who may have committed a double homicide. As O.J. and his friend A. C. Cowlings took to the highway in their Ford Bronco, old audio was released of 911 calls featuring a terrified Nicole Brown Simpson asking for police help as a bellowing O.J., his behavior greatly contrasting with his commercial brand, shouted and slammed doors in the background.

One person who was in high demand to speak about O.J. was Jim Brown. For decades, Brown had been a critic of Simpson's for lacking a social conscience. Also, over the years he had made several statements, which, in the light of the murders, seemed prophetic: that the O.J. the public knew was not the real person, that he "wore the mask."

In *Out of Bounds*, Brown wrote presciently, "I never look at [O. J. Simpson] the way I do a Bill Russell, or a Walter Payton. I talk to those guys, see them speak, I know what I'm hearing is the real man. Too often, I can't say the same about O.J."

After O.J. was arrested and awaiting trial, Andrea Kremer of ESPN was in Brown's home to interview him about the Simpson case. The producer of the segment was Jeremy Schaap, who remembered, "It was clear that Brown did not like or respect O.J. Pretty much the first thing he said in the interview, before he could even be asked a question, was, 'O.J., for once in your life, be a man, and admit what you did.'"

But what has remained with Schaap in the intervening years was something that was said when they were setting up the interview, before the cameras were rolling. "Jim Brown was talking about O.J. and said, 'Man, I don't know about you, but I've never met a man in my life that I couldn't handle, or that intimidated me or gave me any trouble, even. But women will mess you up.' That stuck with me."

It is unclear whether Brown ever actually bought the hype and believed himself to be Superman. But he clearly has always seen women as his own personal kryptonite. Whether women have "messed up" Jim Brown is less important than seeing how he has "messed up" when it has come to these personal relationships.

Racism and toxic masculinity have deeply scarred our society. Resistance to racism has often meant having to assert very traditional definitions of "manhood." Yet because the most traditional avenues to masculinity as defined in U.S. culture—economic self-sufficiency and home ownership—were largely denied to black men, the fields of sports and entertainment (two fields with a lottery's chance of success) have become for too many the markers of excellence and respect. Absent those opportunities, the ways in which a black man could assert that he was in fact "a man" were through that universal cultural marker of male status: the ability to bed and/or control women.

Jim Brown is someone who has used his personal assertion of manhood as a bulwark against racism over the course of his entire life. He is also someone who has gloried in his history of sexual conquest and been accused often of violence against women.

He speaks today and has always spoken about the charges that have accrued over time as a coordinated conspiracy, saying, "My activities can't be attacked, but with my private life it is different. They can take an incident and blow it up. I'm always attacked. They get you in any area they can. Now, you know there isn't a man in this country who hasn't a private life that they could pin some headline on if they wanted to. . . . A lot of papers [carry photos] of me in handcuffs and chains."

"I'm no angel," Brown said to reporter Will Grimsley back during his Cleveland Browns playing days. "If I was a goody-goody, I'd be a psychological wreck by this time. I'd be in a [straitjacket]." But Brown has consistently been adamant that he is innocent of criminal wrongdoing in all instances of violence he has been accused of. "Do you think I could keep throwing girls out windows, knocking policemen forty feet in the air and running down guys on the turnpike without them nailing me for it one day? I'd have to bribe every jury and judge in town. But I've never been convicted. I've just been harassed. I've been hit so much I don't sting anymore. They can call me a 'nigger.' It doesn't bother me. When a controversy comes up, I take it and look my accuser in the eye."

For a very complicated man, this part of his life is simple. As Brown lived this post-football life on a terrain that frustrated his ambitions—whether in the world of sports promotions, the Black Economic Unions, or Hollywood—women were often his pastime, his distraction, his proving ground, and at times the repository for his frustrations. The world of Jim Brown's time was a place that looked the other way, accepted or venerated these kinds of relationships, and never as a rule attempted to hold men accountable for them.

Brown, in his own words, walked "out of football and into the sexual revolution." While older white sportswriters were awed by "the animal" in Jim Brown and black observers saw their Superman, a layer of younger white male journalists, influenced by the politics of the 1960s, saw a kind of synthesis between the Superman and the sexual: he was this stud who also held the power and promise to smash white supremacy. In Jim Brown they saw not only the potential to inspire the fight against racism, but also an ideal of manhood rooted in strength, sex, and swagger.

Journalist and future filmmaker James Toback wrote in his 1971 book *Jim: The Author's Self-Centered Memoir of the Great Jim Brown* that Brown was "a consistent and spectacular warrior . . . a crystallization of physical potency." He went on to write, "Jim Brown was without peer in affording insight into the injection of sexuality into every area of American life and learned tales of freaky scenes, brutality, and an ineluctable erotic flow." For Toback, there was no separation between the joys of sex and violence. This inability to separate the two can be seen as prologue to Toback's life in Hollywood. In 2017, more than two hundred women came forward with stories of his being a serial sexual harasser.

Oliver Stone, who directed Brown in the film *Any Given Sunday*, called him a "Superman in the tradition of Nietzsche's Übermensch. . . . For Nietzsche, the Übermensch carries a heavy load. Knows how to hit. Can take a hit. Incredible force and strength and stamina. Awesome and beautiful and powerful."

Former Syracuse All-American football player turned activist and educator Don McPherson rebukes all these formulations, saying, "The Superman myth is a form of protection. It's protection from having to be examined. One of the ways that power maintains itself is to not be examined. With Jim Brown, his whole thing doesn't get examined: his problems, instances of violence against women—all of that doesn't get examined because at the end of the day, Jim Brown's still a bad motherfucker."

It wasn't just starstruck men, fascinated with his combination of sexuality and ability to kick ass who were giving Brown a pass. An article about Brown by Gloria Steinem published in 1968 only superficially touched on Brown's stormy personal relationships, despite his arrests for violence against women—without convictions—that had taken place in the very recent past. If Steinem didn't care and the New Left didn't care, we should not be surprised that Hollywood and the NFL—only now barely confronting decades of institutional cover-ups of violence against women—didn't care either. Given the history of accusations, the fact that uniformly it is black women who have brought these charges makes the collective lack of concern all the more disturbing.

As McPherson said, "Jim Brown is going to talk about all the racism that he faced, and therefore black men and many so-called well-meaning white people will not examine all of Jim's shit. He just hides behind that badass masculinity. And he has street cred with young black men who can see that Jim's fighting the system. Jim's fighting on our behalf so you can't say shit."

Sex, violence, and power have long walked in lockstep with one another. Whether the man in question is a Kennedy or a camp counselor or a Walmart worker, the same metric of manhood in this area applies: male heterosexual sex brings a measure of authority when in the company of men, which some crave even more than the sex itself. This idea of sex as a powerful symbol of the black revolution was catnip to the middle-aged men who chronicled the struggles of the time. It is readily apparent in the writings of Tom Wolfe, William F. Buckley, and Norman Mailer. But bell hooks put it in more political terms: "White men were attacking black men in the sixties for not fulfilling the patriarchal role when it came to work and family, and black men were telling white men that sexuality was the only real site where manhood mattered and there the black man ruled. . . . Black male public discourse about sexuality pointed the finger at white males and accused them of being pussies who were unable to get it up and keep it up. The black male who could not demolish white male power with weaponry was using his dick to 'bitch slap' white men and by doing so sexually subjugating them. . . . No matter the daily assaults on their man-hood that wound and cripple, the black male is encouraged to believe that sex and sexual healing will assuage his pain."

Jim Brown in so many respects represented this synthesis of the political and the sexual. He was an outspoken leader who also had a very public reputation as a ladies' man, which he was not shy about sharing. It affirmed his cultural weight as some-one who was to be respected.

A Black Economic Union official was quoted in 1971: "Jim's image is founded mainly on sex. His life is supposed to be an orgy from one end of the earth to the other."

Sex is ideally an act of mutual pleasure. But when Brown described his sex life—and he has done so in great detail over the years—it sounds less like sex for pleasure and more like sex for ego and power. Brown has said that his desire to exert dom-inance over women stems from his own absence of control that he felt in relation to women in his infancy.

He wrote that his having grown up being raised by women "might make people think I'd have a lot a problems. I don't know. Maybe I have a lot of problems. But I felt community and I felt loved. Then when I was eight, I went to live with my mother in Great Neck. . . . They say I'm fucked up. Maybe I am."

Brown has written and spoken about this only rarely, but his relationship with his mother remained volatile throughout his life—the periods of calm more akin to walking on eggshells. In high school, he could not control who she dated or what she did and it drove him to solitude, silence, and anger until he eventu-ally found escape in the home of his girlfriend Henrietta Creech. In 1981, Brown's mother was approached by journalist Pete

Dexter for a profile on her son and all she would say was, "He's the only one I got. Things are right between us now and I wouldn't say nothin' to upset that."

Older, or even similar-aged, women never held any appeal for Brown as sexual partners. In *Out of Bounds*, the fifty-three-year-old Brown talked about his romantic preferences: "Physically, between a young girl and an old one, there is no contest. . . . I don't like being told what I'm supposed to want. For instance, I prefer girls who are young. My lady right now is nineteen."

Whether Brown was twenty-five, thirty-five, forty-five, or fifty-five, that remained his preference. He wrote, "When I eat a peach I don't want it overripe. I want that peach when it's peaking."

He also expressed a desire for women who are physically small: "I don't mean mousy small. I mean tight. Petite. Delicate. No excess. Thin legs, nice butt . . . small. When I get into the bedroom, I don't want to see anything that's big like me. That includes big breasts. I don't want big breasts anywhere around me. Keep those big breasts away." He told Steve Rushin of *Sports Illustrated*, "I mess with young women. I know it's bad, but I'm bad."

Dating a younger woman, of course, also ensures a power imbalance of experience and education that otherwise would not exist.

Brown's home has been a place of gang truces and fundraisers for political and civil rights leaders across the decades. In the 1970s, it was also a place to party and have sex in imaginative numbers and combinations, where women were shared and the stories of experimental couplings became Hollywood lore.

Brown has said that his house was a place of "Creative

Orgies." These events were mired in sexual and gender roles that sound less than revolutionary. Brown wrote, "It was our way of life and we had certain rules. . . . The main reason we called them Creative Orgies was that we'd look for women who normally would never even consider going to an orgy. That was our particular quirk. We'd find women who are sweet and seemingly innocent. That's when I started learning about appearances: some of these sweet little innocents turned out to be total freaks! . . . Just between you, me, and the tabloids, I've had up to eight girls in my room, maybe four on my couch and four on my bed. I might have sex in one night with four or five of them. But only if Jim Junior was feeling exceptional. Some people think that makes me a pervert. I think it makes me lucky."

Other memoirists, including Jennifer Pryor, have written descriptions of these parties that include Quaaludes and small groups watching Brown have sex. These stories do not age well. They also sound uncomfortably like something *Sweet Sweetback's Baadasssss Song* was critiquing, with people crowding around to watch Jim Brown, physical specimen, show his prowess without pads.

Then in 1985, in a sensationalized and widely publicized case, a thirty-three-year-old schoolteacher named Margot Tiff claimed that the forty-nine-year-old Brown beat and raped her when she refused to engage in sex with him and another woman. She said that the violence occurred when she got cold feet before the proposed ménage à trois. Because Tiff gave contradictory testimony, Los Angeles prosecutor Dino Fulgoni dropped all charges, saying, "I would not wish anyone to be forced to stand trial with the contradictory nature of the proof that came forth before this court."

Tiff also attempted to sue Brown for $10 million—claiming, according to court documents, that Brown had "battered, tortured, physically and psychologically abused and raped and attempted to rape." This was also thrown out of court. When asked about the incident by *Sport* magazine, Brown reportedly looked "amused" and said, "You must have read about it in the papers, or I don't think you would have come here." *Sport* describes the woman as having "clearly been beaten," but the charges of rape, sexual battery, and assault were dismissed after she "gave confused and inconsistent testimony." This "confusion" included the successful efforts of Brown's lawyer Johnnie Cochran—who later, of course, defended Brown's nemesis O. J. Simpson—to challenge Tiff's assertion of rape since there was only "partial penetration."

Brown described his arrest: "The next morning when I walked to get my paper there were ten policemen there. They handcuffed me without telling me anything. They had a search warrant. They said there was marijuana in my house. They said my companion was involved. At no time until they set me down at a table with my hands behind my back did they tell me what it was all about."

Brown's defense was that he and his partner were the victims, put off by what they called "a lesbian advance" from Tiff, and defended themselves after she became violent. But the charges disappeared. The *Los Angeles Times* described it as a "dramatic courtroom about-face" by Fulgoni when the prosecution dropped the charges.

It is difficult to believe that Brown and a partner would be put off by "a lesbian advance," since that element of group sex was central to the West Hollywood scene. Brown has described these orgies as personal and intimate, even tender, but then wrote in *Out of Bounds*: "At times I desire two girls, or three girls, or one girl—as long as it's new pussy."

Brown went out of his way to make sure his readers knew that when it came to his sexual relationships, his libertine approach was a one-way street. "I'm a double standard man myself," he wrote. "I want to be truly liberated. It's logical. It's fair. And I'm not. I want to freak when I want to, but I don't want my woman to. I want her to be something I'm not willing to be."

Brown also boasted, "Talk all you want about brain power, but the intellectual gets the secondary women. It's the physical giant who gets the premium women."

This pursuit of sexual conquest has been a part of Brown's public life as long as he has had a public life. In his 1968 Alex Haley *Playboy* interview, Brown said, "I have a nickname, 'Hawk,' which comes from having very good eyesight. Visually, I appreciate anything that I consider beautiful—if it's a car, if it's a suit, a painting, a woman or what have you. And the woman I appreciate most is my wife, Sue, who seems to be happy and very much in love with me. I have never denied her and I have never denied those three big babies we have at home in Cleveland. So I'm sure that I'm doing no big damage by looking."

Of course he was doing far more than looking.

Brown justified his sexual life to Steve Rushin in an article published in *Sports Illustrated*: "I know this is America and we like to have our heroes, but hell: Martin Luther King screwing around—people are still in denial about that. The Kennedys, Bobby and John, they womanized. I look at the good and at the bad. Do *I* like a lot of women? Hell, yeah. What bothers me is when people hold on to the falseness of something."

He would go on about his love of young women, telling award-winning journalist Pete Dexter, "Young girls, they touch you. They say what they feel, they do their choosin' from the soul. You come home and pull off your shoes, and she loves you that way, too. I like tight bodies and pretty faces. You bring in Methuselah, if she's got a tight body and a pretty face, that's all right, too. I tell all of them, though, nature's got a plan. There's a pretty girl turning [sixteen] years old every day. It's none of this takin' advantage thing. Marlon Brando said it once, 'I don't want my bitch pushin' me around in my wheelchair.' I feel like that, too. It's not forever. When it's up, it's up. And when I cut a lady loose, she's takin' something away. She's going away knowin' how to deal better. I show her that and maybe it makes her stronger the rest of her life."

In a very odd 1981 article in *Inside Sports* magazine that looked uncritically at the forty-five-year-old Brown, drinking vodka and apple juice from mason jars and picking up young girls on roller skates, Dexter described an exchange between Brown and a "twenty- or twenty-one-year-old girl." They talked for ten minutes and then she said, "I'd like to go with you tonight, but if your thing is, you know, beating up women . . ." He laughed in response to this. "People meet me," he later commented, "they don't know what's goin' on. They're always waitin' for me to jump up and down and kick somebody's ass."

His ex-wife, Sue, put it this way: "Everybody's afraid of that black side of his temper, but who's ever seen it? He doesn't go givin' himself away in public."

This "black side of his temper" has created these many stories of abuse: all involving very young and mostly black women. There was the aforementioned eighteen-year-old Brenda Ayres, the high school dropout who in 1965 accused Brown of assaulting her in a Howard Johnson motel in Cleveland. There was the rape charge filed in 1965 by an Ohio State student who withdrew the charges before it ever came to trial. In 1971, he was accused of battery of two young women. In 1985, he was charged with rape and assault. In 1986, it was assault of his fiancée, Debra Clark. In 1999, it was a domestic disturbance with his twenty-five-year-old wife, Monique; on the 911 tape from the incident, Monique said Brown threatened her, a claim she later recanted.

Not one conviction of violence against women emerged from any of these charges. Yet in almost all of these cases, Brown was not vindicated by a jury as much as by the women in question, who in nearly every instance refused to bring charges after initially calling the police. It should be noted that these matters were not taken seriously by the court system or even much of the feminist left. Gloria Steinem, writing about Brown in 1968, touched on his reputation of violence against women in surprisingly cursory fashion. She mentioned the cases that were brought in and then dismissed, and approvingly quoted an ally of Brown's who said, "Any guy with a reputation like that has got to be blackmail-prone."

Of a high-profile charge of battery, involving a model, brought against Brown in 1968, Steinem wrote: "Movie people either cursed the Los Angeles cops or said he'd be in jail if he weren't a Negro, depending on their political beliefs. Many assumed, with all that money tied up in unreleased pictures, that the fix had gone in somewhere. Meanwhile, the model, a long-time girlfriend of Jim's, kept right on seeing him. And she still is. It's the kind of *Rashomon* story that no one, possibly including the principals, will ever be totally clear on."

Steinem described Brown as someone who "turns up at Hollywood parties and the world's best discotheques in a flowing silk shirt open down the chest, brass-buckled belt, handmade boots, pants so tight it takes him a minute to wedge out a $100 bill."

When pressed about such incidents of violence, Brown said only, "There's been lies written about me, there's been some truth, too. I'm no angel, but what I do, I tell the truth about."

It is not merely that Brown did not take violence against women seriously. Nobody took it seriously. In one interview, Art Modell, former owner of the Cleveland Browns, said with a smile that Brown "got into trouble because of, shall we say, a rough social encounter with a gal, or two, or three."

The cases against Brown are extensive. He has often said that he has "never been convicted of violence against women," which is true. He also laughs and says, "Violence against women . . . shit," as if he cannot believe this still follows him at this point in his life. Yet the cases span the years from 1965 through 1999. It's a remarkable stretch that cannot be written off as just an endless series of law-and-order conspiracies, coincidences, or bad luck.

Brown and others have seen these as politically motivated

attacks attempting to tear down a strong black man. His defenders conflate all the charges with the two times he was in court for physically assaulting other men. The first time, in 1970, he was found not guilty of assault and battery after a 1969 road-rage incident that ended with a man thrown on top of a car. The second was in 1978, when Brown was sentenced to a day in jail and two years' probation for choking and striking his golfing partner Frank Snow. After being cleared in the first case, Brown told a journalist, "This was supposed to kill me. It was supposed to take my black manhood and put it on the ground. But when the jury heard the case, they took less than a half hour to find me not guilty. So I know they are singling me out. But it won't work, because my head won't drop down to my chest. You're going to say that I sound bitter. But I don't sound bitter, man, I'm just real."

Even without convictions of violence against women, there are enough 911 tapes and testimonials to see that this is not a fantasy created by those trying to destroy him.

Debra Clark was fifty-year-old Brown's twenty-one-year-old fiancée. In August 1986, he was released on $5,000 bail three hours after being arrested at 5:15 a.m. as a result of an "incident" with Clark. To judge from photographs, Clark, slender and five feet, five inches tall, was exactly one of those very petite women whom Brown found so attractive. On this occasion, she had a bruised arm and a scratch on her face, as well as a cracked rib. She had called the police from inside Brown's house while armed with a pistol, which she discharged while inside.

A few days later, Clark told police she did not want to press charges. After the incident, *Sport* magazine called and asked Brown if Clark would come to the phone. "He put Debra on the phone. 'Hello,' said a small voice. Brown took the phone back and laughed. 'I don't know what that proved,' he said. 'That voice could have been anybody's.'"

Speaking to me today, Clark says, "What most experts say is that a good relationship must have the eighty/twenty rule. What Jim and I shared was more like ninety-five/five. However, that five percent was like an inferno. . . . I choose to forgive, which was pretty easy to do when you loved someone so intensely. . . . Life is a series of choices, and I choose to get better and not bitter."

It is very difficult to get people who know Brown to speak about this area of his life. They don't deny that gender violence is a part of his past, and none will go on the record to say that they believe it all to be lies made up by racist media. They do believe that the reason people care, however, is highly racialized. They insist that if he were white, then no one would want to examine this part of his history. But this is a part of Jim Brown's narrative. To deny it on the basis of the good works he has done serves to erase Debra Clark. If this part of his history does not matter, then one is also saying that Clark does not matter.

In 1981, Pete Dexter wrote that it is "a fact that Jim Brown scares people. He scares people, and he controls them. The relationships he has—family, friends, women, strangers in the street—are on his own terms. When he says he won't lie and he won't change, that is his integrity and it doesn't shift with the situation."

At eighty-two, even though he is older, more mellow, and more philosophical, Brown still intimidates. Yet people with a distance from him, like Dr. Mark Anthony Neal, have a great deal to say about how to understand the intertwining of his personal and political selves.

"We do hold Jim Brown personally accountable for his behavior. But we also put that behavior in a larger context," says Dr. Neal. "In some ways this violence against women in the 1950s and 1960s was seen as normal. The question for Jim Brown is, how does he go forward from that period of time? How does he own up to any criticism of instances of violence against women in his life and how do we find a way to find a common ground between private and public Jim Brown? Whether we're talking about the musical genius of Miles Davis versus his brutality or a figure like R. Kelly or, today, an athlete like Adrian Peterson or Ray Rice, how do we find that perfect ground that allows us to hold them accountable for their actions but also provides space for redemption that allows them to come back into the black community?"

But Brown has never had to ask for redemption or for reentry into any community. Quite the opposite. He has taken the accusations of assault and used them to paint himself as a victim of a power structure determined to tear him down. The fact that there actually was a power structure that was invested over the course of years in seeing him fall only adds to the confusion many confront when trying to disentangle his private, public, and political lives.

No single case of violence against women has stuck, however, quite like the case of Eva Bohn-Chin, the twenty-two-year-old model who either was thrown or fell from a balcony of a hotel room she was sharing with Brown. After receiving reports of shouting, breaking objects, and screaming inside the hotel room, the police arrived. Two deputies were blocked by Brown, who according to police reports said, "If you're coming in, you're going to have to go over me." Brown later couched what he said to the officers in more political terms, claiming that he shouted, "You big white cops and your goddam system. Everything is against the Negroes. If you're coming in you're going to have to shoot me first. Well, come on ahead, but you're going over me."

He then, again according to police accounts, straight-armed one officer, launching him seven feet backward into a wall. The police on the scene had to call for reinforcements to push him backward and enter the room.

Bohn-Chin lay semiconscious below, from a twenty-foot fall onto concrete, and Brown was arrested on multiple charges including assault on a police officer and "assault with intent to commit murder" against Bohn-Chin.

Except—and one might be sensing a pattern—she did not press charges. Almost immediately, the story became part of Jim Brown's legend and lore. The truth of what actually happened behind those closed doors has mattered less than the oft-repeated phrase "Jim Brown threw a woman off a balcony." Even though Bohn-Chin insisted at the time that she had climbed out on the balcony out of fear of the police and slipped, and even though she continued her relationship with Brown after the incident, the simplest and most violent explanation better fit people's preconceptions of the type of life that Brown led.

*New York Times* journalist Judy Klemesrud wrote about his

career in 1969 and mentioned the incident with an eroticized fascination: "This Jim Brown is usually thought of in terms of bulging biceps . . . paternity suits . . . broken football records . . . beautiful girls falling mysteriously from balconies . . ."

Gloria Steinem even predicted that this could "spice up his screen image; give it an edge of real-life scariness. Because he is potentially the Bad Black Man, and both Negro and white audiences enjoy it."

Once again, Brown was cleared of all charges, including those of assault against a police officer. Brown would comment with mock regret that the incident made him even more of a target of lust, as women sought him out on the basis of the incident. Steinem portrayed him as a victim, writing that because Brown loves women, he "is vulnerable to them."

Brown also painted the attention he received for it in political colors, telling Klemesrud of *The New York Times*: "The cops were after me. They tried to tell her I'd thrown her off the balcony. We had had a fight that night, and neighbors called the cops. Eva was always giving as much as she was taking. If the cops hadn't interfered, she wouldn't have tried to get away down the balcony. The cops had ransacked her apartment a couple times and they had tailed her car. They were after me because I'm free and black and I'm supposed to be arrogant and supposed to be a militant, and I swing loose and free and have been outspoken on racial matters and I don't preach against black militant groups and I'm not humble. Besides, most of these cops are Birchers anyway."

Yet this story has not aged well. Some of that has to do with the changing culture. In 1968 the idea that an abused partner would stay despite the abuse, or refuse to press charges, was neither understood nor explored. The idea, in a world where the police were killing Black Panthers in their homes, that the authorities would go out of their way to frame Jim Brown, was also something that did not seem far-fetched. It rang logical and true.

Sure enough, the balcony incident did not derail Brown's movie career. It also led to a greater demand for Eva Bohn-Chin in the fashion world, showing that in the decades before reality television, infamy has always sold. Helpful to Brown was that Sue, to whom he was still legally married, said, "The day the headlines broke that he was being charged with attempting to murder Eva, I knew he didn't do it. I thought maybe he hit her—he has that temper—but I knew Jim wouldn't try to kill any woman. There's things in him nobody will ever understand, but it isn't that he's mean. He's just who he is."

In Spike Lee's *Jim Brown: All American*, Brown said, "I am going to say something emphatically to you and the world. I never threw Eva Bohn-Chin off of the balcony. It was totally fabricated . . . she tried to get out of the apartment. She tried to get down so the cops would not mess with me."

Yet Lee found the reclusive Bohn-Chin and was able to interview her on camera, the first time she had publicly spoken about the incident. For decades, she had stood by her story that she feared the police, climbed on the balcony, and fell. But when asked by Lee, she says, "He pushed me. He slammed me." She then pointed out scars on her body and said the harrowing words: "I was young, good-looking, a person who loved life. Why would I jump? To become a cripple or whatever? Why would I do this? I am a damaged person."

When one attempts to understand why Jim Brown did not receive the Obama White House honors his friend Bill Russell did, this story is often cited. Yet similar accusations have not proved to be a problem for Donald Trump, who similarly writes off multiple accusations of sexually predatory behavior made against him as some sort of conspiracy narrative or "fake news."

Some of the people closest to Brown, people who have lived with violence and believe his intervention saved their life, do not care. Rockhead Johnson says forcefully, "People say to me, 'You know he threw a girl off the balcony?' And I'm like, 'God damn, you know I went to jail for killing somebody? Or . . . for pulling out a gun, or . . . for shooting somebody in the head? Or I was in jail stabbing people? You're going to tell me that Jim supposedly throwing somebody over a balcony, a small balcony, is more severe than hurting somebody and going to jail for most of my life for it? Y'all are some strange people.'" The difference, though, is that Rockhead had to pay a price for his violence. Not only did Jim Brown not have to pay that price. He has also been protected by friends who look at these charges and dismiss them without any analysis.

His former teammate and dear friend John Wooten said in 2016, "I'm loyal to Jim, and he and a bunch of us from the Browns days remain close friends to this day, so I say this in that context: I don't get into his personal life. But I do think a lot of the troubles Jim went through were invented by people. They took advantage of the fact he was famous. None of us is perfect and we all make mistakes, but I really do believe a lot of that stuff was bullshit. I'm not going further than that."

Yet Brown himself, even while dismissing accusations of

violence against women, has hinted that there is something to them. He told *People* magazine in 1991, "I don't always claim to be the person who's done the right thing, but the media's singled me out as the most brutal cat that ever lived. I try to treat women with respect. The ones that know me like me and trust me."

In a 1994 interview with the Cleveland *Plain Dealer*, in response to a question about his treatment of women, Brown said, "I'm not going to go over all that dried-up s— about women I supposedly beat up. . . . Anything I did regarding the law is part of the record."

It would be one thing if that was all Brown said. But as far as these situations with women, he also speaks about his potential to be victimized and being an easy target. "I'm very vulnerable. I don't have much chance if someone wants to get me."

He is a victim in one respect: a victim of the sports world's inability to own the fact that a big part of jock culture is seeing women as the spoils of gladiatorial combat—"gladiator" being a word Brown often uses for football players.

When we consider the dropping of the charges against Jim Brown, specifically by black women, the words of radio journalist Esther Armah come to mind. She says, "When you're talking about the period of history when Jim Brown would've come to prominence—the 1950s and 1960s—you're talking about witnessing just the state of hostility, aggression, and violence towards black men in every single form. And that negation of life at the hands of white authority was the primary issue for the civil rights movement. It was dealing with racism as it came at you from white authority. And so the lives of women were secondary. Not even were they just negated, but girls were nurtured to understand implicitly that to turn a black man, and to put a black man in the hands of white authority, was to hand him to certain death, and that's something you were unwilling to do. . . . You would more likely be willing to die at the hands of that man than absolutely call any kind of white male authority, because it's really sort of kill or be killed. And at that time, you're talking a resistance to white racism that was all-encompassing. Going to authority was also something for which you would likely be condemned by the community as a whole. And that in a space where white men are the other enemy, all you have is your community. It's not as if you have that other community that you're ever going to go to. And so you are, in a lot of ways, trapped."

The most illustrative example of Brown's attitude toward this question of violence against women, his stubbornness to admit any wrongdoing, his distrust of the state and the ways in which he would fiercely clutch to the idea of his own manhood as a shield, was the case in 2002, when, after smashing the windows of his twenty-five-year-old wife Monique's car in June 1999, Brown found himself for the first time behind bars, at the age of sixty-six. He believed his imprisonment to be so unjust that he stopped eating, shedding twenty-five pounds during his six months in jail. Ironically, given his years of work with prisoners, he was kept segregated from the prison's general population, against his wishes. For all but one hour a day, he was on lockdown in a six-by-fourteen-foot Ventura County Jail cell.

"The prison's rationale for the twenty-three-hour isolation

is that they need to protect me because I'm a celebrity," Brown said at the time. "But it's like being buried in a hole. . . . I have not eaten since I've been here. I'm fasting. I'm on a spiritual fast. That way I am setting the terms of my imprisonment. . . . I'll fight as long as I have breath in my body. That's who I am. That's who I've always been."

It was quite the collision of Brown's greatness and his flaws. Years of antigang work uniquely qualified him to do something positive with his time behind bars and collaborate with fellow inmates, yet he was isolated from this very activity, struck down by his own fame and by a criminal justice system happy to make his time behind bars as terrible as possible.

The awful coda to this story is that if Brown had chosen to accept the original sentence, he would not have had to spend a day in prison. Brown had been charged with making "terroristic threats" against Monique and for vandalism. He was acquitted of the former but not the latter. His sentence was initially not six months of jail time. Instead he was handed four hundred hours of community service or forty hours of cleaning up streets and ordered to pay $1,700 to a domestic abuse charity and a women's shelter and to attend counseling. But he didn't accept that sentence, calling it "mean-spirited and vicious," and chose jail time instead. He said, "I'm going to take six months. You are not going to humiliate me. I'm not going to pick up trash on the freeway."

Brown again painted this entire situation in political terms, telling journalist Jon Saraceno of *USA Today*, "There's no doubt that I'm a political prisoner, but race in America is always under the surface. If I were domesticated, I would be accepted racially. I'd have approval if I stayed in my place. The worst thing an African-American man can do is be as free as those more powerful than he is."

Then he invoked the leitmotif of his political life: "The last thing I'm going to give up is my manhood."

Brown told the press that he should be praised for destroying Monique's car with a shovel, saying, "I went the opposite of domestic violence that night. In anger-management training, they teach you never to hit a person—hit an object. That's what they teach you."

Brown also rejected the idea that he had done anything wrong. "The issue isn't about the safety of women," he said. "It is about [the courts] making a political point. I can deal with any persecution or prosecution. Your enemy wants you to walk one mile, you walk two."

The only person who publicly apologized for the incident was in fact Monique Brown, who testified that she had never felt threatened and that she had authorized her husband to attack the car as a therapeutic form of anger management. She said she had called 911 to humiliate her husband, whom she had suspected of cheating on her. She later said, "I challenged him. I shouldn't have done that."

Monique commented that she should have thought about his history with police: "It made me realize who my husband is. Not who my husband is inside but who he is in America." She also said she should have been more sensitive to the fact that Brown was in a very dark place, his dear friend George Hughley having died in a February 1999 motorcycle accident.

Monique's political explanation for her husband's conviction only amplified what Brown was saying behind bars. He told Jeff Adler of *The Washington Post*, "I could have been a domesticated African and taken what the judge gave me. But I chose to be a man of character."

Brown, very tellingly, does not paint this particular political stand in the traditional language of Black Power. Instead he directs his ire against a powerful cabal of white women, and portrays it as an organized campaign by these women to bring down a prominent man. Brown said, "[Female judge] Dale Fischer is the CEO of a radical and extremist group of white, upper-class women who target men of color, including Jim Brown. Judge Fischer has converted the court into a command post used to wage a war against all men, and black men." He added, speaking about himself in the third person, "Jim Brown has a duty to his people, Americans, to stop a matriarchal corporation from using the bully pulpit to manufacture domestic-violence crimes when they don't exist."

This group he was referring to is the American Inns of Court, a benign legal organization whose mission is to "foster excellence in professionalism, ethics, civility, and legal skills." The board of trustees is about half male.

Brown chose the six months behind bars because above all else he refused to concede that anything he did was connected to domestic violence.

Upon leaving prison, Brown said, "I served my time . . . I did it as a gentleman. The conditions of my [initial] sentence were ridiculous. If I had accepted those conditions I would have been condoning something that could have represented the way that the law was administered for many, many years. . . . The system itself has been corrupted."

Deputy city attorney Grace Lee scoffed at this characterization, calling the affair "a very ordinary case about domestic violence."

But Brown didn't see it as ordinary at all, and his comments at the time bring him back toward using his onetime bulletproof masculinity as a shield. "You cannot take my dignity. You cannot take my manhood," he said. "Fifteen years, twenty years, twenty-seven years Nelson Mandela spent to fight apartheid in South Africa. Only that man did it. Maybe God made me a catalyst, because I know if I go to jail and spend my six months with dignity and pride it's going to mean a lot to the young people I work with around this doggone country."

In court, Detective Brian Gasparian had testified that Monique Brown asked officers not to arrest her husband "after she came to a police station and tearfully told them of a history of abuse in their two-year marriage. . . . Monique Brown was tearful, trembling but open in discussing what she described as incidents of abuse, some of which involved threats on her life. . . . She seemed upset. She was crying. She asked me what was going to happen, if her husband was going to be arrested. I said I didn't know."

Gasparian later said, "She advised me that she didn't want him arrested. . . . She said she wanted me to just take a report in case something were to happen in the future. Her eyes were red. She was kind of shaky."

Outside the courthouse during the trial, Jim and Monique held hands as he again made this a political issue, speaking about the tearing down of men and the overempowerment of women. He railed against domestic violence laws that he said give all the power to women to accuse men who are deemed instantly guilty. He said, "Under these laws she is now the boss of my life forever. . . . She can pick up a phone and call the police and that's it. . . . This law forever makes [men] totally unimportant in our home."

Speaking later, Brown commented, "I can definitely get angry, and I have taken that anger out inappropriately in the past. But I have done so with both men and women. So do I have a problem with women? No. I have had anger, and I'll probably continue to have anger. I just have to not strike out at anyone ever again. I have to be smarter than that, smarter than I was. What I would say is that with wisdom, I will only use my mentality or my spirit aggressively. I will never use my hands [that way] again."

The story was not as explosive, invasive, and damaging to the Browns as it might have been today, in this era of social media and the twenty-four-hour news cycle. Yet there was still a great deal of copy written about the case in the country's biggest newspapers. Brown was also able to control this narrative somewhat by delivering interviews from behind bars to *The New York Times*, *The Washington Post*, and other outlets. But not every columnist was friendly. *USA Today*'s Jon Saraceno went for the jugular with the headline "True Manhood and Perspective Elude Brown." Saraceno eviscerated Brown for his "misogynistic, violent history." Brown, he wrote, "is not yet the man he wants us to believe he is. . . . Personal responsibility and self-control are issues at the core of his long-standing activism. Instead, he chooses to hide behind '60s-style militant rhetoric and black-power salutes, railing against the 'evils of government.' He is out of step with society, black and white. He is missing the message of selflessness he has preached over the decades. . . .

"Choosing jail," Saraceno said, "was not a selfless act by a wronged man but the epitome of self-absorption and martyrdom."

Saraceno is most cruel and betrays his superficial understanding when describing Monique Brown: "She sounds brainwashed, or she's a cover-up artist. Either way, her perspective is skewed. Maybe she's afraid, which is understandable. When she tries to explain away her husband's actions, she is worshipful."

Calling an abuse survivor "a cover-up artist" is shameful, re-victimizing the victim in this case. It's not altogether surprising, however, that this callous way of writing about abuse survivors went unnoticed at the time.

Since the 1999 incident, Brown has not been accused of violence against Monique or any other woman. In the meantime, the power dynamics in his house have changed, as he and Monique have had two children, Aris and Morgan, and Brown has slowed as the years have passed. Monique runs the house. But Jim Brown's value system, at least publicly, has not budged.

There was a fascinating exchange between the media and Brown in 2013 that also revealed a good deal about Brown's stance on violence against women. ESPN asked Brown for his thoughts about Kobe Bryant. In recent years, most people in the sports world genuflect at the mention of Bryant, with his two decades in the NBA. Brown did not. Instead he referred to Bryant's infamous efforts in 2003, after being charged with rape in Eagle, Colorado, to get the local police to investigate his teammate Shaquille O'Neal instead of him. The *Los Angeles Times* quoted a police report that said Bryant told detectives that "he should have done what Shaq does . . . that Shaq would pay his women not to say anything" and already had paid up to a million dollars "for situations like this." (Shaquille O'Neal has never been accused of violence against women and was enraged with Bryant when these reports went public; the rift between the two men lasted for years.)

For Brown, Bryant's being arrested on charges of violence against women was not what disgusted him. It was the snitching. He then connected the snitching to why Bryant would never have been invited to the Ali summit five decades earlier. On *The Arsenio Hall Show,* Brown said that Bryant had thrown Shaquille O'Neal "under the bus" and "is somewhat confused about culture, because he was brought up in another country." (Bryant spent much of his childhood in Italy.) Bryant, Brown went on, "doesn't quite fit what's happening in America. In the days when we had a summit and called the top black athletes together to talk to Muhammad Ali about his status with the armed forces, there were some athletes we didn't call. If I had to call that summit all over, there would be some athletes I wouldn't call. Kobe would be one of them." Once again, it's the snitching, not the alleged violence against women, that makes Bryant unworthy.

Another window into his thinking came in September 2014 when Adrian Peterson, star running back at the time for the Minnesota Vikings, was arrested on charges of abusing his own young son with a stick.

Brown responded to the story by saying, "In this society, there's a thing called child abuse. Adrian lives in a time with women's rights and all that shit. You could get run over standing in front of women when they're talking about their rights, domestic violence and child abuse and shit."

When asked if he had something more to say about domestic violence and violence against women, given his own history, he said, "Yeah, domestic violence is different to me than child abuse. It's strange, but child abuse, to me, would be a deep sickness. I mean there'd be some deep shit going on there if you want to whip the hell out of your kid where your kid would have welts and shit, I don't know what the hell that's about.

"Now, here's my honest feeling about it: child abuse is one thing that's very clear-cut and doesn't carry, in my mind, the same emotion that [abusing] a woman carries. So, I'll put it to you this way: as I grow older, I would not touch anybody. I will not follow anyone into that hole where they are trying to take me where I could get angry and provoke their satisfaction by succumbing to that anger. You need education to learn not to fuck with some shit like that. When you're talking about being in love, being emotional, feeling certain ways, that's some deep shit. And it's not predictable. All rejection is difficult to take and who rejects you more than a fucking woman?

"And since society says there's not two sides to the coin, she'll spit on you or hit you across the knee with a hammer and that's not an excuse for you to hit her. It really isn't. But, in that emotional state, you might knock her out, unless you're at the stage in your development where you're ready to walk [away]. And if she is not [ready to walk away], then you're dealing with two people. You're depending on her to feed you something that's logical that fixes the argument, right? [But] she don't give you nothing that's logical and shit. So then your only alternative is to walk. You have no other recourse but to walk. But then you got ties, legal ties, all kinds of shit that you gotta cooperate with each other on, to work out how to leave each other. That shit's all fucked up. That will screw with you on another level. . . .

"I've never seen a man that was perfect with his woman. I saw two quotes in the paper today by these teammates of Ray Rice. One guy called him a 'piece of shit.' And they put that shit in the damn paper. 'That piece of shit.' Like I said, he's falling into the trap that they lay to assuage the females. . . . If someone spits in your face, someone slaps you, what's going to be the reaction? And individuals don't really want to [talk about what that reaction would be]. They don't really want to address it because what it suggests and what it does is a form of reality that individuals don't want to address."

Brown would not talk about any of the cases that he was involved in over the course of his life. His mind did wander toward speaking about the Ray Rice video. "Did you see that elevator?" he said. "She made some kind of move and it looked like she said something, or spit at him or something. And then she went back and he knocked her out. But the piece of the video that bothered me most wasn't the blow. Did you see how he treated her outside of the elevator? Kicked her with his shoe. Like a piece of fucking trash. Man, what kind of shit is that? Everyone's saying the punch [ruined Rice's reputation]. No, that shit outside the elevator did it for me, from the standpoint of the lack of respect that he showed. She's knocked out now. I don't know what he could have done but he sure could have

done something different than he did. Yeah, I didn't see nothing but disrespect. Disrespect don't appeal to me under any
circumstances. . . . What are the rules in an argument? Leave
the fucking house [laughs]. Get out of Dodge. That's all you
can do."

He then spoke about an article in the Cleveland *Plain Dealer*
comparing him to Ray Rice. He was tickled that people still
felt the need to attack him on a basis that he absolutely believes
is not about his own failings, but is politically motivated. That
narrative still holds in his mind: anything that had been done
to him was also done to tear him down.

"I am honestly trying to do what I can do in this society to
make it better. And I'm long past the stage of needing anyone
to validate me. My thoughts now are about leaving here and my
family and my friends and doing what I can do before I get out
of Dodge myself. And to have someone taking slaps at you, it's
like, 'Damn, man. This is desperation time! You're still fucking
with me? You're fucking with an old man? What kind of shit
is that?'"

He obliquely referred to his years of court cases: "How do I
come at everybody? I just deal with the evidence. I stood up to
my accusers. What you do in this country is you stand up to the
accuser and you go through the process, whatever the process is,
and then if you got to pay the price, you pay the price, and if
you don't, you don't."

Journalist Kevin Powell is someone who has been open,
repentant, and deeply analytical about the topic of violence
against women. Powell explains why he thinks Brown, despite
these rock bottoms, seems so resistant to confront any of this

history. "Unfortunately, as black men we feel a particular kind of weight that's really unexplainable if you're not a black male in this country," he said. "Then if you add into it what you might have gone through with your family—a black family in America with residual effects of slavery and segregation and all of these emotions and insanity that come from that—it makes it very, very difficult to look in the mirror because you're talking about traumatized people. Any group that has been traumatized, I guarantee that you'll find in that community people who are profoundly successful, but also profoundly wounded.

"But what's missing is the ability to pause and do some deep reflection and healing. . . . I think that most men, regardless of race, just don't know how to stop. Because one of the twisted definitions of manhood is that you always have to be doing something. It does not lend itself to critical self-reflection, healing, and being vulnerable or being honest about what's hurting you and causing you pain. And I think that's the case with Jim Brown."

Attempting to discuss this with "critical self-reflection and healing," however, gets undermined by the belief that it is rife with racialized double standards. Academic and bestselling author Michael Eric Dyson said, "There's a racial aspect to the perspective on personal flaws. The magical appeal of black pathology is that the public narrative always ascribes greater power to black misfortune and black misconduct. So now Michael Vick becomes the face of dogfighting. Adrian Peterson, the face of brutal practices of disciplining your children. Ray Rice, of violence against women. And so on . . . Racism and racial barriers can always be held up when black people are candidates to represent American pathology."

Dr. Harry Edwards has done remarkable work in recent years on gender issues and has also been a close friend of Jim Brown's. He stated: "What makes heroes heroic is the fact that they are human and yet are able to accomplish and contribute these extraordinary things. And far too often, because the public in general, and people with a vested interest in certain outcomes in particular—in other words people who want to see African-American men fail—want to find a reason to discount that greatness. They will go to human frailties, and say, 'See there? He's not what he claims to be.' I mean, they said that about Dr. King. The reality is that what is at the very heart of the heroic contribution—someone who comes from among us, walks off into that dark and frightening forest of challenges, and comes back having achieved the height of expectations, of possibilities—is that they came from among us. Jim Brown didn't descend upon this earth from some alien planet. He came from among us. And the fact of his humanity means there are going to be frailties, shortcomings, and so forth. It's human beings who are heroic, because they are everyday people just like the rest of us who manage, through some gift, greatness, capability, sometimes through sheer determination, to do extraordinary things.

"I don't discount or ignore any issues that may have tarnished, or have appeared to tarnish, Jim Brown in terms of wiping out some illusion of utter perfection. I take those as part of his humanity, understanding that it's probably the case that we don't even know and completely understand what those imperfections and frailties really were or amounted to. What we have is what was put out there, oftentimes by people who are literally interested in not just discounting his achievements and accomplishments, but in discounting *him*."

This can be true and yet we also have to acknowledge that there is a deep degree of enabling that takes place with this kind of response. The contradictory part of these various defenses, however, is Jim Brown's refusal to publicly recognize any of his own frailties. He does not confront this part of his history, and because he's a public figure who built his political reputation as someone who fights injustice, this has undoubtedly hurt him. But it also creates a chorus of people who marvel at his indomitability. It creates admirers who have interpreted one man's refusal to partake in one of the most difficult public acts in American life—admitting political and personal wrongs—to be a badge of honor. But this ignores the fact that part of what made Malcolm X so remarkable—such a role model as a human being—was that he very publicly shifted his views on race, struggle, and resistance. He went from preaching a doctrine of black self-help and self-defense against white devils to a mass international resistance to oppression. A similar argument applies to Dr. King, who shifted his views on the scope of his struggle and publicly stated that he would never again speak solely against southern racism or what today some call "black-on-black violence" when the root causes of both extended far deeper. He said, "I knew that I could never again raise my voice against the violence of the oppressed in the ghettos without having first spoken clearly to the greatest purveyor of violence in the world today—my own government."

Brown never did that, and it's a weakness, when compared with these other great men. Ossie Davis said, "Malcolm is our manhood." Jim Brown may be Superman, but being a real flesh-and-blood man is much more difficult. The tragedy is that many will support a Jim Brown more for aspiring to be Superman than for scrutinizing himself. The message from our culture is that real men don't reflect on anything. Most of us cannot live our lives in such blinkered fashion, so we need that Superman, that exemplar, that symbol that says our own emotional constipation is not only understandable, but even noble. There is an appetite, a craving, for that Jim Brown, and that's why he is celebrated for being the last man standing.

# EIGHT

# LAST MAN STANDING

—

The thing is that, when you are a popular athlete, and you accept the money and the fame, and you become a front person for those who have the power, a culture dies. You're doing a great injustice to young kids that are coming up. I never wanted to be a representation of anything less than a man if young kids were going to come up emulating me.

—*Jim Brown*

*You are Scott Raab, journalist and lifelong son of Cleveland. Your city hasn't seen a championship since the 1964 Cleveland Browns, led by Jim Brown. You were at that game as a boy and have kept that ticket stub in your wallet for fifty-two years, waiting for that next title from someone, anyone . . . the Browns, the Indians, the Cavaliers . . . anyone who could remind the world that Cleveland was once known not as a punch line, but as the City of Champions. You think it will be the Cleveland Cavaliers, but then their star, LeBron James, goes to Miami and breaks your heart. You even write a book,* The Whore of Akron, *about how*

*LeBron turned his back on a city that needed him more than South Beach ever would. But then LeBron shocks the world and comes back to Cleveland. That wasn't supposed to happen! People leave Cleveland. They don't come back. In his second year back home, LeBron does the impossible, leading Cleveland back from three games to one against the best regular-season team of all time, the Golden State Warriors. LeBron leads both teams over seven games in points, rebounds, assists, blocks, and steals. He's a man among boys, a physical marvel reminiscent of that other physical marvel who brought the Browns a title in 1964.*

*You finally take that 1964 ticket stub out of your wallet, and you better believe you are there on the day of the great parade after the Cavs win it all: a parade five decades in the making. The crowd swells even beyond initial estimates. A million and a half people line the streets, and there are even people rappelling down the sides of the city's buildings so they can get a closer view. It's almost perfect, and then, the icing on the cake: there's Jim Brown riding on top of a car, sitting in a chair and soaking in the cheers, his wife and children at his side.*

*Cleveland has its title. The City of Champions, Believeland, is alive again. The moment gets ratcheted up even further: Jim Brown is tasked with handing the NBA championship trophy, in front of what seems like the entire city of Cleveland, to LeBron James on a massive stage where the whole Cavs team, in varying degrees of inebriation, is in a state of delirium. When Brown takes the stage, several players, including LeBron, seem to snap out of their shirtless reverie and take Brown by each arm to help him across the stage, but the old man doesn't need it. He is flying. The people of Cleveland have been cheering him for hours. He is a hero. He is embraced. At age eighty, he is imbibing a combination of love, worship, and respect. No controversies. No scandals. Just undistilled legend in the flesh.*

IT'S GAME THREE OF THE 2015 NBA FINALS, WITH THE
Cleveland Cavaliers and the Golden State Warriors tied at one
game apiece. The Cavs are at home in Cleveland after two
games in Oakland, attempting to finally remove the "God
hates Cleveland" curse from the city. No Cleveland sports
team has won a title since that day in 1964 when the Browns
shut out those powerhouse Baltimore Colts 27–0. The current
star of Cleveland, LeBron "King" James, a person so physically
imposing he looks like our twenty-first-century incarnation of
the "Greek god in African skin," took a moment before the
start of the game to turn to a man sitting courtside. In front of
the raucous packed house and a national television audience,
the King bowed. LeBron James was paying respect to the only
person one could imagine him bowing to: Jim Brown. "It was
one of my greatest sports moments," Brown said afterward. "I
had no concept that LeBron even knew I was at the game.
And when he made his gesture, it was just a great thing for an
old guy."

Being the "last man standing" from a rebellious era has soft-
ened his volcanic history and turned Brown into the person the
media go to as a way to understand the present. After the historic 2008 election of Senator Barack Obama to the presidency,
Brown was ESPN's prime-time, central choice to discuss the
significance of the moment. Remembrances of time in jail or a
woman allegedly thrown from a balcony fade as he sits in the
winter of his life, his body hunched over that imposing cane.
This fire-breathing dragon from another era is now fawned

over by today's masters of the universe who grew up either watching his exploits or hearing about them from their parents or grandparents.

Tom Farrey, former ESPN reporter and now director of the sports wing of the Aspen Institute, spoke about what it was like when Brown arrived among the various movers and shakers attending the Aspen Ideas Festival in 2012. "It's quite a gathering," said Farrey, "a pretty exclusive crowd . . . so as you're walking around there are folks who aren't easily impressed. But Jim Brown created more buzz than anybody I've seen there, in a select group with people like President Clinton and Bill Gates. I remember him at a cocktail party on the first night of the event and he's out on the deck, and he and I are talking and these college kids are coming up and asking him for autographs and photos, and older folks are craning their neck and looking at this old lion that they grew up with. There is an aura around him."

When his eightieth birthday passed on February 17, 2016, the Cleveland Browns, the team with whom he had battled for so many years, announced that they would be building a statue of their greatest player in front of the stadium.

Jimmy Haslam, the current Browns owner, said, "It is only fitting that one of the most iconic professional football players and members of Cleveland and the Browns is commemorated with this statue, as he will always be such a permanent fixture in our city."

Even this was met with some controversy. Cleveland *Plain Dealer* columnist Bill Livingston wrote in outrageous fashion, "Brown is idolized because of the strict division [that] most hold between his actions on the field and off. Fans and media members downplayed players' off-field incidents until they erupted into the headlines in the worst possible way, as with O. J. Simpson and Aaron Hernandez."

Comparing Jim Brown, whatever his sins, to Simpson and Hernandez just gives more ammunition to those who uncritically defend Brown and feel that he is held to a double standard.

Yet these kinds of critiques were less resonant than the general applause and appreciation for an eighty-year-old legend, especially in Cleveland. Brown says, "I am entrenched in that city. The city I like doesn't live, for me, through the media. I have friendships there that are friendships for life. I have many associates there. . . . The way that I live is based upon cultivating those relationships, and nobody can ever take that away."

It is not surprising that Brown is finally getting this kind of due. With Ali having been unable to speak at great length in the last several decades of his life and Bill Russell largely reclusive, Jim Brown has had to carry the mantle of his era.

Brown was the interview of choice when Ali died in June 2016. He traveled to Louisville to mourn his late friend and speak about his legacy. Ali, Brown said, "was able to use the spotlight like nobody else in history. He represented what a man should be in America. . . . He made people accept him as a man, as an equal, and he was not afraid to represent himself in that way. That's what I loved about him."

Brown had for years taken a position that Ali was so beloved "because he had gotten sick and he was so much easier to take in a state of sickness. That young, fiery, energetic, bold person was no longer there. He became a global caricature, because

Muhammad Ali was no longer that youngster who could come into a room and light it up."

It is statements like this that contribute to Brown's aura of "last man standing," but he has earned this reputation because he is seen as still fighting the fight. There are so many athletes who were political in the 1960s and 1970s but stepped out of the struggle once it had fallen out of fashion. Brown has never stopped entering the fray, even if his political opinions have confused or angered former admirers and detractors alike.

He says, "There is no way that I could stop being in the struggle, because if I wasn't in the struggle, the struggle would be in me. You're talking about a lifetime. I'm eighty years old. In the next ten years I might be rolling out of here. The only thing I know now is that the best shot that I have to leave a mark is to be as decent a person as I can be. People say to me, 'Well, get ready for the history books! You're going to join them!' Well, that shit doesn't excite me. When I'm dead, how somebody wants to remember me is up to them. I won't remember shit. I don't have any questions for myself. All I know is that the only thing I'm not sure about is how it's going to feel to die."

Brown doesn't want people to genuflect in front of him. He doesn't want people to visit his home like he's some kind of a pontiff. He still wants to have the debate, the conversation, the argument to push his particular conception of social justice forward. He is a critic of the United States but also someone who loves this country. Just as in 1968, he saw no contradiction to endorsing Richard Nixon and dialoguing with Huey Newton. That conception is contradictory to many, but clear as glass to him.

"They all say that America is the greatest country in the world," he says. "Well, I think that, too. I travel, and I like it here better than anywhere else. I respect freedom and democracy . . . or as much of it as I can get. But one day, I would like to see America face up to fulfilling those promises that it makes. It's not difficult for that to happen, because"—and here he might as well be describing what so many people have wanted him to do—"it's almost as if you just say, 'Look, man, I apologize for the mistakes I made and how I treated you, and I'll try to be a better person. I will be a better person. I will be a better country; I will be a better political system. And I'll try to do the right things, but I need your help. It's a form of forgiveness. Let's move forward with what we have and make it better. And this is for all people who've decided that we have a place in how that dream is written—the dream of freedom in America.' But the cover-up still stays there: the lack of acknowledgment of the crimes of the past and how they affect our present. . . . It's like me telling you I've been perfect. How? I cannot be perfect. But if I tell you about how I've been perfect, I'd miss things I've done that I really regret."

This tacit acknowledgment of his own duality, as well as the country's, allowed him to support Colin Kaepernick "a hundred percent" but also to be his critic, saying, "I want to be in his corner, and I do think, 'God bless him.' [But] I'm going to give you the real deal: I'm an American. I don't desecrate my flag and my national anthem. I'm not gonna do anything against the flag and national anthem. I'm going to work within those situations. But this is my country, and I'll work out the problems, but I'll do it in an intelligent manner." He makes these comments with little regard for the fact that they give ammunition to people who hate Colin Kaepernick, as well as people who, in decades past, would have hated Jim Brown.

Brown has constructed his own brand of patriotism that attempts to profit from the opportunities available but rejects silence in the face of racism. If Jim Brown, as Public Enemy once dreamed in the liner notes to their album *Greatest Misses*, could be president, he says he would do it, "inside out." He muses, "If I was in the White House, I would go to the bottom, where the poor people are, and try to engage them. I would work out with them what they could do, and then I would show them what the government would do. I would join into a partnership with the poor people and let them be my allies in a plan that's aimed at their spirit and then fight from that kind of a position. For example, if I were president of the United States, I would have already talked to me."

He laughs in a way that is laced with sadness. "I would have meetings with groups of people on a basic level, and we would be talking about the safety of our communities and the education of our kids, and give them a direction."

He would also argue that "we have to be intelligent enough to understand that there's not a quick fix. We'd have to work toward the future with our young people. We have to look at some socialistic methodologies to give the poor population a chance to become a part of the system. The fundamentals need to be taught. So, if Amer-I-Can met with LeBron, LeBron probably would have a hard time separating his importance from our intelligence. Certain other athletes that are my friends are just the opposite. Young ones, too. They study, they're smart. They know what an elder is, they know we have to pass the torch."

Although he believes that all young athletes need to be more educated before they open their mouths, he has a great deal of respect for LeBron James and what he is doing in the city of Cleveland. When asked about LeBron's organizing his team at the time, the Miami Heat, to stand with the family of Trayvon Martin after he was killed by George Zimmerman, Brown says, "You never want to criticize a guy for almost any gesture and I'm glad he did it. But, from the standpoint of utilizing his effectiveness, he's wasting his time." Brown catches himself and brings it down a notch. "It's good, it's good. I'm not the one who should be judging, you know. It is a good thing. Better to be conscious and raise consciousness than do nothing."

He thinks that LeBron has the ability to achieve his own stated goal of becoming "a global icon like Muhammad Ali," but "he would really have to step out. You always have to talk about Ali in terms of the true capacity of everything he did and everyone he reached. You can say that you want to make a lot of money, and you can achieve that. But you can't achieve character or status. That comes from the inside and that is proven by your deeds. That has to be who you are. You can't just say 'I want to be like Ali' and be like Ali. It has to be part of your makeup. LeBron might have the financial wherewithal. He may have the physical wherewithal. But how does he develop the emotional and psychological wherewithal to sustain an Ali-type presence? I do think a person like Mr. James is showing himself to be a thinking leader, and that's fantastic. It takes high-profile athletes to call attention to social issues and step out so players can follow that lead and create a collective voice."

Brown is still merciless in his assessment of today's black athletes who remain silent. During the civil rights movement, Jackie Robinson would repeat in his speeches: "If I had to choose tomorrow between the Baseball Hall of Fame and full citizenship for my people, I would choose full citizenship time and again." Brown said, "Yeah, that sums it up. It seems like almost every black athlete should feel that way, but they don't."

In 2002, asked by *Sports Illustrated* what athletes he admired, Brown said, "Compared with a Bill Russell? Nobody. . . . Can I tell you something? Everybody does good things, but I'm talking about making major changes in the educational system that would impact an entire race. I'm talking about stopping these young gang members from killing one another. I'm talking about keeping prisons from overflowing. I'm not talking about teaching black kids to golf and get to country clubs. Come on! That's wonderful to do, but Tiger [Woods] makes enough money that he could change many more things that are important to black kids than learning to golf. . . . I don't talk to very many [young black athletes]. I give them their space because they have a right to do what they want to do in this country. Most of them already feel they know more than I know. They make more money, and they've got more power. They're relevant today because they create profits for owners. That's it. Michael Jordan brings millions of dollars when he shows up in an arena. Since money is how we judge people, he's very valuable. But while that's happening, Rome is burning within the black community."

He says that "it's a constant struggle because there's the real America and there's the America that pretends. We like to take the posture that we are holier than thou in so many cases, yet we have the legacy of slavery. But then we have the legacy of people who fought slavery. America is a great country when you understand how to live it. I've lived in so many different areas—from really having a great time in Miami to being a friend of Hugh Hefner's, to having young gangbangers in my house for the last twenty years and [never having] them pull a gun on me, to [having] young people come back to my house after years and say that I've helped them turn their lives around, to having a relationship for years with my old high school coach. All these things are relevant. The good times, the helping people, the old connections, they all give me hope. They are all relevant."

"Relevant" is really the defining word for Jim Brown. He still has a great deal to say about the current generation of black ballplayers and their political obligations.

Brown actually feels hopeful about the political courage of this new generation of athletes. "The thing that I feel most [excited] about is the emerging of young players that are intelligently protesting what they feel are injustices, their willingness to step up and recognize that there has to be some changes in the methodology of engagement with citizens and police. . . . When these young people stand up and risk their careers, that's a good sign for everything and all of us. They have the power of bringing attention to the issues."

For Brown, it's still imperative for athletes to lead by example, and he wants athletes not to reject America but to use their wealth as a bridge to the poor who are left behind. "Regardless of what else we do, young black men in this country have to understand that they have a responsibility. They cannot be the enemy in their own neighborhoods and usurp the effort of good people that are trying to make things work."

He has supported both Democrats and Republicans in his life. The legislative agendas that disturb him the most—mass incarceration, prison privatization, and get-tough-on-crime mandatory sentencing for nonviolent offenses—are issues both parties have supported to differing degrees.

"It's a losing cause. It can feel that way. It's like a chess game out there. White America has allowed itself to be hoodwinked into being the bad guy. You know how America functions? They get poor people saying, 'I'm an Appalachian, and I'm white, and I'm a little better than you because you are brown or black.' The propaganda machine says, 'Jim Brown is anti-white.' I don't know how to be anti-white. What do you do to be anti-white? I'm struggling to be myself. I'm an American citizen, I pay my taxes, and I want my damn rights. Now tell me another American that doesn't want that. The bullshit is based upon superiority: the need to appear superior is in our streets. Take Ferguson: they know that police officer didn't have to kill that boy. And he left him in the street for so many hours afterwards, too. And they basically rule in favor of the police. You can accept that as right, but that shit is wrong."

Brown continues, on Ferguson and police violence: "If you don't get your hands up fast enough, if you stumble and it looks like you're coming at the police, they're going to shoot you down. It's all part of that need for that feeling of superiority. I don't know too many African-American men that dislike white people—I know a lot of them that dislike what white people do. But I don't know any of them that just hate white people. That's not our real nature. We hate the things that people do in the name of being white, and wonder why they do it. If you study slavery, and look at the humiliation that was doled out on a helpless slave, why would someone need to take a hopeless person and inflict cruelty on them when they can't fight back or do anything? What need is in that human being?"

He then goes back to that article in the Cleveland *Plain Dealer* about his past violence against women, as if it were an itch he can't quite scratch away. "It's crazy, [the article] was kind of a hit job because it exposes things that didn't need to be exposed, and it puts an old man right in the center of something."

One can't escape the feeling when speaking to Jim Brown that there is this gap: that he was so hard for so long, so unforgiving of those around him, and so neglectful—as generations of men have been—to his own children, that he has paid a greater personal price for that than the wounds potentially caused by a thousand *Plain Dealer* articles.

Michael Eric Dyson said, "It would be helpful to the broader community, especially the black people, for a valuable icon like Jim Brown to wrestle in public with some of the demons that have plagued his own existence."

That ain't happening. Brown says, "The last thing I'm going to give up is my manhood." More likely, it will leave his body only when he leaves this earth. At that moment, he will finally be unburdened from that crushing weight. This is a deeply held conviction for Brown. He says, "Keep your principles even if it hurts. Especially when it hurts."

Is that how Jim Brown defines "manhood"? He says, "Being a man is about taking responsibility. Everyone has different definitions and I do not have the be-all, end-all on this. But it means that you stand for something. You take responsibility for your home. Let your children figure out their own lives. And you don't dance. You never dance."

"You never dance." To Brown that means that you never lower yourself for people in power. You never become a jive-ass entertainer when you can stand up and be respected as a man. Yet there is another dimension to saying "you never dance." It's the dimension heard in the words of early feminist revolutionary Emma Goldman, who once said, "If I can't dance, I don't want to be part of your revolution," or the title of Norman Mailer's bestselling book *Tough Guys Don't Dance*. Jim Brown went to all the discos, wore the naked-lady medallion, and did all the steps, but he didn't dance. He didn't unclench. He didn't let go. He couldn't.

He tells a story about his dear friend Bill Russell. "His wife died [in 2013], and he was suffering, man. And he likes to drive, so he asked me if I would take a trip with him across the country. He was going to go down to Dr. J's [Julius Erving] house. So we drove, man. Cross-country. And just related. He wanted to talk to someone that he could truly talk to. When Bill and I talk, we share different things on a certain kind of level. And we are so arrogant—we don't think anybody else is going to understand it. And when we have a conversation, we say, 'What else did you learn, man?' Those are the things in my life that I'm pleased about."

It would be special to learn what they discussed, to hear these icons come down from Mount Olympus and share their pain, to let the rest of us know that there is no shame in hurting. But that is not going to happen.

Jim Brown refuses to let go, to be "soft." Many have suffered for this choice. But he has suffered as well; he suffered because of a brand of manhood that doesn't create fully realized "men" as much as it creates people in need of rescue, people who are nearly incapable of extending their arms and asking for help. Jim Brown the football player certainly knew how to extend his arm and send a 250-pound man into the bleachers. He also extended his arm to push people away, and never really stopped.

There are young female protesters leading the social justice movements of the twenty-first century. In Ferguson, they marched with signs that paid respect to the Memphis sanitation workers of decades ago. But the signs now read, "I am a WOMAN!" They are now carrying the torch of Jim Brown's lifelong fight against injustice with a flair and determination that is inspiring people across the country. They are climbing hundred-foot poles and tearing down Confederate flags. They are pulling down statues that pay homage to the men who owned and traded their ancestors. They will not wait. They are taking the best of the tradition of self-assertion in the face of racism, making it their own, and discarding the rest. That knowledge should comfort Jim Brown. Even if he was never able to free himself from either the burden of this country or his own history, the next generation just might be able to take the weight.

# AFTERWORD

—

*You are Jim Brown and it has been a hell of a year. The Cleveland curse is over and the torch has been passed, it's the City of Champions once again. LeBron James finally dragged the Cavaliers, as well as the city of Cleveland, with its ample psychological baggage, across the finish line and at long last brought a title home. You hand the title to LeBron on stage in front of a city showering you with unvarnished love.*

*Four months later, a statue of you is erected in front of the Browns Stadium; twenty years late, but better than never. Your friend Muhammad Ali finally left this earth, and the sports world turned to you for guidance to help understand his legacy. A new generation of athletes is finally speaking out and it's making a difference, proving wrong all the people who have said for decades that you were selling ideas long past their due date and that the need for activist athletes was something that died with the 1960s. The media are revering you as never before. You*

*are basking in the warmth of their respectful attentions. You see that you
are featured in an exhibit at the new Smithsonian National Museum of
African American History and Culture. People are genuflecting in your
presence these days, but it's not enough. You don't want genuflection;
you want a reckoning. There are still grievances to nurse. You see Kareem Abdul-Jabbar—the man whom you once knew as "the serious
kid" Lew Alcindor, whom you let sit next to you at the Ali Summit,
fifty years ago—being given a Presidential Medal of Freedom by President Obama. You see Michael Jordan, the man you've been dragging
for thirty years for never doing enough for the community, get a medal as
well. You see this first black president—a man who would not be there
without your sacrifice—but he never puts a medal around your neck.
You believe he won't reach out to you because "the people around him
are scared." They can't get over the "bullshit with the women."*

*The phone rings. It's Donald Trump. You have met him over the
years at various golf and charity events. He wants you by his side as he
prepares for his presidential inauguration. He doesn't care about any of
the past female bullshit. Like his other sports supporters—Bob Knight,
Mike Tyson, your friend Bill Belichick—this is a man's man. You tell
him that you think he's run "the greatest campaign in history." He
wants you in Washington, D.C. He wants you on CNN to talk about
how he has no problems with "the blacks." He asks you to defend him
against all those old civil rights movement folks like John Lewis who are
speaking about him is if he is the reincarnation of George Wallace. He
speaks about economic development in the black community. He promises resources and investment. It reminds you of the promises Richard
Nixon made right to your face in 1968, before the Southern Strategy
took him away from the community economic empowerment he promised. He makes pledges that would tempt the Savior. You know that to*

*accept his hand means that you will now be on the opposite side of some of your oldest and dearest allies. Kareem, Dr. John Carlos, Dr. Harry Edwards, and your late friend Muhammad Ali have all called for active resistance to Donald Trump's agenda. Are you really prepared at this point in your life to be that isolated, that reviled, and to tear down all the idol-making and hagiography that have been constructed around you over the last year? Goddamn right. You don't just want that. You need it. It's not a sacrifice. It's your gasoline. It makes you run. In fact, the thought of their hatred and the contempt of the media that have always wanted to tear you down is irresistible. You go on CNN. You say that you heard John Lewis "cry the blues about Mr. Trump and [say] that it's an illegitimate presidency—I take offense to that." You mock his civil rights marches as "parades." It's a line you've been using for decades. People don't know that you have always had this contempt for these civil rights charlatans. They are going to learn. You read what people are saying about you: that you must have Alzheimer's, that you sold out, that Trump must have paid you off. The arrows are coming at you, just like in the 1950s, except this time it isn't from the racists, the bigots. It's from the black community. It's from your old allies. It's from people who have spent the last sixty years defending you. Your face appears in what outsiders must think is a grimace. But it's a smile that comes from somewhere deep and ancient, and you say, "This is glory." Again. You matter.*

## ACKNOWLEDGMENTS

—

This book took years to write, and there is no way I could have done it without the assistance, support, and friendship of the following people. Thank you, Peter Gethers, for your editorial insights. Thank you, James Schamus and Anthony Arnove, for introducing me to Pete Gethers! Thank you to my literary agent, Scott Waxman, who at times worked pro bono as a psychotherapist. Thank you to Brant Rumble, my editor at Blue Rider, as well as Terezia Cicelova, Anna Jardine, and Maureen Klier. Thank you to the Lannan Foundation and especially Patrick Lannan and Sarah Knopp for providing indispensable assistance. Thank you to researchers and transcribers Alex Rubin Holt, Daniel Suarez, Tim Horsey, and Dan Baker, and especially librarian extraordinaire Leonidas Mallias. Thank you, Brian Baughan, for your editorial advice. Thank you to Katrina vanden Heuvel, Annie Shields, Peter Rothberg, and all my other colleagues at *The Nation* for your marathon patience as I attempted to get this done. Thank you to Michele, Sasha, and Jacob: the three best people I know. And last, thank you, Jim Brown. Thank you for living a life worth examining, a life that holds lessons that are essential in the fight for a more just future.

# INDEX

---